ATLANTIC'S LAST STOP

COURAGE, FOLLY, AND LIES IN THE WHITE STAR LINE'S WORST DISASTER BEFORE *TITANIC*

BOB CHAULK

NIMBUS
PUBLISHING
— NIMBUS.CA —

Nimbus Publishing Limited
3660 Strawberry Hill Street, Halifax, NS, B3K 5A9
(902) 455-4286 nimbus.ca

Printed and bound in Canada
NB1482

Editor: Angela Mombourquette
Design: Rudi Tusek
Cover design: Jenn Embree
Many photos from the author's collection are courtesy the estate
    of Greg Cochkanoff.
Cover image: From *Harper's Weekly*, April 19, 1873.

Library and Archives Canada Cataloguing in Publication

Title: Atlantic's last stop : courage, folly, and lies in the White Star Line's worst
    disaster before Titanic / Bob Chaulk.
Names: Chaulk, Bob, author.
Description: Includes bibliographical references.
Identifiers: Canadiana (print) 20210215674 | Canadiana (ebook) 20210215704 |
    ISBN 9781774710104 (softcover) | ISBN 9781774710111 (EPUB)
Subjects: LCSH: Atlantic (Ship : 1870-1873) | LCSH: Shipwrecks—Nova Scotia—
    History—19th century.
Classification: LCC G530.A84 C53 2021 | DDC 910.9163/44—dc23

Nimbus Publishing acknowledges the financial support for its publishing activities from the Government of Canada, the Canada Council for the Arts, and from the Province of Nova Scotia. We are pleased to work in partnership with the Province of Nova Scotia to develop and promote our creative industries for the benefit of all Nova Scotians.

Dedicated to the memory of the men and women
of Meaghers Island, Ryans Island, and Lower Prospect,
whose lives were thrown into turmoil
by the arrival of some four hundred men who
had to be rescued from the sea, resuscitated,
warmed, accommodated, nursed, fed, and clothed.

Next morning when the sun arose, as the angry billows swelled,
The people on the Prospect shore a fearful sight beheld.
The rocks around were strewn with dead as each wave broke o'er,
Bearing its load to be laid with sorrow on the shore.

John Boutilier
The Atlantic Ballad (1885)

TABLE OF CONTENTS

CHAPTER 1

THE ISMAYS

The great credit of the unexampled success of the White Star Line is undoubtedly due to Mr. T. H. Ismay...who has so admirably overcome the difficulties which were presented to him in the enterprise of the White Star Line.

The Nautical Magazine *for 1876*

On April 21, 1863, Henry Ismay Metcalfe went to sea. It was an important and inevitable milestone in the life of a sixteen-year-old male from a seafaring family. Henry's vocation was to become a master mariner, like his father and brother. For the next four years he sailed the world aboard the 700-ton clipper *Birkby*, which had been built at Ritson and Sons shipyard in his hometown of Maryport, England.

Maryport was on the northern extremity of the Irish Sea and formed a triangle with two important cities. About 150 miles to the west in Northern Ireland was Belfast, poised to become one of the world's great shipbuilding centres. The same distance to the south, at the mouth of the Mersey River, sat the historic seaport of Liverpool. Both these places would hold prominence in Henry's life. Connections were everything in those days. The expression "It's not what you know but who you know," defined how things were done. Henry's father,

George, a shipowner himself, was, no doubt, acquainted with the *Birkby*'s owners, Hayton and Simpson, and would have arranged for his son to start his seafaring career on one of their ships.

Thomas Henry Ismay was another son of Maryport who would be important in Henry's life. He was Metcalfe's first cousin, ten years his senior, and already a prominent name among Liverpool shipowners. Thomas's father, Joseph Ismay, and Henry's mother, Ruth Ismay, were brother and sister. Thomas had also started his career at age sixteen—as an apprentice with the Liverpool ship brokerage firm of Imrie, Tomlinson, and Company. When the apprenticeship ended, he too went to sea to gain first-hand experience of the ocean and the operation of ships. He had no intention of remaining a sailor. Upon his return to Liverpool, he went into business and in 1858, at the age of twenty-one, he became a partner with Philip Nelson, a friend of his father. The firm of shipowners and insurance brokers was called Nelson, Ismay, and Company. Nelson retired five years later, in 1863, and the new firm of T. H. Ismay and Company came into being.

By then, Thomas Ismay was owner or part owner of dozens of world-ranging ships, some of which flew the flag of a company called the White Star Line of Packets. Packet ships originated with the post office. They carried the mail, always travelling on an established route on a published schedule—something that seems obvious today but was unusual in the mid-1800s. The line had been around since 1845, trading mostly with Australia. Like many shipping firms of the day, its owners were faced with two innovations that would forever change travel on the oceans: wooden ships were giving way to iron ships, and sails were giving way to steam engines, resulting in bigger and faster ships. Thomas Ismay would be an agent of those changes, which would precipitate an unprecedented magnitude of disaster—disaster that Thomas and his son Bruce would both experience.

The transition to iron and steam was expensive and difficult, and the White Star Line's owners chose a bad time to attempt the change. The Royal Bank of Liverpool failed in 1867, and Henry Wilson, the White Star Line's principal shareholder, was bankrupted. He was forced to divest himself of the money-losing firm. Never one to miss an opportunity, young Thomas Ismay purchased the name, flag, and goodwill of the defunct company at fire-sale prices, with the plan to eventually succeed where Wilson had failed—by acquiring passenger steamships to operate on the crowded but lucrative North Atlantic. The market was dominated at that time by Cunard, a company started by the visionary Samuel Cunard of Halifax, Nova Scotia.

At that time, Thomas Ismay's cousin, Henry Metcalfe, passed the requirements for the British Board of Trade certificate for second mate. On April 23, 1867, at the age of nineteen, Metcalfe became qualified to serve as an officer on an ocean-going ship registered anywhere in the British Empire.

A year later, on March 21, 1868, Thomas Ismay inaugurated his new business by dispatching to Melbourne the 750-ton iron sailing ship *Explorer*.[1] By this time, the total sailing tonnage of his firm amounted to nearly 40,000 tons—between thirty and forty ships—engaged in trading with Australia, California, the west coast of South America, the River Plate in Argentina, India, the West Indies, and Mexico. On board as second mate of the *Explorer* was his cousin Henry Metcalfe. As Ismay had benefitted from family connections, he did his duty by seeing that his cousin did also. The voyage was auspicious for both of them.

Thomas Ismay was ambitious and shrewd. He wasn't satisfied to own shares of wooden sailing ships. While he was happy enough to carry goods to and from Australia as long as it was profitable, his real vision was for taking emigrants to America. There was a rising tide of migration to the New World and Ismay saw a lot of opportunity. Though he was reasonably wealthy by this time, building ships of the size and sophistication he wanted would take some major financing and dealmaking.

He already had a business relationship with German-born financier Gustav Schwabe, an astute and generous Liverpool merchant who had no children and who chose to pour his energy and fortune into his nieces and nephews and the arts. He had helped Ismay with the financing for the White Star Line purchase. Schwabe's nephew Gustav Wolff was the junior partner in a Belfast shipbuilding firm with Edward Harland, whom Schwabe had also helped to get into his business. Harland and Wolff was facing severe financial difficulties because of a couple of bad deals and it had a partially completed vessel whose owner had recently declared bankruptcy. The ship was available and Ismay required more vessels to grow his business. Schwabe provided the financing and Ismay soon received his first vessel in what would be a long association with Harland and Wolff. They named the 600-ton iron barque *Broughton* after Schwabe's Liverpool home, Broughton Hall.

A barque was a common type of large sailing ship in the days of sail, with three or more masts carrying big, puffy sails that stretched from side to side across the ship. A barque was square-rigged, as opposed to modern recreational sailboats that are fore-and-aft–rigged, with the sails oriented along the length of the vessel. A 300-ton barque was small, a 600-tonner was respectable, and a 2,000-ton barque was enormous. They were ideal for going to and from Australia, but were not suitable for the emigrant trade on the North Atlantic. However, Thomas Ismay had cemented a vital business relationship. Over a game of billiards with Schwabe and his nephew, the three worked out a deal whereby Schwabe would provide the funding for Ismay to turn the White Star Line into a steamship company. There was one proviso, to which Ismay agreed: Harland and Wolff would build the ships.

On March 20, 1869, Henry Metcalfe walked aboard the barque *Explorer*. He was the newly minted chief officer of the ship, bound again for Melbourne. Ten days earlier, he had earned his First Mate's certificate, making him second in command to the captain. Unlike previous trips, this one would be less auspicious.

Six weeks out, at 3:20 A.M. on April 21, the ship was off the coast of Brazil. Metcalfe had command as officer of the watch, on a clear night with light winds. Suddenly, a ship appeared out of the darkness. They collided with the French barque, *Bretagne*, bound from Buenos Aires to Bordeaux with a general cargo. The *Explorer*'s captain, Edward Trumble, was instantly on deck and in command. Seeing that the smaller wooden French ship was seriously damaged, he ordered the *Explorer* stopped and sent a boat to her assistance. The *Bretagne* sank within ten minutes. An hour and a half later, the rescue boat returned, towing *Bretagne*'s lifeboat with a few survivors aboard, including the captain's wife. The captain, first mate, and three others had perished.

With nine survivors aboard the *Explorer*, Captain Trumble headed towards Brazil. When he got within sight of the coast off the town of Bahia, he put the survivors back into the *Bretagne*'s boat, provided water, provisions, and spare oars, and sent them on their way. He then continued to Melbourne, where he reported the incident.

An inquiry convened, and the evidence against Metcalfe was damning. The man at the helm testified that Metcalfe had been asleep on top of the chicken coop when the collision occurred. It was not the helmsman's fault because he was at the back of the ship behind masts, ropes, and sails, relying on the officer whose job it was to see the oncoming ship and guide the helmsman to avoid a collision. Instead, one of the inquiry's examiners declared, the accident "occurred through the want of care and attention on the part of the chief mate in not keeping a due and vigilant watch."[2] In its decision, the inquiry board found,

> *Mr. Metcalf, the chief officer of the Explorer, to have been*
> *guilty of negligence of duty as officer of the watch on the 21st*
> *of April last. The court therefore suspends Mr. Metcalf's certificate as*
> *first mate (No. 85,180) for a period of twelve calendar mouths from*
> *this date.*[3]

ON JULY 30, 1869, WHILE METCALFE WAS AT SEA RETURNING TO ENGLAND, Harland and Wolff received an order for a new steamship, to be called *Oceanic*. It would be the first of many passenger-ship orders for the White Star Line. The relationship would last for more than sixty years. With shipowner G. Hamilton Fletcher and other investors, Ismay formed the Oceanic Steam Navigation Company on September 6, 1869. Henry Metcalfe's brother, the Reverend Middleton Metcalfe, was a minority shareholder.

Thomas Ismay had apprenticed with Imrie, Tomlinson, and Company. Upon the death of his father in 1870, William Imrie Jr. decided to merge with Ismay. They formed Ismay, Imrie, and Company, with Imrie managing the sailing ships under the name of North Western Shipping Company and Ismay and Fletcher managing the Oceanic

Steam Navigation Company.[4] All the vessels would fly the flag of the White Star Line. That was the name most people would come to recognize. The venture became a huge success and four decades later, when the number of North Atlantic shipping lines had been winnowed down, Cunard and White Star were at the top. After Thomas Ismay died on November 23, 1889, his son Bruce became the managing director. In 1912, he would be a passenger on the only voyage of the White Star Line's newest ship, *Titanic*, securing a seat in one of the scarce lifeboats when the big ship went down.

Henry Metcalfe was ashore until his certificate was reinstated on July 25, 1870, and he returned to sea aboard Ismay's 650-ton barque, *Singapore*. Meanwhile, the SS *Oceanic*, the first of four new ships on order from Harland and Wolff, was launched in August 1870. Three months after that, on November 26, 1870, the *Atlantic* was launched. Many shipping companies at the time used a theme in the names for their vessels. Ismay gave all his liners names ending with "–ic." The first four ships were called *Oceanic*, *Atlantic*, *Baltic*, and *Republic*. That number grew to six when *Adriatic* and *Celtic* were launched in rapid succession.

Oceanic went into service to great acclaim. It was a transformational time for transatlantic passenger travel and for Thomas Ismay. To command his first steamship, he chose Captain Digby Murray, later to become Sir Digby Murray. One of the most significant sailors in the history of the White Star Line, Murray took all the *Oceanic*-class ships on their maiden voyages to New York. He had been at sea since the age of fifteen, when he had gone into the Royal Navy, and had "retired" five years later, going on to a distinguished maritime career.

Under Murray's capable command, the *Oceanic* arrived in New York on March 29, 1871. The next day, the *New York Times* welcomed her:

> *The steam-ship Oceanic, of the White Star Line of steamers between this port and Liverpool arrived here yesterday, beating the time of the City of Washington, sailing the same day, and that of the Cunard steamer Calabria—the latter by some forty hours. The Oceanic elicited the admiration of all who saw her steam up the harbor, as she is the largest steam-ship ever in these waters with the single exception of the Great Eastern.*

The commander of this steamer is Capt. Digby Murray, who remains here as Port Captain. The first officer is Capt. Thompson, who will hereafter command her, and the second officer is Capt. [Hamilton] Perry, who goes back as first officer and will return in command of the next ship, the Atlantic.

The article then sallied forth with a multiplicity of superlatives not limited to: enormous, fastest, extremely fine, comfortable, exceedingly lofty, not to be surpassed, most modern, lavish, very best, and culminating with:

One great feature in connection with the accommodation for the steerage passengers is that there are separate and distinct lavatories below for married men and women, single women and single men, and all necessity for coming on deck is done away with.[5]

An exceedingly lofty ship, indeed. *The Nautical Magazine* later reported that fifty thousand people came out to see the *Oceanic* on its first visit.[6]

Less than three months later, *Atlantic* arrived in New York. Meanwhile, Henry Metcalfe continued his quest to become a master mariner. On February 7, 1872, at the age of twenty-four, he received a Master's certificate, giving him the credentials to be captain of a British Empire ship. Immediately, Ismay signed Metcalfe as captain of the 800-ton barque *Compadre*, and on February 21, 1872, Metcalfe set sail for San Francisco on an eleven-month voyage. Under his command were two officers and a crew of fifteen, including two men from Maryport—Thomas Ismay was a loyal employer of sailors from his hometown.

Two weeks out, at 3:30 A.M. on March 6, Metcalfe lost a crewman when twenty-three-year-old John Flatman fell from high in the rigging and broke his neck.[7] The half hour between 3:00 and 3:30 A.M. was an unlucky time for Metcalfe. He had sunk the *Bretagne* at 3:20 A.M., with the loss of five lives, and

> Twenty-four sounds young to be the captain of a ship, but it's not even as young as New Brunswick native Molly Kool who, in April 1939, became the first North American female holder of a Captain's certificate (and the second in the world). She was twenty-three.

Deserting was an easy way to emigrate to another part of the world, so desertions were common. For example, twelve of the fifteen able seamen aboard the famous tea clipper *Cutty Sark* deserted on a trip to Australia in 1876.

now he had lost another man at 3:30 A.M. Worse was to come.

On July 20, while they were in San Francisco, five of the crew disappeared overnight and did not return. Then, on August 1, three more left, and by August 10, eleven men had deserted. Twelve of his crew of fifteen were gone. He replaced some of them, but they also left—and by the time he got back to Liverpool in January 1873, fourteen had deserted and one man had died, for a 100-percent turnover in the crew.[8]

For Thomas Ismay, the failures of his young cousin were minor compared with the challenges of his new enterprise. Just finding a place for his ships to consistently tie up required tedious and complex negotiations with the Mersey Docks and Harbours Board. White Star Line's ships were finally allocated a berth in 1872 at West Waterloo Dock.[9]

Just days after the *Compadre* had sailed, Ismay heard from Digby Murray the news that he had almost lost the brand new *Republic* in a

Atlantic's sister ship *Republic* loading passengers from the tender *Traffic* at Liverpool circa 1873. *Traffic*'s funnel shows just forward of the mainmast, second from left. (National Maritime Museum, Greenwich, London)

hurricane off New York. Later, Murray would describe it as the worst passage he had ever made across the Atlantic.

We encountered a terrific gale. Our decks were swept, all boats but two were entirely destroyed, the engine room skylight smashed and driven down on top of the cylinders....

Mr. Williams, the second officer, whose pluck and endurance has been beyond all praise, while securing a sail over the fidlay [the entrance to the stoke-hole on deck], great quantities of water having gone down and put out the lee fires, was caught by No. 4 boat as it was dashed a perfect wreck inboard, one of the davits unshipping and coming with it, and crushed against the railing round the funnel.

His left thigh broke a little above the knee; his left ankle was dislocated; we fear some of his ribs broke. We trust the accident may not prove fatal, but time only will tell us; he shows amazing pluck, and is at present doing well. If he does not recover he will be a very great loss to the company, for men like him are very few and far between.[10]

Murray noted that the new ship was now unfit for passengers and suggested returning empty, as the *Atlantic* was to arrive soon and could take their passengers to Liverpool.

Second Officer James Agnew Williams spent several months in hospital in New York and recovered. Ismay was happy to get his star officer back and promoted him to chief officer on the *Celtic*.

DESPITE TWO BLACK MARKS ON METCALFE'S RECORD, ISMAY HIRED HIS cousin back to be an officer on the nineteenth voyage of the *Atlantic*, due to depart for New York on March 20, 1873. Unlike Metcalfe's previous ships, which had a captain and two officers, this vessel had five deck officers, seven engineers, a purser, a doctor, and a chief steward in charge of a staff of nearly forty.

In the *Liverpool Mercury* on February 8, 1873, the regular sailing ad for White Star Line included a new name. Captain Benjamin Gleadell

```
"WHITE STAR LINE"
─────
UNITED STATES MAIL STEAMERS
─────

              Tons         Captain
OCEANIC..........3707 ..........E.J. WATTS BRISTOW
ATLANTIC ........3707 ..........JAMES AGNEW WILLIAMS
BALTIC..............3707 ..........CHARLES W. KENNEDY
REPUBLIC ........3707 ..........BENJAMIN GLEADELL
ADRIATIC ........3888 ..........HAMILTON PERRY
CELTIC ..............3888 ..........W.H. THOMPSON
GERMANIC........ ___        {Building}
BRITANNIC        ___        {Building}
       WEEKLY SERVICE TO NEW YORK
               ─────

Sailing from LIVERPOOL every Thursday and calling at
  Queenstown on Friday to embark Passengers.
The following well-known full powered Steamers are intended
           to sail from Liverpool:—
ATLANTIC .......... FOR NEW YORK ........ Thursday, Feb. 13
REPUBLIC.......... For New York........... Thursday, Feb. 20
ADRIATIC .......... For New York........... Thursday, Feb. 27
BALTIC............... For New York........... Thursday, Mar. 6
CELTIC ............... For New York........... Thursday, Mar. 13
ATLANTIC ......... For New York........... Thursday, Mar. 20
REPUBLIC.......... For New York........... Thursday, Mar. 27
ADRIATIC ......... For New York........... Thursday, April  3
     Returning from NEW YORK every Saturday.
     These steamships afford the very best accommodations to all
classes of passengers, and have accomplished quick and
regular passages between this country and America.
     The staterooms, with saloon and smoking rooms are placed
amidships, and cabin passengers are thus removed from the
noise and motion experienced at the after part of the vessel.
     Passengers are booked to all parts of the States, Canada,
India, etc. at moderate through rates.
     Steerage rates as low as by any other line.
     A surgeon and stewardess carried in each ship.
     Drafts issued on New York for sums not exceeding £10 free.
     Freight payable here or in New York at Shippers' option.
     Loading berth—West Waterloo Dock.
     Saloon passage 18 Guineas and 21 Guineas. Return Tickets
35 Guineas.
     NOTICE—On and after the 1st of July, Saloon Fares will be
£21 and £25. Return Tickets, £40.
     For Freight or Passage apply at the Company's Office, 7,
East India-avenue, London, E.O. ; 19 Broadway, New York ;
and 96, Market-street, Chicago ; in Queenstown to James
Scott & Co. ; or to
          ISMAY, IMRIE, & CO,.
          10. Water-street, Liverpool

The ATLANTIC will sail for New York on Thursday next,
February 13. The Saloon Passengers embark in a steam tender
from the Prince's Landing Stage, at noon.
```

Re-creation of the *Liverpool Mercury* ad from February 8, 1873, advertising the *Atlantic*'s final trip to New York on March 20. It also advertises what turned out to be Captain Williams's only two trips as a White Star Line captain.

had moved from the *Atlantic* to the *Republic*. James Agnew Williams would take the *Atlantic* out on the weekly sailing to New York, departing February 13. The Ships were on a five-week rotation, which meant Captain Williams's second departure for New York would be on March 20.

Metcalfe was now third in command, after Captain James Williams—whom Metcalfe observed to be walking with a limp which required the use of a cane—and Chief Officer William Kidley. Subordinate to Metcalfe were Third Officer Cornelius Brady and Fourth Officer John Brown.

Brady, who was nearly three years older than Metcalfe, had received his Master's certificate in November 1870, and had already been captain of a steamship sailing out of Liverpool. Like many officers, he was willing to take the demotion to get with one of the crack Atlantic passenger lines. Brown also had a Master's certificate, which he received prior to joining the *Atlantic*, and had been ten years at sea, serving as an officer for three and a half years. Metcalfe was younger and less experienced than Brady, who was a very capable officer, as events would prove. Not only had Ismay hired his cousin back; he'd wedged him into the pecking order ahead of a more experienced man, despite Metcalfe's poor record.

Born in Cork, Ireland, in 1840, Captain Williams was the son of David Williams, of a Welsh family with a long association with the sea. He received his First Mate certification on Jan. 3, 1862, and his Extra Master's certification on Dec 17, 1871. He served his early apprenticeship in vessels of the Guion Line out of Liverpool. He had risen to be an officer and captain of several of their ships, including the *Manhattan, Nevada, Wisconsin,* and *Colorado.* In 1867 he married Elizabeth Uttley and in 1873 they had three children. By then, Williams was thirty-three years old and had earned the highest certificate of competency a British mariner could attain.

On departure day, some crew shuffling took place and John Firth came over from the *Republic* to replace Kidley as Chief Officer of the *Atlantic,* arriving at 9:00 A.M. It would be only his second voyage with the White Star Line. Previously, he had commanded ships on the Mediterranean and India trade routes. At forty-three, he was the oldest of the officers.

On its nineteenth crossing, the *Atlantic* had a captain about to start his second voyage, a chief officer on his first, a fourth officer on his second trip, and second and third officers on their third. Nobody among the deck officers could claim to have an intimate knowledge of the *Atlantic* and its ways—or of one another. The relationship between the captain and the chief engineer, who had joined the ship as third engineer and was also on his second voyage as chief, would have especially significant consequences.

CHAPTER 2

A First-Class Vessel

*Many gentlemen on board, who have crossed the ocean repeatedly,
declared they had never seen anything comparable with it before, and
that it really initiates a new era in ocean navigation.*

Rev. A. A. *Willits*
The Atlantic Extra

Fortunately, some of the crew members were familiar with the
ship. John Foxley, the chief engineer, was on his seventeenth
voyage on the *Atlantic*, his second as chief engineer. Unlike many
of the crew, the stewards were valuable representatives of the line,
responsible for the customer experience, so the company hung onto
the best of them. Among this select group was Irving Stuttaford, a
twenty-one-year-old Canadian from Kingston, Ontario, who had gone
to sea at age sixteen, probably on the Great Lakes, after being orphaned.

Of the more than 150 on the crew, there were also three women,
who served as stewardesses. Among their number was Frances McNally,
known to everybody as Fanny. She was a widow, working to support
her children. With very slim employment options, she'd had to leave
them at home in Belfast in the care of her mother.

By the spring of 1873, Thomas Ismay had six steamships plying the
North Atlantic, with two more under construction. Four decades had
passed since Samuel Cunard had inaugurated transatlantic scheduled

steamship service. The benefits of travelling on a steamship were enormous, not the least of which was being able to depart and arrive at a more-or-less predictable time. Now, expectant relatives could be waiting at the dock as their loved ones arrived, united again after years of separation. For $33 a head, an immigrant who had experienced modest financial success in North America could buy a prepaid certificate and send for family members. Ismay's ships were lowering prices and raising the possibilities.[1]

The *Atlantic* was a state-of-the-art vessel, the second built for the Oceanic Steam Navigation Company. The very latest in steam technology, the *Oceanic* class vessels each had two engines driving a three-bladed propeller. That soon changed to four blades, as Harland and Wolff continued to improve on their revolutionary designs. Four huge steel masts towered above the decks. Though they were capable of carrying a vast spread of sail, the *Atlantic*, like all the *Oceanic*-class ships, was first and foremost a steamship, powered by coal that heated water into steam to drive the engines. Previous steamers had essentially been sailing ships with an engine and a paddlewheel on each side, but these new designs from Harland and Wolff had the hulls of modern motor ships. Gone were the cumbersome paddlewheels and the rounded hulls that enabled the ship to lean while under sail; their replacements were flat-bottomed, straight-sided ships driven by propellers. The sails that supplemented the engines would be gone from the next generation of ships.

Little did Ismay or anybody realize that steamships had set into motion something that would have serious, if not drastic, consequences for the earth. The exhaust from coal-burning ships began the first large-scale assault on the earth's atmosphere, as vast amounts of coal went up in smoke and ascended to the heavens, slowly changing climates and heating the atmosphere. The steamship was the first motorized means of transportation devised by humans, soon leading to other big polluters like trains, automobiles, and aircraft.

From Ismay's perspective, the future was bright. Ever-increasing numbers of Europeans wanted to get to the New World and he planned to expand his company as fast as the workers in Belfast could build ships for him.

But what was a trip on these vessels like? In much of the writing about ships of this period the words "luxury" and "luxurious" tend to pop up. Yet to call any steamship of the 1870s luxurious would be a stretch.

Even though the *New York Times* may have gushed about the *Oceanic*, saying, "These steam-ships have been designed to afford the very best accommodation to all classes of passengers," they never used the word luxurious. What was the voyage like for the top class of traveller, those in saloon class?

The *Atlantic* had steam heating in the passenger areas, for the steerage as well as the saloon-class passengers. It was a big step forward. Instead of having to find a stove or fireplace to sit by, passengers received heat that was delivered by pipes to all parts of the ship where they were domiciled. That was the upside. The downside was that the pipes sometimes expanded and contracted, which caused clanking and rumbling. There was no thermostat with which to set a desired temperature; somebody turned a valve and the steam heating was either on or off. Then there was the rumble from the engines, which had been placed amidships where the rolling and pitching of the ship provided the least inconvenience. However, all ships rolled and pitched, and so did these.

Perhaps the biggest improvement of these vessels was the use of propellers instead of paddlewheels, although the props had a lot of teething problems. They made the ships more manoeuvrable, more efficient, more economical—all good things, of course. But, these benefits accrued to the company. Did they improve the trip for the passengers? Some experienced travellers of the day still preferred paddlewheels, which made the ships more stable. Propeller-driven vessels had a tendency to roll from side to side because they were narrow, and the propellers caused them to vibrate. Improvements like bilge keels were still three decades away and stabilizers much further in the future.

During winter, passengers were stuck indoors most of the time. In the spring, especially off the Grand Banks of Newfoundland, the droning of the foghorn went on for days as the ships tried to avoid colliding with other vessels or running over fishing boats while feeling their way through the fog. And, of course, there was the danger of icebergs, as those travelling on the *Titanic* would eventually discover. By any measure, travel aboard these steamships was certainly not a cruise, although it may have been better during in the summer months before the August gales or autumn hurricane season moved in. (And remember that ships received no hurricane forecasts in those days.)

Almost everybody in the steerage, as it was called, was an emigrant. The term "steerage" originated from the days of sailing ships when the cheapest fare placed you on the lowest deck in the stern, through which the steering lines ran to connect the rudder to the wheel on the deck above. One of the questions that the official inspecting the *Atlantic* had to answer was, "Are the wheels and chains so guarded as to prevent injury to passengers?"[2]

Unlike the steerage folk, saloon-class passengers slept in cabins. The *Atlantic* was built to carry 952 in the steerage and somewhere around 84 saloon-class passengers. Saloon class and those travelling therein gave the ship a certain panache, but the bread and butter of the business was the transporting of emigrants to the New World, almost exclusively to the United States in the case of the White Star Line. They might get almost three times the fare for saloon-class passengers, but there were twenty-three times as many steerage passengers aboard on this journey—and they could carry far more bodies per cubic foot in the steerage. The densely populated steerage was about eighty-five percent filled while the cabins were less than half full.

The company had unused capacity to fill so, with the coming of the fifth and sixth White Star Line ships, *Adriatic* and *Celtic*, they advertised "superior accommodation for a limited number of second cabin passengers."[3] The names soon changed to first, second, and third class, to allow for this new middle group and to get away from the historically negative connotation associated with the steerage.

The saloon passengers had more room to move about during their waking hours. Outdoors, they had some private deck space so they didn't have to associate with the lower classes; the interior walls and floors were more attractive, with marble, carpets, and the like, and the food was better. There was a printed list of who was among their group so they could get to know one another, and they were generally more comfortable.

Their sleeping hours were spent in a cabin instead of a dormitory. The *Atlantic* had two-, three-, and four-bed staterooms that also contained a sink with hot and cold water, but no toilet. For that, they had to walk down a corridor to one of the eight toilets that could be a significant distance away. That meant walking through public spaces, which were often occupied until well after midnight. Obviously, this was not an option for the women. At night, they would reach under the bed for the chamber pot.

Saloon passengers ate at a long table that was shared with many others, but they were not expected to provide their own dishes and cutlery like the steerage folk had been obliged to do until just a year before.[4] Everybody dressed for dinner, which consisted of things like roast beef and was served by stewards, unlike the steerage passengers who had to line up. Saloon passengers had access to a bar and a smoking room and there was a piano, a library, and two fireplaces. The ladies had their own saloon, to which they were often expected to retire after dinner, while the men relaxed with their cigars and port.

Steerage passengers lived in a large open area, part of which was divided into closet-like compartments, each containing fifteen bunks—five together on three levels. The bunks were two feet wide and they abutted one another, with a four-inch-high board separating them. These passengers had to enter the bed from the foot and crawl towards the head.[5] This was considered an improvement over past configurations. Like the saloon passengers, they had to share a toilet. In their case, if the ship was full, each person shared a toilet with forty-five other people, whereas the saloon passengers shared a toilet with half that many.

So although it would be fair to say that in some ways the saloon passengers experienced luxury according to the standards of the day, they were a small percentage of the overall complement of passengers.

In addition to the steerage and saloon passengers, there was another group aboard—the officers and crew. On occasion in the past, crew members and steerage passengers had had to endure exceptionally bad treatment at the hands of unscrupulous shipowners and captains. In the nineteenth century, the British government enacted legislation for their protection. The Passenger Act spelled out in detail how emigrants on ships were to be treated and the Merchant Shipping Act did the same for the crew, as well as laying out the requirements for the ship and its operation. All of this was administered by the Board of Trade, which certified mariners, inspected ships, and generally kept an eye on anything having to do with merchant shipping.

Saloon-class travellers did not require protection. They had money, but most of the emigrants had to save, sometimes for years, to scrape up the $30 a head for the transatlantic passage. After they had sold everything they owned, some had enough for a new start in America. Those with assets converted them into gold, usually in the form of British gold sovereigns, which consisted of one quarter-ounce of gold in a coin the size of a Canadian or American 25-cent piece. They sewed them into their clothing. Whatever garment held the money was not removed for the whole voyage. William Westwell, a printer from East Lancashire, was reported to have had £30 in gold with him, and travelling companions William Clegg and James Lee had £20 apiece.[6]

Before the *Atlantic* departed Liverpool, it was subjected to a thorough inspection. From stem-post to gudgeon, William Geary, assistant emigration officer for the Port of Liverpool, examined everything required to get the passengers and crew safely to New York.[7] The condition of the ship and its machinery, fuel, provisions, and emergency equipment, including firefighting gear, lifeboats, distress rockets, and floatation devices, all received precise inspection.

Like all ships of the day, the *Atlantic* did not have enough lifeboats. There were ten, ranging in size from nineteen- to thirty-two feet long.[8] The biggest scandal in the greatest transatlantic steamship disaster—the other White Star Line ship, *Titanic*—was that it had been woefully underequipped with lifeboats and fifteen hundred people died needlessly. The law stipulated how much lifeboat capacity a ship was required to provide. It was not based on one seat per passenger carried; it was based on the volume of carrying space aboard, with one hundred cubic feet equating to one ton. The law said that a ship must carry, not boats or seats, but "cubic feet" of lifeboat space. It was assumed that a passenger ship would never be able to save every passenger in the event of a disaster—there was simply not enough space aboard for all those boats.

The ten boats on the *Atlantic* totalled 5,778 cubic feet, which was well over the 3,600 feet that the law specified. It was estimated that these boats could carry five hundred to six hundred people in fine weather and four hundred in rough weather, enough to save about half those aboard if there were a full load.[9] It is unclear what was supposed to happen if the weather changed from calm to rough after they took to the boats. Did they jettison some of the occupants?

Dr. William Spooner, medical officer at Liverpool for the inspection of passengers and passenger ships, inspected everything having to do with the health of passengers—things such as toilets, ventilation, medical supplies, and food provisions.[10] Adolphus Large, the shore steward for White Star Line, received the provisions from the victualling firm of William Rogers and Company, and saw to their stowage aboard.[11] For this trip, the *Atlantic* carried provisions sufficient to feed 50 saloon passengers, 700 steerage, and 143 crew for thirty-two days. It also carried fifteen thousand gallons of fresh water and had the capacity to distill sixteen hundred gallons every twenty-four hours. In addition to the needs of those aboard, water was required for creating steam to drive the engines. It was constantly recycled after it exited the cylinders, but there was wastage, so the eleven boilers had to be topped up to keep the engines operating.

The furnaces that generated the heat to make the steam also had to be fed. The trimmers carried the coal from the storage bunkers to the firemen, who shovelled it into the furnaces. It was not uncommon for 350 baskets, each containing fifty to seventy-five pounds of coal, to be used in a four-hour shift.[12]

Richards, Power, and Company of Swansea, Wales, supplied sixty-three railway carloads of coal for sixteen days' steaming.[13] The trip to New York normally took ten to twelve days. Coal was delivered to the ship while it was tied at the West Waterloo Dock and later when anchored in the Mersey River off Prince's Landing Stage.[14] Barge-like vessels called lighters or flats, with names like *Eleanor*, *Rose*, and *Amelia*, delivered in excess of one hundred tons each per load. Their captains lived aboard with their families to keep an eye on their valuable cargoes and to always be available when called upon. One after another, they tied up to the side of the ship and remained for six to eight hours

A steamship at anchor (circa 1905) while receiving coal from lighters, showing the manner in which the *Atlantic* was refuelled. (COURTESY TOM LYNSKEY)

while a dozen men filled and passed up baskets, each containing fifty or more pounds of coal.[15] White Star Line workers took the baskets aboard through doors in the side of the ship's hull, starting at the after bunkers and moving forward.[16] Eight hundred forty-seven tons of coal went aboard to supplement what remained from the previous trip.[17] That required almost thirty-five hundred baskets to be filled aboard the flats, passed up the ladders, carried to the bunkers and dumped—a slow, dirty, labour-intensive job that was continuously occurring with a ship or two somewhere in Liverpool harbour. For what would be the ship's final trip, the *Atlantic* started coaling on the morning of March 13, 1873, and completed just before midnight on the evening of March 19—a full week.[18]

A ton of Aberdare South Wales coal occupied forty-three cubic feet; a ton of Lancashire coal took up forty-five cubic feet.[19] Both kinds were used. On the last voyage, the *Atlantic* carried 967 tons, which occupied a shade over forty-two thousand cubic feet of space on the ship—enough to fill two large two-storey houses.

There was no fuel gauge to track consumption. Every basketful had to be counted as it was carried from the bunkers to the furnaces, and marked on a tally board in the boiler room. Each day, the chief engineer read the board, updated his records, and gave the captain a report of the amount remaining. To make that report accurate, it was essential that he know the amount aboard upon departure. It was also essential that every basket be accounted for. That was expecting a lot from overworked, unmotivated men who trudged back and forth hour after hour from the bunkers to the furnaces with basket after basket, tolerating often unbearable dust and heat.

To complicate matters, coal was used in places besides the boilers feeding the engines—the galley stoves, the water distillers, the ship's heating system, the "donkey boiler" that provided steam to the small engines used to hoist cargo aboard—some while the ship was still in port. It all had to be accounted for if the captain were to have an accurate report upon which to base his decisions.

Chapter 3

The Leaving of Liverpool

Our exit was attended with every prospect of a successful voyage as we left old England's happy shores amidst gentle zephyrs and genial sunbeams shining on a calm sea. We sailed gently down the channel and finally took our last lingering look at the distant shore, leaving behind us in obscurity the land of our birth.[1]

Thomas Moffatt
Steerage passenger

At the Prince's Landing Stage, the passengers boarded the steam tender *Traffic*—in service between 1872 and 1896—and were taken to the ship as it lay anchored in the stream. Young couples like James Bateman and his wife, Rosa, went aboard, as did William Glenfield and his new wife, Annie. He had done well in America and had returned to England for their wedding. Thirty-seven-year-old Henry Dry, a bricklayer from Basingstoke, went without his family. His wife, Jane, was to come later with the children when he got established and had money to send for their passage. Many of the unaccompanied men, like master carpenter David Boswell, were single and looking to improve their lot in a new land.

After W. C. Reeves, the emigration officer for the Port of Liverpool, had given his final approval,[2] the *Atlantic* departed Liverpool on its nineteenth voyage on March 20, 1873. There were 615 passengers

Passengers boarding the tender *Traffic* at the Prince's Landing Stage in Liverpool. The *Atlantic* is in the background at upper right. (COURTESY TOM LYNSKEY)

aboard. The vessel left Liverpool just after 2:00 P.M. and entered the Irish Sea, rounding Holyhead and skirting Ireland's south coast, en route to Queenstown, Ireland. With fair winds, the captain ordered the sails set. They reached Queenstown—known today by its ancient name of Cobh (pronounced Cove)—at nine o'clock the next morning.

They dropped anchor and picked up another 175 passengers, including Mary Ryan and her nine children, Annie Nicholson with her three, Mary Tracy with four, and Mary Shea with two.[3] Their husbands would have gone ahead, perhaps even by years, depending on their financial situations. After the tender *Jackal* had ferried them out to the ship, Captain Williams sent a message ashore to be forwarded by undersea cable to Liverpool:

REPORT *of Captain Williams*

White Star Line of Mail Steamers, Steamship "Atlantic"
Queenstown, 21 March, 1873

Gentlemen:
The "Atlantic" passed the Rock at 2:35 P.M. yesterday, and Roche's
Point at 8:45 A.M.; had moderate southeast wind down, with clear
weather. Passengers all well; engines working well; coals better; aver-
aged 40 revolutions down. Will pass Roche's Point outwards about
10:30 A.M.

Messrs. Ismay, Imrie & Co.
(signed) J. A. Williams[4]

They left Queenstown at
10:30 A.M. and commenced the
trip across the Atlantic Ocean.
G. W. Cann, of the White Star
Line passenger department, later
reported that there were 790 passengers aboard, of whom 32 were
saloon class—mostly Americans
returning home from travelling in

Steam tender *Jackal* taking passengers to a steamship at Queenstown. (COURTESY TOM LYNSKEY)

Europe. The rest were steerage class, the majority being emigrants
heading to a new life in a new world. There were 673 adults, 90 children, and 27 infants.[5] Officers and crew amounted to 152,[6] which took
the total to 942. Up to 14 stowaways were later discovered, and it is
believed that 2 babies were born along the way, based on comments
made by survivors to newspapers.[7] Adding those in brings the total
to 956 souls aboard when the ship arrived off Nova Scotia. (For more
information about those aboard, see Appendix D, page 243.)

As Ireland slowly faded behind the stern, passengers and crew
settled into their shipboard routines. There were two more days of
fair weather, with a steady wind from the east. With all sails set and
the engines humming, *Atlantic* carried its passengers, crew, and cargo
on their way. Years later, steerage passenger Thomas Moffatt would
record an account of his experiences aboard the *Atlantic*. Of this portion
of the trip, he wrote, "The sea remained unchanged, everything went
on pleasantly and delightful as fine weather and fair breezes tend to
make ocean life enjoyable."[8]

The next day, Saturday, March 22, Chief Engineer John Foxley gave the captain a written report detailing the amount of coal on board. Knowing how much coal remained was a matter of life and death on a steamship carrying almost a thousand people on the North Atlantic in winter. The White Star Line required chief engineers on their ships to report to the captain daily on the amount remaining. Foxley's report noted that 120 tons remained from the previous trip from New York, and 847 tons of new stock had been loaded in Liverpool. Eighty tons had been used in port before departure, mostly to provide power to load the cargo, but also to provide heat and cooking for the few aboard and to move the ship within the harbour.[9]

The next day, with winter barely over, the weather began to deteriorate. It was, after all, the stormiest time of year on the ever-stormy North Atlantic. Thus began what the captain called, "three very severe days' weather."[10] There was nothing to do but barge ahead across the ocean. The ship was built to handle it.

Thomas Moffatt later wrote,

> It seemed as if we were alternately on the mountain top and then in the valley beneath. There was many a longing look and wishful sigh for home. Such remarks as "We shall never reach our destination" and others of a similar character were often uttered during this very depressing condition. Days became tedious and nights became restless and irksome, and especially so by being compelled to remain for days below deck. The decks became impassable by the waves which were continually going over them so that we had to remain without food some time. Fear and dismay were seen on the countenances of all....
>
> One or two persons became temporarily deranged, and some of the crew received injuries, so that for three or four days we experienced the inconveniences, the intense anxiety, and dangers attending a storm at sea.[11]

The storm also meant the ship was unable to maintain the speed required to stay on schedule, even though fuel was being consumed at an unprecedented rate.

The weather had turned sour so quickly that some of the sails got torn before they could be taken in. A huge wave came aboard and smashed Lifeboat #4. On Wednesday, the 26th, the ship travelled only 118 miles, one-third the progress of the previous Saturday. At some point along the way, on the 25th or 26th, the salt fish and potatoes, which were stored on deck, got washed overboard.[12] That may sound innocent enough, but it was the period of Lent; Friday would soon arrive and there were a lot of Roman Catholics aboard who were expecting fish. Within a little more than a week, some would be telling newspapers that the White Star Line did not have sufficient provisions aboard.

There was no further mention of coal reports from Foxley until Friday, March 28, when he reported that the coal supply was down to 319 tons.[13] That was a huge drop from the 887 tons they'd supposedly had when leaving Liverpool. Williams was shocked. It was low-quality coal, Foxley complained, and the ship was gobbling it up at an alarming rate.

The first thought that went through Williams's mind was, "What if worse comes to worst and we have to refuel?" The logical choice was Halifax, Nova Scotia, which was getting closer by the day. It was the known backup for US-bound ships under stress. (It still is. On January 4, 2020, the Cunard liner *Queen Mary 2* put in with a medical emergency while en route to Southampton.) No White Star Line ship had ever had to go there, but Williams tucked the option away in his mind and started issuing orders to cut back.[14] He told Chief Steward Hugh Christie to have the cooking fires lit as late as they could get away with and put out as early as he could. The next day—Saturday—he told Foxley to reduce consumption to as little as he could manage, leaving it to his discretion. The sails were put back up. The stress was taking a toll on Williams and he was having trouble sleeping.[15] On Sunday, he broached with Chief Officer Firth the idea of going into Halifax.

On Monday morning he told Foxley to get the opinions of his engineers regarding how much coal remained and not to just rely on his own judgement. Williams was probably inclined to take a look himself, but was unable to do so because of the injury he had sustained on the *Republic*, which continued to limit his mobility. Foxley reported back between noon and 1:00 P.M. Williams was conferring with Firth in the chart room. He presented Williams with a slip of paper, which the captain read and passed to the chief officer, while commenting how bad it would be for the *Atlantic* to be the first White Star Line ship to go into Halifax after having run so successfully during eighteen voyages.

"Better sure than sorry," Firth replied.[16]

"That is so," said Williams. "The chances of getting into New York successfully must be taken against the chances of finding ourselves off Nantucket Shoals without coal."

He grilled Foxley, asking if he could have made an error in his calculations. Foxley replied that there were 127 tons aboard and that was it. By now they were, as the captain put it, "under the Nova Scotia coast." It was almost calm, and with the barometer falling, that meant there was more windy weather in store. He asked for opinions and the others felt they had no choice but to divert to Halifax.

That settled it. He issued the order and the ship turned north towards Halifax, 170 miles away.

WITH THE DECISION MADE, THERE WAS NO REASON TO CONTINUE SKIMPING on the coal. Get to Halifax, get refuelled, and get going as quickly as possible. It was a simple and obvious plan. The captain ordered full steam ahead. In the boiler room, baskets of coal were trundled to the furnaces and the engineer on duty pushed the firemen to pick up the pace as they shovelled the coal into the *Atlantic*'s twenty furnaces, the sweat dripping off their grimy chins. The fires responded, heating more water in the ten boilers, driving up the pressure of the steam that went to the two engines.[17] Soon, the propeller's four blades were throwing the water astern with a renewed sense of purpose. By mid-afternoon, everything was humming as the big ship drove her way through the bright white waves breaking along her left side.

Dinner was served as the darkness came and the passengers started thinking of sleep. They would awaken in the morning in the New World! It was not New York but it was still exciting. In the saloon, the cabin-class men retired with their cigars and glasses of port. Children in steerage were put to bed, after which people talked quietly, played dominoes or chess, mended clothing, and prayed for a safe arrival.

Up on the bridge, Chief Officer Firth shared the final watch of the day with Third Officer Brady. When midnight came, they handed command of the ship over to Second Officer Metcalfe and Fourth Officer Brown. Brady repeated to Metcalfe the orders from the captain: keep a lookout for loose ice, and in the event of seeing a fixed light to get it two points on the port bow—approximately their 11 o'clock position— and call the captain immediately. Under no circumstances was he to be called later than 3:00 A.M.

The captain returned to the chart room to update the *Atlantic*'s position. He determined that they were forty-eight miles from the Sambro light-

Men shovelling coal into the furnaces. While these men were often referred to as "stokers," the White Star Line called them "firemen." (COURTESY TOM LYNSKEY)

house, whose beam separated the harbour approaches from the forbidding rocks of the Sambro Ledges, an area of granite islands and reefs to the left, west of the route into Halifax Harbour. The need for the light was so obvious that on day one of the first session of the General Assembly of Nova Scotia—October 2, 1758—an act had been passed to build the lighthouse. It was paid for with £1,000 from the duties paid on alcoholic beverages, and a tax on vessels entering the harbour. Today, it is the oldest operating lighthouse in the Western Hemisphere, sitting atop Sambro Island.[18]

Captain Williams's intention was that when the light was sighted and he was awakened, he would stop the ship and wait until daylight to fire a blue rocket into the sky that would call for a harbour pilot. Only one of the five navigating officers, Third Officer Brady, had ever been in Halifax Harbour. Even in daylight, he would not have been able to thread the needle among the unseen rocks and shoals, having to first line the ship up to the left of Portuguese Shoal, squeeze between Neverfail and Lichfield Shoals, steer clear of Mars Rock, stay off the Lighthouse Bank, and realign the ship to get around Georges Island without striking Middle Ground or Ives Knoll.

Williams knew he could count on several pilots to be cruising the harbour mouth waiting for a ship to hail. At that time, there were ninety qualified pilots providing service in and out of Halifax Harbour. He ordered his steward to bring him a cup of cocoa at 2:40 A.M. and retired to a cot in the chart room, behind the man at the helm.

The ship was now under the command of Second Officer Henry Metcalfe, the senior officer of the watch.

IT WAS A LARGE, MODERN STEAMSHIP THAT METCALFE, NOW ON HIS THIRD trip as second officer, was guiding through the darkness in the pre-dawn hours of April 1, 1873. The *Explorer* had been 750 tons but the *Atlantic* was more than 3,700 tons. It was 437 feet long and 41 feet wide. When Metcalfe stood on the bridge directing the ship's way forward, he was nearly five stories above the surface of the water. The bridge was outdoors, without a roof or shelter of any kind, and was the highest part of the ship except for the masts.

Ships of that period had not evolved to the point where they had buildings atop one another the way modern cruise ships are built. The deck on top of the hull had two single-storey buildings stretching along 150 feet of the amidships area. They shared one roof, which provided an extra deck for saloon passengers above the main deck. There were two smaller deckhouses forward and two aft of this duplex building.

The passengers, officers, and crew were berthed in the hull, which had over three hundred round windows called scuttles—today they are called portholes—running from stem to stern along two decks, as well as thick glass skylights inserted into the main deck flooring to provide additional light. On top of the large deckhouse was a smaller building that contained the chart room and the wheelhouse. In front of and above the wheelhouse stood the bridge. While the quartermaster at the helm looked forward to steer the ship, he could only see the bottom of the bridge. He received orders from the officer on the bridge through a speaking tube.

Despite the biting cold, Metcalfe spent the entire watch on the bridge, perhaps to prevent himself from dozing off again like he had on the *Explorer*, but also, no doubt, because he expected to see the light at any moment. There were no instruments to help them see through the darkness, so lookouts were posted throughout the *Atlantic* to watch for other vessels or anything that might endanger the ship. On the other side of the bridge from Metcalfe was Patrick Kiely, who took his position on the starboard, or right, side of the bridge at 2:00 A.M. He had been to Halifax on a Cunard ship the previous May. About ninety feet forward of the bridge was Joseph Carroll on the number one deckhouse, where he also started at 2:00 A.M. The most forward of the lookouts, he had also been to Halifax four years previously. In the stern was Quartermaster Charles Roylance. He was stationed in a building called the aft wheelhouse.

The *Atlantic* was equipped with steam-assisted steering, recently invented by John McFarlane Gray, and built by the Vauxhall Foundry in Liverpool. It was first used aboard the SS *City of Brussels* of the Inman Line.[19] Such big ships would have been extremely difficult to handle using the traditional manual method of moving the rudder. Having power steering meant that the helm no longer had to be located far astern above the rudder. For backup, there was a traditional steering mechanism in the stern and a quartermaster—in this case, Roylance— was kept on duty in case of failure of the steam system. He also served as a stern lookout.

In addition to the officers and lookouts on the *Atlantic* that night, another fifteen of the crew were on duty cleaning the decks and other parts of the ship.[20] Nearly one thousand people caused a lot of wear and tear throughout the day, so every night a squad went to work making everything—well, shipshape.

As the lookouts looked, the steersman steered, the swabbers swabbed, and the captain slept, something was happening to the *Atlantic* unbeknownst to those tasked with ensuring her safe passage to Halifax.

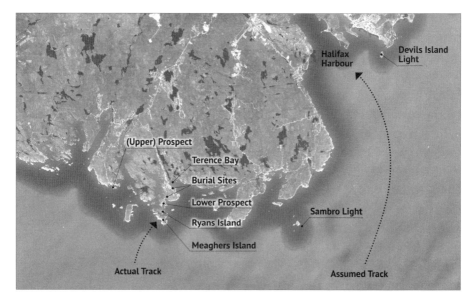

Labels on image: Halifax Harbour; Devils Island Light; (Upper) Prospect; Terence Bay; Burial Sites; Lower Prospect; Sambro Light; Ryans Island; Meaghers Island; Actual Track; Assumed Track

Atlantic's lookouts assumed the ship was on course to enter Halifax Harbour; in fact, the current had pushed the ship some twelve miles off course to the left, much closer to land than anyone realized.

Powerful currents sweep the coastline of Nova Scotia, fuelled by the immense amount of water running in and out of the Bay of Fundy. Twice a day, the tides raise and then lower the water level the height of a six-storey building, tearing at the shoreline and gouging away anything that is not a granite cliff or island. Now they had quietly but relentlessly carried the *Atlantic* sideways until it was no longer pointing into the great funnel that narrows to Halifax Harbour. Instead, the ship was aimed at the wide Chebucto Peninsula that pushes out between the harbour and St. Margarets Bay.

The vessel was twelve miles off course and the land was closer than anybody realized—or was willing to believe.

CHAPTER 4

THE CAPTAIN'S COCOA

Oh, my God! What will my poor children do? [1]

> *Fanny McNally*
> *Stewardess*

Captain Williams did not get to sleep when he intended that night, thanks to a curious journalist. Cyrus Fisher had decided to visit and quiz him about the ship and how they had become so low on coal that this major diversion was necessary. Fisher finally left around half past midnight and Williams lay down on the cot in the chart room, fully clothed, within talking distance of the man at the wheel. His plan was to sleep for a couple of hours, then drink his cocoa and smoke a cigar before starting to give orders at three o'clock.

He awakened at 2:00 A.M., got up and took a look around, and then went back to sleep.

The man at the wheel was Quartermaster Robert Thomas. He had been to Halifax several times in the past and knew that they were approaching a low, rocky coast that was difficult to see at night. He took the wheel at 2:00 A.M., thirteen hours after they had diverted to Halifax. The Nova Scotia shoreline was not far away and he later claimed to have suggested to Second Officer Metcalfe that they were closing in on it. Metcalfe brushed him off. They had not seen the Sambro light;

how could they be nearing land? Neither of them knew that the ship was now dramatically off course, and the light, instead of being ahead and to the left, was now directly off the right side of the ship.

It was close enough to be seen but none of the lookouts saw it.

Thomas later claimed to have argued with Metcalfe that they ought to slow down; Metcalfe, he said, was hesitant. When asked later if Metcalfe had the authority to slow the ship down, the captain replied, "Every officer in charge has full power to change course or reverse the engines and stop the ship in case of danger without referring to the captain."[2]

Williams also said that no officer would tolerate such impertinence from a quartermaster and he didn't believe that the exchange had taken place, but steerage passenger John Holland of Standish, Lancashire, happened to be within earshot and he heard them:

> *I was on deck about an hour and twenty minutes before the ship struck and overheard the quartermaster tell the second officer that he was "too near the land" and the reply was that he [the quartermaster] was "neither a captain nor a mate," and that "he knew too much." I heard this myself, and I thought the second officer was under the influence of liquor.*[3]

A few minutes later, the captain's steward arrived with the cocoa the captain had ordered. Fourth Officer Brown had no idea why the steward would show up at that hour, with cocoa, expecting the captain to be roused. In a letter to the Board of Trade a month later, he noted, "I had no orders to let the captain's boy call the captain, nor yet orders to call the captain at any stated time myself; the second officer, who was on the bridge, and was in charge of the deck, had the orders."[4]

He sent the steward up to the bridge to ask Metcalfe, who told him to take the cocoa away; he would awaken the captain at three o'clock, as ordered.

It was a strange response. He seemed to know nothing about it either—or he was overriding the captain's order. It was obvious that the steward had been ordered to arrive with cocoa for the captain; why else would he be there near 3:00 A.M.? Metcalfe didn't know it, but in sending the steward away, he set the stage for the destruction of the *Atlantic* and its occupants.

Both Metcalfe and Brown were fixated on seeing the light. But lights go out, ships go off course, people don't pay attention when they're supposed to, and human eyes don't see what they're expecting to see. The captain had said that they would see the light by 3:00 A.M., and if they did not, they were to call him. A child could understand such a plan.

They did not see the light. Metcalfe did not call the captain. The ship forged ahead into the darkness.

What was in Metcalfe's mind at this point? His response to Thomas seems to indicate that he was frozen with indecision. With virtually all his experience having been on sailing ships, now he was in command of the biggest and fastest ship he had ever sailed on, at night and off the usual track. Had he ever been called upon to make a decision about the handling of such a big and complex vessel?

The logical course of action in this uncertain state of affairs, as any ship's officer knows, would be to call the captain—especially if he had been ordered to! But let us suppose Metcalfe felt he had everything under control because he had a plan of action. The next step in that plan would be to stop the ship, or at least to slow down and check the depth of the water. By comparing the depth to the nautical chart of the area they could then get a reasonable estimate of how far they were from the land—the less water, the closer they would be. With that information, he could then issue the appropriate orders to ensure the safety of the ship.

Exactly how useful would checking the depth have been? Two hundred forty years previously, a ship called the *Saint Pierre* had been in the mid-Atlantic, navigating in dense fog. The captain, Samuel de Champlain, was on his twenty-seventh voyage across the Atlantic to New France, a place already called Quebec. In the words of historian David Hackett Fischer,

> He ordered out the deep-sea lead and on April 26, 1633, the leadsman found the bottom at 45 fathoms, or 270 feet. The lead brought up a few bits of sand and shell embedded in a pocket of tallow on its hollow

*bottom. A skilled seaman could learn much from these telltale signs
by sight and smell, and even taste. Champlain studied the evidence
and reckoned from long experience that they were 12 leagues onto the
Grand Banks in the latitude of 45 degrees 30 minutes. Even in the fog
he was able to identify his position with uncanny accuracy.*[5]

Would Metcalfe have been able to do that? Very unlikely. The
captain? Probably.

METCALFE FINALLY DECIDED TO CALL WILLIAMS AT 3:12 A.M., BUT HE NEVER
had a chance to actually do it.[6] Out of the darkness came the voice of
Joseph Carroll, the lookout on the forward deckhouse, as he screamed
out, "Breakers Ahead!" Frighteningly close in front of them was a
line of whitewater where waves were striking the cliffs on the shore.
Suddenly Metcalfe came alive. Orders were shouted, the wheel spun
around, engines reversed.

But there was no reversing the events beginning to unfold. For
every person aboard, the next hours would be the most terrifying of
their lives. For the majority, it would be the end of their lives.

"I was awakened from my sleep by three very sharp shocks, following in quick succession, with intervals, as near as I can judge, of
perhaps two minutes," saloon passenger Henry Herzel later explained.
He continued:

*I didn't leave my berth when the first blow was struck, as I had no
thought of such a thing as shipwreck, and stayed still until after the second. The first shock was a sharp knock that made a crashing noise, and
shook the whole ship. The ship seemed to stick fast for a moment, and
the engines stopped for a short time and then started working again.
The vessel then struck a second time and the engines stopped working
completely.*[7]

The engineers shut the engines down and Chief Engineer Foxley
opened the valves to release the pressure from the boilers, lest the

cold water striking the hot metal cause them to explode. The terrifying hissing and clouds of steam added to the confusion and darkness. Distress rockets flew into the air like fireworks as Quartermaster John Speakman signalled to any person or ship in the area. It was their only way to signal and they had no way of knowing whether a single pair of eyes even saw it.

The ship struck twice offshore, the granite rocks tearing through the ship's bottom, before the bow grounded. Water poured in and began to sink the stern, where the single women were berthed. They were the first to die—and every one of them perished.

And so, the carnage began, in absolute darkness and utter pandemonium, with the clanking and groaning of the still-shifting ship and the smashing of the waves against its sides.

AT THIS POINT, THE SHIP WAS MORE OR less parallel to the land, which was on the right. In this tenuous, half-sunk position, people poured onto the deck. These were the men, women, and children who had been berthed amidships in the family quarters. That area was now flooding as they scrambled up the narrow stairways to the deck. Most did not make it. Those who did were told to move forward to the bow area, which was high and dry. But there were too many of them and the deck was falling beneath their feet. It was soon awash, and the big waves swept many away to their deaths. Some of these men could have survived—but only if they'd left their wives and children behind. That they could not do, and it cost them their lives.

One of the oldest people aboard, Caroline Wood perished with her family, including her five grandchildren. (COURTESY JANET BLUNT)

Lewis Cooke was one such man. Travelling in the steerage with him was one of the oldest passengers aboard. Caroline Wood, seventy-two, from Sussex, had married in 1823 and had nine children, at least four of whom she had already buried. Her husband, John, a tanner, had died in 1857 and she was living with her daughter Anne and Anne's husband, Lewis. After nine years of marriage, they had five children. Cooke's income of eighteen shillings (equivalent to less than $100 in today's money) per week as a railway porter was not sustaining them so, with trepidation and hope, they had decided to start over in Chicago. They were travelling with several other families from the little town of Lewes. Their children, Caroline, eight, Frederick, seven, John, five, Edith, three, and George, one, all perished with their parents and grandmother.[8]

John Gilbert, a twenty-year-old steward from London, later reported that he...

...ran up the companionway and found the stewardess, Mrs. McNally, crying bitterly. She had one lifebelt on, and I offered her the one I had and she accepted. I then fastened the one she had on tighter around her body, and was proceeding to adjust the other one when the ship commenced to thump heavily on the rock and I rushed on the saloon deck, telling the stewardess to get into the rigging as it was her only chance. She appeared to be bereft of reason and would not listen to me.[9]

That is all we know of Fanny McNally. Her children had already lost their father. At home in Belfast, her mother, Jane Thompson, died three weeks later, probably from the grief of losing her daughter.[10] The *Irish Times* printed a brief article on December 3, 1873, reporting that Fanny's daughter Henrietta was being admitted to the Masonic Female Orphan School in Belfast.

"Take to the rigging!" The frantic order was repeated by the captain. That was the only quick way to get above the rising waters, but it meant climbing the footropes that led up the masts—easy enough for fit sailors, less so for ordinary folk, older people, and women in long nightgowns. Steerage passengers James Bateman and his wife Rosa, "ran to the rigging, and had just caught hold of it when the ship fell on her side and left us both hanging by our hands, but I managed to get my feet on the rail, and so helped my wife up."[11]

In Herzel's words, "The ship started to roll after about ten minutes and the ends of the yardarms were in the water."

The *Atlantic* was rolling towards the left side, about to turn over, when it stopped, sliding off the rock and grounding again on a ledge, spilling many who had made it to the deck into the icy waters. In the words of one newspaper: "Walking up the deck of the vessel was as difficult as climbing up the side of a house. Many attempting the task slid off into the sea."[12] If they could swim, it did them no good, for the dead 437-foot-long ship was between them and the land, if there was any land; there was no way for them to tell. Among those lost were twenty-three members of three families from the Swiss village of Movelier.[13] Within minutes there were dozens of people in the rigging—the youngest and the fittest males.

In the words of Thomas Moffatt:

The sea was now breaking over her and...as I was wildly traversing the sea-washed deck, I apprehended the thought that life with us would soon have an end, and that my evident fate was sealed. Having reached this side of the ship, I soon got into the rigging where I remained for a good while. It was whilst here that I witnessed such scenes and experienced such sensations as I never shall forget.[14]

Launching the lifeboats—big, heavy things, some of which could hold sixty people—was all but impossible. The five on the left side were swamped or smashed in by the waves striking the side of the ship. The five on the landward side were immobile against the deckhouses. All of them were soon lost and Metcalfe was last seen trying to launch one. In the captain's words:

The Second Officer was in the starboard lifeboat. I carried two ladies [Mrs. Louise Merritt and her sister, Annie Scrymser] and placed them with him and returned for more. Before I got as far as the saloon entrance, I found the ship going over still further. I managed to get hold

of the weather rails and got back to the lifeboat. I took the ladies and
placed them in the main rigging and went back. I called to the Second
Officer to come out as the boat would roll over, which she did in a few
minutes, carrying him with her and thirty or forty men."[15]

If the captain was able to see the danger, Second Officer Metcalfe
should have seen it, too. This fatal error of judgement was the last in
a string of unfortunate decisions. It is evidence of the power of the
sea that this heavy boat, loaded with the weight of all those men, was
flipped over and destroyed. Metcalfe, and all those with him, died.

Saloon passenger Samuel Vick, of North Carolina, later described
the situation of the remaining survivors:

It was now four o'clock, one hour after the vessel had struck, and
nothing could be heard or seen but the men in the rigging and the
mournful whining of the wind. Those who had thus far survived were
almost frozen, and as no succor appeared to be coming, one by one
the passengers relaxed their hold and dropped into eternity. Some
who were up in the mizzen top as they fell from their positions car-
ried several of those beneath them along, and they, too, were num-
bered among the lost. Minute after minute made the position of the
living more precarious, and I believe not a soul on board the vessel
had the faintest hope.[16]

With the lifeboats gone, there was no choice but to swim for
the shore. That was an option only a handful of the youngest and
fittest could even attempt, and most who tried did not make it. The
captain ordered Third Officer Brady to try to get a rope to the rock
the ship had struck. It was to the right of the ship's bow. Brady gave
Quartermaster Edward Owens a life jacket and tied a rope around his
waist. Owens plunged in and swam to the rock, but the cold water
had sapped his strength and he was in danger of succumbing, so they
hauled him back. Quartermaster John Speakman tried next. He got
there and managed to climb up, only to discover an unconscious
crewman had gotten there ahead of him. He awoke him with a kick
and together they secured the rope and hauled Brady over.

That rock came to be known as Golden Rule Rock, although there is no reason why a nondescript rock close to land, that was not a hazard to navigation, should have had a name at all. In his report to Liverpool, Captain Williams gave the wrong location as the place of the disaster. He said it happened on "Marr's Rock off Marr's Head." Some say that the locals called *that* rock Golden Rule Rock. It is a prominent rock that could easily have had a name. The newspapers subsequently referred to Golden Rule Rock without realizing they were talking about a different rock—and the name has stuck to the rock that took the *Atlantic* down.

On that rock a great deal of heartache and heroism played out— heroism that went unrecognized in any formal way at the time. It started with Quartermaster Owens. He could have swum for shore like others did, but he tied the rope around his waist and nearly died trying to get onto the rock. When he failed, Quartermaster Speakman went, and, finally, Third Officer Brady was across. These three admittedly desperate men did what they did for one reason only—to save

The rock that came to be called Golden Rule Rock. Even on a peaceful summer day there can be significant turbulence at the wreck site. (AUTHOR PHOTO)

the lives of others. Fourth Officer John Brown, Steerage passenger William Hoy, and others would later receive mention for their selfless efforts to help men get onto the rock and stay alive.

More men got across and soon additional lines (some reports say up to four more) were strung in the belief that Golden Rule Rock would be their deliverance, but the water was too cold, the distance too far, and the way from the rock to shore too treacherous. Those who made it to the rock got stuck there, and as more desperate men hauled themselves across from the ship it was soon overcrowded. To make matters worse, the tide was rising and the surface of the rock started to disappear under water. They had clawed their way from the ship only to find themselves worse off.

CHAPTER 5

Angels in the Night

The third time the boat came alongside, Christianson, who could no longer maintain his hold on the rope, fell into the sea. The boat put back and he was drawn up from the water. On arriving at the beach he was unable to walk and two men took him into their arms and carried him to a fisherman's cottage.

New York Herald
April 7, 1873

If there is such a thing as a lucky place to have a shipwreck, the *Atlantic* had ended up there, for there was a family living nearby—and no ordinary family, as events would soon prove.

Michael Clancy awoke with a start. He had heard a crash and clatter, and now there was a loud hissing noise. He got up and peered out the window of his house, tucked into a cove on the leeward side of Meaghers Island (which is pronounced, and sometimes spelled, Marrs Island). Streaks of light from the distress rockets leapt into the air west of his house, on the outward side of the island. Others were soon up and the house was in an uproar. Was it the Second Coming? They had never seen anything like it.

In the time it took to get dressed, Clancy was outdoors facing the piercing wind that was a normal part of his family's life on the little island. With his brother Edmund and son, Michael, he started the half-mile walk from their tranquil cove on the north side towards the sound. They had to contend with large granite boulders, thick brush, snow, and ice, which made for hard going. They rarely went over there at that time of year because it was a grim, unforgiving space of bare granite and ice-covered boulders that sloped into the waters. They could hear the waves breaking as they approached the exposed shoreline and clouds of steam brushed past on the wind, but they could see nothing in the darkness; only the ridge leading to the shore. Suddenly, a shape appeared in front of them! A ghost? They held the lantern up for a closer look. It was a sopping, freezing, staggering man, more dead than alive. Quartermaster Robert Thomas had just swum ashore from the grounded ship, a superhuman effort in the icy, churning waters.

From up in the rigging, Thomas Moffatt was one of many who saw Clancy's light, a first hint that there might be hope for a rescue. He later wrote,

> In the early dawn whilst intently gazing on land, I discovered a group of men, gathered on an intervening rock, who had got there by means of a rope, which had been carried by one of the crew. Whilst in this dangerous and hopeless condition, we felt an inspiration of joy, as we saw a light approaching on the land, but this infusion of joy did not last long as the light again disappeared and melancholy despair returned of ever being rescued from impending fate.[1]

He did not know that they were returning to Clancy's house, where Clancy's twenty-eight-year-old daughter, Sarah Jane, gave Thomas dry clothes and put him next to the stove to thaw out. Meanwhile, a dog appeared on the shore, so the survivors knew there must be somebody living nearby. Thomas was the first in an exodus that would flow through Clancy's house—later referred to by the captain as "a hut"—the only dwelling on the island. The village of Lower Prospect was about to be thrown into turmoil the likes of which it had never before experienced and has not seen since.

Sarah Jane's mother, Jane (Coolen), had a disability and Sarah Jane and her husband, John O'Reilly, lived with them while she cared for her. John was away, working in Boston. Sarah Jane had two children of her own—Mary, aged five, and James, two—so she already had her hands full. In the hours following, hundreds of anguished people would descend on her in the middle of the night.

There were almost a dozen people living in Clancy's tiny house. Besides Sarah Jane's children and her parents, there was her sister Elizabeth, brothers Michael and James, and uncle Edmund and cousin Alex. There was also a boy named Eddie Mullins, probably another relative. Clancy sent Eddie to row to Ryans Island nearby to awaken Edmund Ryan, who would spread the word about the shipwreck.[2]

Fortunately for Eddie, his little dory was on the sheltered side of Meaghers Island. Through the blackness, he rowed across the cove, watching the outline of the trees against the western sky to find the narrow entrance to Norris Gut. He passed Norris Island, crossed the gut, and found a wharf. He tied the dory on and climbed up the hill with the news. Forty-nine-year-old Edmund Ryan moved quickly, rounding up Patrick Dollard and Richard Norris. He primed a musket and fired a couple of shots to alert the people on the mainland that something was up. Then he and his brother headed to the wreck to see what they could do.

As they came over the rise they beheld utter chaos and devastation. Offshore in the darkness they could make out the biggest ship they had ever seen, half sunken, and being walloped by huge waves. A few people languished on the rocks, too exhausted to get up after having somehow gotten to dry land. There were bodies everywhere in the water. There was a large flat rock between the ship and the shore with ropes coming from the ship. Men were in the water, trying to pull themselves across, but the cold water was too much for many of them and they were falling away from the ropes. Between the rock and the shore was a shallow gulley that the whitewater surged through. One of the officers, with Clancy's help, was getting a rope organized from the rock to the shore, trying to haul men to the land. It was a death trap, but a few were beating the odds. Unfortunately, in order to get them out, somebody had to get into the water to help them.

It was still dark, around 4:30 A.M., when Edmund Ryan arrived at the site. He and his wife, Elizabeth, lived with their three children on Ryans

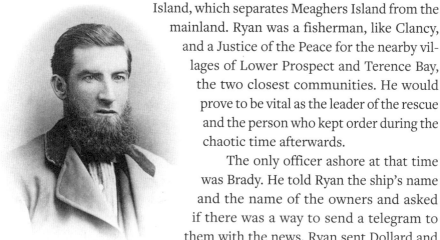

Island, which separates Meaghers Island from the mainland. Ryan was a fisherman, like Clancy, and a Justice of the Peace for the nearby villages of Lower Prospect and Terence Bay, the two closest communities. He would prove to be vital as the leader of the rescue and the person who kept order during the chaotic time afterwards.

The only officer ashore at that time was Brady. He told Ryan the ship's name and the name of the owners and asked if there was a way to send a telegram to them with the news. Ryan sent Dollard and Norris ashore to see Samuel Blackburn Sr., the sixty-one-year-old post office keeper at Lower Prospect, whose wife, Mary, had been born at nearby Oak Island.[3] They carried a note that Brady had written in the White Star Line's private code, to be taken to Halifax and then telegraphed to Ismay, Imrie, and Company in New York.

Third Officer Cornelius Brady, a man possessed of an ardent sense of duty and selflessness as well as uncommon stamina. (NS Archives, Notman Studio Nova Scotia, no. 1983-310 #90100)

Ryan also instructed them to get the neighbours up and tell them all to bring their boats. Many would be needed to help get survivors to the mainland.

Samuel Blackburn ran the post office from his house like his father, William, before him had, and received mail once a week. This night's news required the quickest possible delivery, so a courier immediately left Lower Prospect on horseback.[4] It would be an arduous journey in the snow.

Edmund Ryan and Michael Clancy sized up the situation. They could see hundreds of men hanging onto the ship, on the overturned side where they had clambered when it rolled. Now, they were marooned, all their energy being expended in trying not to tumble down the sloping ship's side into the water. A few of the youngest and strongest were hauling themselves along the rope from the ship to the rock, where steerage passenger William Hoy was on his belly making a superhuman effort to get them up onto the flat, but slimy, surface. His hands, constantly in the cold water, eventually became useless and he got a few more people up by clenching their clothing between his teeth.[5] Ryan and Clancy helped land a few men who were coming ashore from the rock but, even though it was a short distance, the shallow water between the rock and the shore was very violent, and most who tried to cross were perishing. Faced with no better choice, some were choosing the worst option of all—attempting to swim from the ship directly to the shore, like Quartermaster Thomas had done. Hardly any of them made it.

Irving Stuttaford, the Canadian steward, may have been among those who did make it. That is the opinion of his great-granddaughter, Elizabeth Church of Halifax, a long-distance swimmer herself, as was her father.

It quickly became obvious to Clancy and Ryan that they had to get a boat. With Brady's help, they returned to Clancy's wharf, fished his dory out of the water, and dragged it through the woods and over the rocks. In 1873, for people living near the sea, and especially on an island, a dory was the only form of transportation. Fourteen feet long and rowed by one or two people, it was the workboat of east coast fishermen. Easy and cheap to build, dories were reliable and tough, and with their seats taken out they could be stacked five or six high for easy transport aboard fishing schooners originating in New England and Atlantic Canada.

They managed to get it launched, but within minutes it nearly swamped. It would not be suitable as a rescue boat. They had to find something bigger to handle the waves breaking against the shoreline and coursing among the rocks.

That was a tall order. All the fishing boats had been stored for the winter, turned over and covered with boughs or put indoors. Wooden boats dry out when they're out of the water, so when they get put back, they leak until the planks have had time to absorb water to swell them and fill the gaps. Otherwise, somebody would have to constantly bail.

Fortunately, Lower Prospect resident James Coolen had taken his seine boat out early that year, and he arrived with other men from Lower Prospect, the closest community on the mainland.

Seine boats like those used in the rescue can still be seen along the coast. This one is at Peggys Cove. (AUTHOR PHOTO)

Almost twice the length of a dory, the seine boat was a common tool of the local inshore fishermen. The seas around Nova Scotia swarmed every summer with vast schools of herring and mackerel. The most efficient way to catch them was with a seine—a net, with a drawstring at the bottom, which encircled the school, after which the drawstring was tightened, trapping the fish inside. The narrow, twenty-four-foot seine boat was purpose-built for the job. With its rounded sides, it could be tipped almost to the rails while the catch was scooped out of the seine and in over the gunwales using long-handled dipnets.

By this point, the men on the wreck had been hanging on for almost three hours. After the initial violent crash, death and mayhem had been all around them as people tried to save themselves, but after the initial period of activity, those who could had climbed into the rigging while others hung onto the side of the hull, immobile. Now, cold and exhausted, some of them began to fall off into the water and expire. Brady, ashore and wanting to give them hope, painted a sign—"Boats coming"—and held it up into the grey dawn. A muted cheer went up from those on the ship who could manage it.

The rescue boat was heavy and it would take a dozen or more men to coax it across the island. The few survivors languishing around on land were too far gone to be of any help but Brady managed to round up a few volunteers from among them to supplement the locals, and they started manhandling the thing towards the wreck site. Having to haul it uphill, over brush-covered boulders the size of beach balls, each man lifting and pushing eighty to a hundred pounds while trying not to break a leg, made matters worse; the boat then had to be eased down the other side and into the huge waves that were pounding against the cliffs, drenching the men with bone-chilling spray.

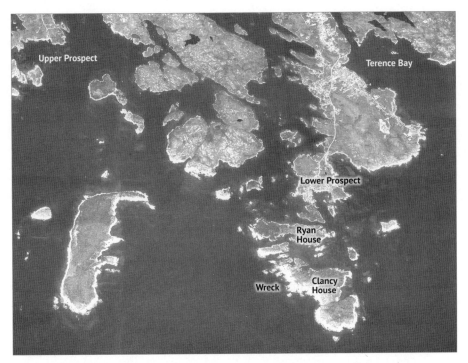

The rescue boats were dragged from Clancy's wharf to the wreck site. All the rescue men from Ryans Island, Lower Prospect, and Upper Prospect had to arrive first at Clancy's.

On the first trip, only James Coolen and Edmund Ryan's brother Dennis manned the boat. Others were reluctant to board because of the high seas and the rocks, but they were soon joined by Patrick Dollard, Edmund's cousin Frank Ryan, and John Blackburn, the twenty-four-year-old son of the post-office keeper. Edmund's other cousin Stephen Ryan, and John Blackburn's brother Samuel Jr. stood by with Clancy's dory in case of an upset.

At 6:00 A.M. they began taking loads of eight to ten survivors from the rock to the island. Once ashore, they then had to get them out of the boat and onto the land without demolishing the boat—or the men. Challenging as that was, it was better than the rope, so that option was soon abandoned.

From the vantage point of the men still on the ship, those on the rock were practically ashore. At least they had solid ground under their feet. They started yelling for the boat to come for them, before the ship came apart. What they didn't realize, which the fishermen did, was that the rising tide would soon cover the rock. The wind was also picking up so, even though they were closer to shore, their situation was more urgent.

Captain Williams was desperate. It was obvious that one rescue boat would not be enough. He waved and screamed until they finally took notice and went out to the ship. Over the roar of the surf he yelled something that caused Dennis Ryan to look at Coolen, who returned his incredulous gaze.

Daylight was finally arriving. By then, 450 to 500 people had died and a near-equal number were still alive. Some were ashore and some had managed to get to the rock, but the majority were still on the ship. Dennis Ryan looked towards the shore and was relieved to see Michael Clancy's seine boat being lugged over the crest and down towards the water. In the gang labouring at it were the O'Brien brothers and Tom Twohig, a fine young fellow from Pennant, across the bay, who had designs on the O'Briens' sister, Kate. The job was daunting. Only one boat could go to the rock in the tight conditions under which they were working.

CHAPTER 6

So Near and Yet So Far

You gentlemen of New York, who only know of this terrible disaster by reading of it, cannot imagine the feelings of the survivors on board, as they gazed at the terrible reality on the deck. There were no screams of women; no yelling men. Every one stood still and was silent. Those who died made no noise except as their bodies fell to the deck.

Samuel Vick
Saloon passenger[1]

If you were to visit the wreck site on a sunny day in summer and get an understanding of where the *Atlantic* lay and see Golden Rule Rock and the shoreline, you would probably find yourself wondering how it was that so many people perished when they were so close to shore.

It was a combination of reasons. Though it was not stormy, it was dark, cold, and disorienting. Everything happened so fast that there was little time to react. Getting to the deck was dangerous in itself. Then, the water was wild, and, finally, the shoreline was anything but welcoming. When daylight came and swimming for it perhaps looked doable for some, all were too cold and diminished to even think about attempting it. By that time, the rescue was finally coming together, anyway.

With the dawn, those on shore could take in the extent of the disaster. In front of them lay the *Atlantic*, broken and sinking. The back half was already underwater, as were the port rails. Four huge steel masts pointed out to sea, like giant cannons on a battlefield. Only the forward half of the ship's starboard side was above water. Clustered upon it were most of the men who were still alive. The rest were up in the rigging of the mizzen-mast, the third mast back from the bow. Its base was submerged, so they were stuck there, with no shelter from the bitterly cold winds. Charles Flanly, of Paterson, New Jersey, was one of them. He was just seventeen or eighteen years old, returning from visiting relatives in Ireland.

Also there was Rosa Bateman, who would be the last woman to die. She had told her husband, James, that she could not go any further and urged him to save himself. In company with Flanly and First Officer John Firth, she was well up the mast, standing on footropes—called ratlines—stretched between the steel cables that ran down to the side of the ship and held the mast up. When the stern began to settle under the water, Firth took to the rigging, urging those around him up as far as they could go. As a seaman, he instinctively knew that the higher the better, given that they had no idea how far the stern had to go down before coming to rest on the bottom of the sea. Mrs. Bateman was dressed only in her nightclothes. Flanly wrapped his jacket around her and did his best to comfort her, but the fact that she had gotten into the rigging simply delayed the inevitable.

They were aware the ship could roll over at any time. To complicate matters, with the stern on the bottom and the bow more than four hundred feet away out of the water, there was a huge amount of stress on the centre of the ship. The weight of the boilers, engines, cargo, ballast, and other heavy machinery that drove the vessel all conspired to snap the hull amidships and send it and everybody aboard to the bottom.

The words of Chief Officer John Firth describe what he saw from atop the mizzen-mast:

When daylight came I counted 32 persons in the mizzen mast rigging with me, including one woman. When these saw that there were lines between the ship and the shore many of them attempted to go forward to the lines, and in doing so were washed overboard and drowned.

Many reached the shore by the aid of the lines and the fishermen's boats rescued many more.[2]

It was a big and confusing scene. The people in the rigging were cut off, out over the water like flies in a web, looking in towards the ship. Firth would have been the person farthest from the land and, therefore, the most difficult to rescue.

In the rigging below Firth, Thomas Moffatt had been watching the same scenarios and he decided to see if he could get to the area where the rescue boats picked up survivors:

> *After they had taken several to the shore, I resolved to make an attempt to reach the land, being in the rigging for four or five hours....I began to descend the rigging and soon got on the side of the ship which was now in an inclined position. As the water was occasionally going over the sides, I halted a moment or two, and during the interval which elapsed between the repeating waves, I quickly passed to that part of the ship where the boats were coming. I had not to remain any time scarcely before I was assisted into the boat by the captain who stationed himself at the junction to prevent persons from crowding the boats.*
>
> *In a few minutes after this I was enabled to place my feet on terra firma which from experience I had thoroughly learned to appreciate. As I looked back on the wreck and saw the place from which I had been mercifully delivered I could not help feeling gratitude to God, for his kind and providential dealings towards me.*[3]

By 6:30 A.M., Twohig and the O'Brien brothers, James and Michael Jr., had Clancy's boat in the water and were joined by William Lacey and Patrick Dollard at the oars. Coolen's boat was ashore with a load of survivors and Dennis Ryan took the opportunity to tell his brother Edmund and James Coolen what the captain had yelled across to him—that he would pay $500 for every boatload of survivors taken ashore from the ship.[4] That was an astounding amount of money for the time and it is surprising that they took him at his word. Sadly, they would come to regret their trust in this stranger who had appeared on their doorsteps and thrown their lives into turmoil.

Captain Williams was very much in charge, despite the considerable pain he was experiencing from having had his hip and ribs broken during the hurricane when he was second officer on the *Republic*. It is difficult to picture him with his cane, managing to stay upright and direct the rescue while men were sliding off into the water—and even to block people who were trying to jump the queue. Whether he had the authority to make such an offer is moot, but others heard him, too, some saying it was £500 and other reports saying it was $500. It was much talked about when word of the offer made it to shore.

In a letter to the owners, Williams wrote simply, "I succeeded, fearing the ship would part and slide into deep water, in getting the boats to take on shore men from the ship first and many were saved who, if left there till the last, would have perished from exhaustion."[5] He would have known, because it almost happened to him.

Though they were hardened fishermen, many of the men crewing the rescue boats were greatly tested by the conditions. Dollard soon left Clancy's boat and his place was taken by Alex Brophy, who made one trip before he, too, left, owing, as he said, "to the manner in which the men whom we were trying to save, crowded into the boat."[6] The *Acadian Recorder* newspaper reported that when the boats came alongside to pick up survivors, sailors from the ship's crew knocked passengers down and jumped into the boats themselves. On one occasion they swarmed one of the boats, and by the time the fishermen could get away there were fourteen of them aboard in addition to the boat's crew. It's a testament to the skill of the boatmen that they did not swamp or turn over.

For the safety of all concerned, the captain told the rescuers to stop coming right up to the wreck. Instead, they stayed off and one of the men crewing the boat would throw a rope into the crowd. Whoever caught it had to jump into the water and get hauled to the boat. That sounds like a dangerous response to the problem but later testimony stated that not a single person was lost getting in and out of the boats.

The words of saloon passenger Samuel Vick describe his rescue:

About two hours after the vessel struck, Officer Brady, with a number of others, was at the left side of the steamer calling on those above them to drop into the sea, and they would be picked up. This order was obeyed by many in the rigging, myself among the rest. My limbs were so benumbed with cold that I was unable to move either up or down, and it appeared as though my fingers were frozen to the ropes. I, however, let go of my hold, and closing my eyes let myself fall. I felt almost unconscious as I did it, and in a second I knew I was in the sea, but felt immediately afterwards the efforts of the officers dragging me into the boat. To be brief with the matter, I at last reached shore and then for the first time wished that I had perished with the others. I am naturally a nervous man and not very rugged and the dreadful ordeal I had passed through made me utterly regardless of life.[7]

In the mind of Samuel Vick, who would later engage the *Atlantic*'s chief bedroom steward to care for him on the trip to New York, only the heroic Brady could have rescued him, assisted by other officers, not run-of-the-mill fishermen. Brady may have been aboard the boat because he was everywhere that night, including at the oars of the

A Currier and Ives print showing the grounded *Atlantic*. The presence of the rescue boat between the mizzen and jigger masts is in keeping with passenger Samuel Vick's description of his rescue.

rescue boats, but Vick was, in fact, pulled out of the water by the fishermen.

Transferring these men from the ship to the boat under the conditions prevailing that morning was no simple matter, and having to pull them out of the water only made the job harder. (Getting a buoyant scuba diver into a boat on a rough day is hard enough. One minute you have hold of him and suddenly the boat lurches up on a wave while the diver drops into the trough, and if you're not quick to let go, you get hauled overboard or the diver gets smacked on the head by the boat. A twenty- to twenty-four-foot boat can smash down and kill a man if it hits him in the right place. A diver is comfortable in the water, and most have the presence of mind to let go and push away from the boat. A scared, exhausted non-swimmer in freezing water is another matter altogether. It would take at least two, if not three men working hard, to get him aboard.)

To steady the boats, they strung lines from shore to the ship. This not only shortened the travel time back and forth but it enabled the rowers to get their oars out of the water and out of the way so they could give all their attention to the man in the water while a couple of rescuers held the rope. Then, when they got ashore, holding the rope kept the boat off and away from the rocks.

Getting out of the boat and navigating the huge, slimy, surf-washed boulders on shore was the climax of a brutal and bruising fight for life. It's incredible that anyone pulled it off.

CHAPTER 7

I Was a Stranger and You Took Me In

I visited the house of Clancy, at which the sufferers were first relieved and as he told me of the drowning, of the shrieks, of the moans, of the haggard, frenzied, half-crazed people who crowded into his house, the tears ran down his face in streams.

New York Tribune
April 8, 1873

I n 1873, the people living in communities like Lower Prospect were surviving—and that was about all. The houses were little and most families were big. Children slept three and four to a bed, which they didn't mind because it provided company in the absolute darkness, and warmth in the freezing house. There was no electricity or running water or indoor plumbing. Everyone went to bed early to avoid wasting candles or the fish oil that fuelled the lamps.

All the accessible trees had been cut for fuel years before so residents relied on coal as much as wood to get them through the winter. The only heat came from a low stove in the kitchen or a fireplace—the most inefficient means known to try to heat a house. Many mornings in winter, there would be frost on the floor and ice on the drinking water in the barrel. The toilet was in an outbuilding behind the house or at the outer end of the wharf.

The thin soil provided little more than hay for the animals and potatoes for the people. In the fall, they put away all their food for the winter, and the long and hungry month of March had just come to an end. Supplies were low. Many would have been living on bread, molasses, salt pork, and tea, and their growing sons and daughters often left the table hungry. Despite that, most readily shared what they had until it was gone.

On the night of the shipwreck, the people who had been rescued were taken to Michael Clancy's house, the only shelter on the island. It was jammed with suffering survivors. Sarah Jane and her sister were furiously feeding fuel to the stove and boiling water, scrounging for dry clothing as fast as they could, and coaxing their meagre resources along. They welcomed boatload after boatload, did a quick triage, and helped them in while encouraging those already there to leave the comfort of their father's little home. The beds in the house were filled with the worst cases and food and fuel were running low, despite being restocked from other houses on the mainland.

As soon as they were mobile, the men were put into a boat and rowed a short distance to Edmund or Dennis Ryan's house on Ryans Island. There, Ryan's wife, Elizabeth, and daughters Emma and Ellen fed them and arranged for their distribution throughout the community. At the home of Michael O'Brien, whose sons were in the rescue boats, his grown daughters Agatha and Kate also saw to the comfort of survivors. They had lost their fifty-six-year-old mother, Catherine, a year and a half before, and both still lived at home, taking care of the two youngest boys: Andrew, fifteen, and Charles, eleven.

Typical of the reactions of survivors after being saved were the words of saloon-class passenger Freeman Marckwald:

> At daybreak, a fisherman's boat came out and rescued a number of us, and landed us on Meagher's Island. A handful of the people there warmly welcomed us. They gave us food and clothing and did all for us that they could. Edmund Ryan, Dennis Ryan, and their wives were especially active in ministering to our wants.[1]

Eight to ten drenched people, most barely alive, were coming ashore every ten minutes or so, being hauled out of the boats by men who were sometimes up to their waists in the frigid water, and who were trying not to get thrust under the boats that were careening about.

Clancy's house was so jammed with soggy people that he had to bore holes in the floor to drain the water that kept getting dragged in on the survivors. Though she was, as one newspaper described her, a "little slip of a woman, being...only five feet in height,"[2] Sarah Jane maintained order and kept things moving. More than anything, these men had to be warmed up, so there was a constant rotation around the stove. As soon as they were able to move they had to leave the house—usually unwillingly—to make room for others. Edmund Ryan said he had to constantly chase them out of Clancy's house and outbuildings so they could cram new arrivals in.

Many years after her heroic efforts in caring for hundreds of exhausted people, Sarah Jane O'Reilly relaxes with her granddaughter Gladys while wearing the engraved gold locket she received from the people of Chicago.

Thomas Moffatt's narrative bears that out, as he comes ashore and goes first to Clancy's house and then to Ryans Island:

The next thing I had to do was to follow those who were wending their way to habitation, but not knowing whither I went, I followed on alone for some time, keeping at a little distance from those who were going before. The path was almost obscured by the depth of snow which was lying on the ground. At last we reached a dwelling house, and I with the others entered it, but it was so crowded that I could not so much as see the fire and I should not exaggerate at all, if I say that there were three or four inches of water on the floor which had completely dripped from the persons of those who had been and were there present.

I did not remain there any time scarcely, but on leaving the house I was accosted by an inhabitant of the place and he informed me that I was to follow him. I did so but I had not to walk far before we came to an inlet of water, on the margin of which I saw a few boats collected together, and I soon learned that I, with the rest, had to seat ourselves in one of them and be taken to another part of that settlement. It was greatly against my feelings to have anything to do with boats just then. We had a safe transit across the water, and the little boat soon got to its destination.

We were there conducted to a fisherman's cottage but as there were only three or four inhabited dwellings in that locality, the living rooms became crowded. Here were assembled representatives of varied nations. Our conveniences were also few, as you may suppose, for we had to pass the night sometimes sitting and sometimes standing. All the provisions that could be obtained when equally distributed constituted but a small allowance for each individual. The food that we ate, from the time that we took our evening's repast on board the Atlantic *[Monday evening] until the Wednesday afternoon was comparatively very little.*[3]

Boats that had been stowed away for the winter were hurriedly turned over and launched, requiring frequent bailing until the dry planks soaked up enough water to swell them tight. Teams of men and boys were at the oars, shuttling back and forth between the two islands and the mainland, away from the high winds and waves that the rescue boats were contending with on the outer side of Meaghers Island.

In the homes of Lower Prospect, fires were in, warming houses that had turned cold overnight, and heating water for buckets of tea, sometimes sweetened with sugar but more often with molasses.

By April 5, the situation was critical for some and the *Halifax Morning Chronicle* had to come to their rescue:

While the charitable public are thinking of how they can aid the survivors of the disaster, they should remember the people of Prospect. We do not now refer to the acts of bravery which may merit rewards, but to the fact that the fishermen's families gave all the provisions they had to the shipwrecked people, and in many instances are now themselves in actual want. There could be no better way to manifest sympathy in the matter than to send down to Prospect a quantity of provisions to refill the larders which were so cheerily emptied to feed the distressed people. This is an important matter, and should be attended to at once.[4]

It was attended to and the people soon had enough to get them to the fishing season.

CHAPTER 8

THE KINDNESS
OF STRANGERS

*We were treated well, and every care taken of us by the fishermen on
shore, especially by the Clancys. That's a splendid, brave girl, that
daughter of his.*[1]

James McAllister
Engine room crew

With 8:00 A.M. approaching, about 230 men were ashore but
a couple of hundred more were still marooned offshore.
The tide was rising and the rock's surface was shrinking, squeezing
the men seeking refuge. The channel between the rock and shore was
widening and becoming more violent as more water barged through
the gap. Golden Rule Rock would soon be underwater.

The rising water also buoyed the grounded ship, which, instead
of providing some relief, strained the amidships section even more.
The wind was still blowing directly onto the left side and as the water
rose, the ship was moved about instead of lying firmly on the bottom.
This constant twisting of its tortured frame put the *Atlantic* at greater
risk of coming apart.

The two boats were shuttling back and forth to the *Atlantic* and
the rock, getting violently thrown around by the waves that came over
the ship and also thrashed about as these same waves deflected back

off the shore. It was this wave action that killed several who tried the swim from the ship to the shore. When they got to the shore, the waves threw them upon the rocks and then hauled them back into the water and repeated the cycle. Rowing was difficult, especially in the confined space near the rock, and pulling desperate, terrified men out of the water, one after another, was exhausting.

The two rescue crews were struggling. They regularly swapped men in and out of the boats but, while a respite from the hard work was welcome, stopping only made them colder.

In the nick of time, a boatload of men arrived from Upper Prospect, the largest of the three communities. These were hearty Irishmen, many of them relatives of the families in Lower Prospect. Even though Lower Prospect and Terence Bay were closer to the wreck site, their way is blocked by islands. The people of Upper Prospect, despite being more than three miles from the wreck, had a clear view across the water. There are accounts of Thomas Coolen having seen the distress flares.[2] He knew something was amiss and woke some others. At daylight, Nicholas Christian, a prominent businessman and Justice of the Peace, was awakened by his brother Patrick with a story that a ship was aground at Meaghers Island. At first he had been reluctant to believe his brother because it was April Fool's Day. Patrick produced a telescope and, lo and behold, there was indeed a ship on the rocks, and a big one at that.

Nicholas and Patrick headed to their father's stage, where a suitable boat was available, and started fitting it out with gear. Extra oars, rope, sails, water, salt pork, and bread went aboard. They didn't expect to be using the sail because, with the wind in their favour, it was faster to row. Along with Samuel White, Patrick and Thomas Duggan, and William Selig, they slipped through the narrow opening at the entrance to the little harbour and steered for the scene. Christian reported:

> It blew so hard and there was so heavy a sea on, that although the
> wind was fair and the distance only about three miles, we could not
> go down by the usual and direct course, but had to go around about
> inside islands. All the boats from Upper Prospect went inside, as well as
> ours. We landed at Michael Clancy's stage on the east side of Meagher's

Island, the wreck being on the west side, and went across without loss of time to the scene of the wreck.[3]

A stage was a fishing premises, consisting of a wharf and several buildings.

Other boats soon followed Christian's, one of them carrying nine-year-old Tom Hamm of Upper Prospect.[4] In those days, kids were expected to pitch in when there was work to be done, and there was plenty on this day. Now, with more men available, another seine boat could be crewed to bolster the rescue. Edmund Ryan's was closest and it was soon being bumped and coaxed over the boulders and through the underbrush. The arrival of the Upper Prospect men gave the effort a second wind. Over the next hour and a half they made eighteen trips to the rock, racing against the incoming tide.

At about 8:30, Dennis Ryan, one of the two men in the first rescue boat, was feeling the effects of the three hours of continuous effort while constantly getting drenched by the icy water. He needed a break. He got relieved from the first boat and went home, taking with him the ship's doctor, Thomas Cuppage, who was at death's door from the cold and in need of immediate attention. Clancy's house was jammed full. Now that there were more people helping out, they were deflecting the worst cases over to the Ryans. Dennis Ryan later said that the doctor "was restored by very vigorous measures taken by me and members of my family."[5] He spent three nights at their house, finally getting to Halifax on Friday, April 4.

After getting out of his wet clothes and having something to eat, Dennis returned to the wreck site at around 9:30, as the rescue was just wrapping up. Barely ten minutes after the last man was taken off the rock, the tide was high and the rock was being swept by waves as the water covered it. They had saved everybody who had been trapped on the rock and on the bow of the wreck.

The captain was one of the last to go ashore. With just seventeen people left aboard, Williams was carried off the dead ship and placed into a boat. He left the chief officer, John Firth, behind in the rigging, but he had done all he could to atone for losing his ship. There were two others up there with Firth—Rosa, by now dead, and Charles Flanly.

The wreck site. The small boat is above where the bow was grounded on an underwater ledge after it slid off the rock. Survivors pulled themselves on the rope to get to the rock, but conditions prevented them from getting ashore. The boat is oriented as the wreck lies on the bottom. Ryans Island is in the background, with Lower Prospect behind it. The Clancy house was in the small cove upper right. (CHRIS DEVANNEY)

Efforts had already been made to save them but to no avail. To get to them the boat would have to go to the outside of the wreck and venture under the unstable mizzen-mast, which was hanging precariously out over the sea above a swill of cabling, ropes, cargo, and bodies, with the three huge yardarms poised to crash down on anything that came near. They would have to wait until the tide fell and the wind died down.

CHAPTER 9

THE LONG WATCH

*Our boat made an attempt to go to the men in the mizzen rigging when
we finished with the others but the tide was high and we could not go
near enough to them to take them off.* [1]

Thomas Twohig
Rescue boat crew

T
he situation for all the survivors had been dire, but for Firth
and Flanly it was pretty much hopeless. The cable shrouds
were straining mightily to keep the 110-foot steel mast in the air out
over the water—and them with it—as it pointed out toward the horizon. When the ship was on an even keel, the shrouds on both sides
kept the mast balanced upright, but with the ship nearly on its left
side the whole weight of the mast was on the starboard shrouds and
that weight was so great they could spring at any time—and Firth
knew it. Fixed to the side of the disintegrating ship, each shroud was
attached to the mast at a different location. The first of nine shrouds
was attached halfway up the mast and the last was almost up to the
truck, where the battered flag fluttered feebly. Firth and Flanly owed
their lives to this staggered arrangement, because it balanced the
strain on the whole mast and kept it from breaking off somewhere
along its length, but if those shrouds were to let go, the men would

The man in the lower left holds the shrouds that support the masts. On the other side of the ship, Firth and others climbed to safety as that area was flooding. (SOURCE UNKNOWN)

be doomed. The steel mast, unlike a wooden one, which would float, would plummet to the bottom and take them with it.

Before the daylight came, they had been so isolated upon their perch that they did not know who was alive and who was dead. They didn't even know there was a rope going to the rock. As soon as the rescue boats arrived with the dawn, Firth and Flanly started yelling for them to come to their aid, but the boats had more than they could handle, dealing with the hundreds of survivors that could be readily taken to safety. They could only watch helplessly as the thirty-two people that Firth had counted below them in the rigging either got washed off or got to a boat. With the daylight, they saw men trying to pull themselves on the rope to the rock, some making it and others succumbing to the intensely cold water.

They had watched with jealousy and despair as boatload after boatload went ashore to safety and hope. They saw the last of the men leave the disappearing rock and envied their immense relief in knowing that the encroaching sea did not possess them any longer. They saw the captain get put aboard a boat and the last of the men finally leave them in their great loneliness, so near to redemption and so far from it. On the outside of the wreck, a large American schooner lay to, as the crew watched the goings on, but they could not come near and they did not attempt to launch a rescue.[2] In Firth's own terse words, "At last all had either been washed off or rescued except myself, the woman and a boy. The sea had become so rough that the boats could not venture near us."[3]

A couple of boats tried to get them but it was impossible. The waves were too high and would have rammed the boats under the mast and all its entanglements. Nicholas Christian later testified, "I saw some men go to the point and hail the men in the mizzen rigging telling them to wait until the tide would fall and they would get them off."[4]

There was no other way. Inch by agonizing inch, the submerged rock—salvation for some and death for others—slowly revealed its U-shape again. First, its slimy flat top, then the dark yellow-green marine growth, and then its steep sides, draped in the long slippery seaweed that had caused such distress to those trying to claw their way through it.

From their refuge in the rigging, it became clear to the marooned pair that the rescue was over. The exhausted men pulled their boats up and fires were lit to warm anybody left on the shoreline—cozy, inviting fires at which they stared pathetically. Boatloads of survivors were departing the island for Lower Prospect, Terence Bay, and Upper Prospect, where they would be received into small but welcoming houses. There they found warmth and were served bread and tea with molasses or jam. In some houses, they might have received whatever dried fish, potatoes, salt pork, and beans that remained after the long winter, all spread out on oil-clothed tables. Worn-out men soon sank into the beds of the householders who had just vacated them and were rescued by sweet sleep, a brief respite from the havoc and trauma, the terrible groaning of the dying ship, and the screams of dying people.

Though he too was suffering from exhaustion, Firth kept waving and yelling, hoping against hope that the rescuers would pull off a miracle. He knew the captain was alive; he saw Fourth Officer Brown on the rock helping with the rescue. Third Officer Brady seemed to be everywhere, and had returned to the ship several times to confer with the captain. Foxley had gone ashore. But there was no sign of the second officer. And not far below him was the body of the purser, Ambrose Worthington, his head jammed between the rails of the ship as he hung over the side. He had not seen Hugh Christie, the chief steward, and suspected that he had probably perished. Firth was the last officer left alive on the ship. Surely, they would not leave a fellow sailor to die.

The hours crawled by. Rosa Bateman, who had kept everybody's spirits up through the dark night by leading them in prayer and singing hymns, was now silent in death. Firth and Flanly had tied her to the rigging to keep her from falling. Her body hung limp, kept in place by the ropes. Nearby was the body of a steward, wearing one of the cork lifebuoys that had drowned many of those who had put them on incorrectly.

The *New York Times* reported Mrs. Bateman's story:

> *Among the steerage passengers who gained the deck were a young Englishman and his wife and child. Just after they got into the mizzen rigging a wave snatched away the child. Immediately afterwards an order came from the captain for all who could do so to get into the fore-rigging, because that part of the vessel was higher and less exposed. The young woman said that she was too much exhausted to attempt to move, but entreated her husband to go and save himself. He did so but Mr. Firth, the Chief Officer, refused to leave her, stood by her until she died and...then it became impossible for him to shift to a place of safety.*[5]

It raises the question: if she was too exhausted to move, how did she manage to stay alive? The *Times* could only have gotten that detail from Bateman himself, a convenient way to justify having deserted her. Samuel Vick described it this way:

> *In the rigging of the vessel [Firth] lashed the only steerage woman who reached the deck, that she might be saved; but the poor woman died of cold, fright and exhaustion, and when the first streak of daylight came she was bent and motionless, her chin resting on her chest.*[6]

Firth himself made no claim to have stood by her. He spoke of her courage but said nothing to uphold his own. With the instincts of a survivor, he was determined to stay where he was until somebody rescued him, as confirmed by passenger John Holland, who told the *New York Herald*:

> *He was not there trying to save her, but he was there because he had not, up to that time, had a chance to get off. He was one of the first to go up the rigging and the last to come down.*[7]

Rosa's husband wrote a letter to a newspaper in England to let family know of her death. He made no mention of having deserted her, but in a carefully worded narrative gave the facts about her death while making it sound like he had remained with her in her final hours:

> *After hanging six hours in the rigging, my wife began to lose the use of her limbs, then grew delirious and foamed at the mouth, and after nearly nine hours she fell dead from cold. The only chance left for me was to get from the mizzen rigging to the front of the ship....Thank God, I crossed safely and was saved by a boat.*[8]

It defies belief that it took her nine hours to die. She was in her nightclothes. She was probably unconscious before daylight, as Samuel Vick said.

THE WINDS HAD QUIETED DOWN SLIGHTLY BUT THE SEA WAS STILL VERY active. As he surveyed the scene on shore, Firth saw a new man arrive. People were coming and going, but this man caught his interest. He was tall and carried himself differently from the fishermen. He seemed to know them all and said hello as he walked to the edge of the shore and surveyed the situation. The fishermen seemed to show him a certain deference, some of them even removing their caps. He walked over to the man who appeared to be in charge—Edmund Ryan. They talked briefly and the man pointed up at Firth. They had a brief exchange, pointing at the wreck. The conversation seemed animated. Surely it was about him and those in the rigging with him.

He did not take his eyes off them. They finished their conversation, but then, after one final look their way, the tall man walked back from the shore and over the rise. The chief officer settled back. More disappointment. Time passed as he wondered how much longer he could hang on. Then, an hour or so after he first arrived, the man reappeared and spoke again to Ryan. They both looked again towards Firth, who waved as frantically as his exhausted body would allow, to let them know he was still alive. He told Flanly to wave.

Ryan walked among the remaining boat crews and then five of the men gathered around a boat. Others started shoving it off as they got aboard with the tall man, each picking up an oar and placing it between the thole pins.

Oh, glory! Was it finally happening?

CHAPTER 10

THE LAST SURVIVOR

At two o'clock in the afternoon, after we had been in the rigging 10 hours, the Rev Mr. Ancient, the Church of England clergyman, whose noble conduct I shall never forget while I live, got a crew of four men to row him out to the wreck. The woman, after bearing up with remarkable strength under her great trials, had died two hours before Mr. Ancient arrived.[1]

John Firth
Chief Officer

With Samuel White, James Power, Patrick Duggan, and John Slaunwhite at the oars, and the tall stranger, Rev. William Ancient, leading them, the boat passed around the battered bow and to the outside of the wreck. Also aboard, according to Ancient, was an unnamed and unruly drunk, who had decided they could not manage without him. It wasn't stormy, but the wind blew hard and cold, as it always does on the Atlantic Ocean in winter and spring. Firth and Flanly watched them intently, like starving men watching food being ladled onto a plate.

They didn't go to the logical spot—the mizzen-mast—to effect a rescue but stayed off, closer to the bow. They were taking forever! Ancient kept urging the crew to get the boat alongside the wreck but they started yelling to Firth and Flanly, telling them to go forward to where they could pick them up. That was not practical because the base of the mizzen-mast was submerged and it was nearly a hundred feet forward to where the deck came out of the water.

The wind had tempered a bit but the water was still rough and they were stopped so long that Firth began to lose heart again. He knew he could drop at any minute, like many before him had. Just then Flanly decided he had waited long enough. Firth argued with him to hang on a bit longer but he took the lifebuoy off the body of a steward who had lashed himself to the rigging and strapped it around himself. He later explained,

> *I crawled down the rigging and got on the rail along the side of the deck. Three waves washed over me, the third taking me along with it. I could not sink with the belt, and almost insensible was I, when a fisher-men's boat, pushing up to me, took me in and I indistinctly remember being landed on the shore...and carried to a fisher's house.*[2]

William Ancient had managed to snatch and hold him. There was no time to get him aboard; they had to get the boat clear first. Once out of danger, they hauled him into the boat and kept going.

Firth was now alone on the ship. He felt his heart sink as they rowed back towards the bow and on towards the shore. They were giving up!

In fact, Ancient had no intention of giving up, even if it did look hopeless. Once their passenger was ashore, they immediately turned the boat around, rowing back out to the lee side of the ship across from where they had picked Flanly up. The crew again yelled and beckoned for Firth to jump in but his response caught them by surprise: he couldn't swim.

A lively discussion ensued between one of the rowers and the stranger. John Hooper Slaunwhite, from Terence Bay, was afraid of

> The name and age of the first person rescued by Ancient's boat was incorrectly reported to have been John Hanley (often misspelled John Hindley), the only child definitively known to have survived the wreck.[3] The legend lingers to this day, but there is conclusive evidence that it was, in fact, Charles Flanly. Hanley had been rescued by steerage passenger Richard Reynolds, who'd pulled him up through a porthole, as John himself confirmed days later. [4]

losing his beloved pastor. William Ancient was the ex–Royal Navy man who had come to their tiny community from England, got a church built, started a school, preached the gospel, baptized their babies, married their children, and buried their parents. Whatever the job, he got it done. He reassured Slaunwhite and then, to Firth's amazement, he stepped onto the rickety wreck and climbed the sloping side to the rail. He went up the rigging of the mainmast and came down with two long pieces of rope, one of which he tied to the wreck in case he should get washed off. He wrapped the other over his shoulder. With the rope in his hands, he proceeded towards the stern, atop the sloping rail to the submerged base of the mizzen-mast, tying the long rope at intervals along the length of the ship as he went, to help him get back with Firth in tow.

There, he lashed himself on, shouted up to Firth and threw him the other rope. Firth tied it around himself and started down the ratlines. As soon as he moved, his exhausted legs gave out and he plunged into the maelstrom. Ancient managed to hang on to him as he bounced along the wreck, screaming that his two legs had been broken. "Never mind your shins, man," Ancient yelled. "It's your life we're after!" He somehow got the rather corpulent Firth out of the water and onto the rail. They worked their way to the bow where the boat picked them up.

It was mid-afternoon on April 1, 1873. The last person alive was off the ship and was being helped towards Clancy's house—but Sarah Jane turned him away.

Years later, she described Firth's condition:

The last two men saved were benumbed with cold and could not have lived much longer; one was put to bed. I gave the other hot drinks and told Mr. Ryan to take the man to his house as our house was packed full, could not hold another person.

The man I write of, Mr. Firth, turned to Mr. Ryan and said: "If you take care of me, I will give you a hundred dollars."[5]

That would be $2,000 in today's money.

They were words of desperation from a man who had been defying death's embrace for too long. After all he had been through—the wait, seeing so many perish, losing Rosa, the on-again off-again nature of the rescue, seeing Charles Flanly almost drown, the sea finally clutching him when he fell in—being turned out at the very door of deliverance was more than he could stand.

So, like hundreds before him, John Firth was rowed across the tickle to Edmund Ryan's house, the last survivor that Elizabeth and her daughters cobbled back together. Two hours later, the bow, resting on the rock, supporting the weight of the ship and the twisting of the heavy masts out over the water, broke off from the rest of the ship before it finished rolling over and sank. The builder, Edward Harland, later said that "she twisted her nose off." The sea had completed the destruction fourteen hours after the *Atlantic* grounded.

Did Elizabeth's husband ever see the $100? It is unlikely; Firth would not have had that kind of money with him.

Did the captain or the White Star Line ever come good on the $500 or £500 per load, as the captain had promised as he stood on the disintegrating ship with nobody to turn to but a dozen strangers who appeared out of the night? They did not.

The men in those three boats were their salvation, as were so many of the local people. Even though forty or fifty survivors got ashore on their own, their survival depended on the locals. If they had struck on an uninhabited shore, especially an uninhabited island, they would have faced a bleak future indeed and the death count, bad though it was, would have been much higher.

The survivors were now spread out among all the available homes in the nearby communities. There were forty-six houses in Lower Prospect and Terence Bay combined. Adding that number again for Upper Prospect means that roughly four people were doled out to each house. It was not that neat and tidy, of course. Some took a dozen or more and others did not take any. Those closest to the wreck—the Clancys, Ryans, O'Briens, Blackburns, and Coolens—had multiple family members on the scene and are mentioned most often in the records.

By midday that day, Simon Harrie of Terence Bay was leading the steadfast third officer, Cornelius Brady, on foot to Halifax. They left around 1:00 P.M. Later that afternoon, John Foxley, with some of his engineers and a few passengers—around a dozen people, all told—followed their footsteps, in snow they reported to be a foot or more deep. It was a long trudge. Near Hatchet Lake, they rested at Strawhouse, on Court Hill Farm, a well-known stopping place for travellers. It was operated by Thomas Drysdale and his wife, Mary Ann Umlah.[6] Local resident Ed Holt advised that the Strawhouse was located where St. Timothy's Church stands today.

The going was too hard for some and they ended up spending the night, either there or at a house perhaps in Brookside or Goodwood.

The second group arrived in Halifax at 10:30 P.M. on April 1, the day of the wreck.[7] The mayor, James Duggan, had been alerted by Brady's arrival earlier and preparations were already underway for the second part of the rescue: getting the survivors to Halifax.

CHAPTER 11

STOP THE PRESSES!

It is our painful duty this morning to record the most terrible marine disaster that has ever occurred on our coast.

Halifax Morning Chronicle
April 2, 1873

The first details about the disaster came from the pen of William S. Fielding, the twenty-five-year-old reporter for the *Halifax Morning Chronicle*. He got the scoop from Brady, tracking him down on the night of April 1 and getting the story into Halifax homes by breakfast the next morning.

The leading evening newspaper, the *Daily Acadian Recorder,* had stopped the presses the day before. Brady had not yet arrived in Halifax but they had the bare bones of the story, and in a single paragraph they had the name of the ship, the name of the line, where it had left from, and where it was headed. That was all they could get from their source so they were forced to make the biggest understatement of the whole story: "It is rumored that lives were lost."[1] Their source was likely the courier or somebody in the telegraph office.

Around the same time, Thomas Ismay got an overseas telegram from James Sparks, the company's agent in New York, to whom Brady had sent the news, and the *Times* in London got wind of it. They, of course, rushed it to the street. Another telegram arrived on Thomas Ismay's desk, this one from the Board of Trade. He promptly responded:

Atlantic mistook lights and struck rocks near Halifax, Two A.M. Tuesday; rolled over into deep water; sank immediately; 250 saved themselves by clinging to rigging; were taken off by fishermen; 700, including women and children, drowned; no names known as yet; survivors will be landed at Halifax, Wednesday afternoon; cared for by Cunard.

Much of the information was inaccurate and represented estimates made by Brady. At that point it was impossible for anybody to have a clear picture of the situation, but those incorrect details have been quoted and reprinted over and over in the century and a half that has elapsed.

The next day, steerage passenger Henry Dry wrote to his wife, Jane, in Basingstoke:

Our lives were saved and they were so kind to us but we have lost everything except what we stand in. I have the only old shirt on what I left home in. The only thing saved was my watch and that I must part with to get me a sheet. But, Dear Wife, I hope you will have some kind friends to give you a bit of bread, and my dear little children, kiss them all for me and accept my love from your dear husband. It will be some time before I will be able to write home for we have nearly 2 thousand miles to go now.

Henry Dry, Steerage Survivor[2]

Steerage passenger James Bateman had too many people to inform, so he wrote to a newspaper, the Guernsey *Star*, ending with:

There were seven of us in all—my wife, five cousins and myself; but I alone am saved to tell the awful tale. Dear Sir, I cannot write to all my friends; but I thought if I sent to you you might get it published in the papers, and so everyone would know.

It was printed three weeks later.[3]

Overnight, two steamships were made ready to depart from Halifax for the wreck site. The first was the SS *Lady Head*, a government vessel named after the wife of Sir Edmund Walker Head, the Governor General of Canada from 1854 to 1861. It travelled in company with the Cunard steamer *Delta*. Carrying food, clothing, and other essentials, they departed Halifax at 3:00 A.M. on April 2, accompanied by the steam tug *Goliah*. The intent was to arrive at daybreak to allow for the maximum amount of daylight. Nobody knew what to expect.

Fielding reported,

When Mr. Brady left Prospect at noon, all who were alive on the steamer had been rescued except the Chief Officer, Mr. Firth. He was still in the rigging, holding on for life, and crying for assistance, but the sea had become so rough that no boat could venture out.

Journalist William S. Fielding was the first to get the story for the *Halifax Morning Chronicle*. (NS ARCHIVES, NOTMAN STUDIO, NO. 1983-310 #91952)

Having missed the dramatic rescue, Brady was unaware that Firth was safely ashore, and when Fielding asked if he would survive, Brady replied, "I fear not. He must have been almost exhausted when I left, and he could hardly hold out until the sea became calm enough for a boat to venture out. I tried to get some volunteers to go, but all said it would be certain death."[4]

Fielding's reporting created a sensation and sent his career into overdrive. His work over the following weeks was competent and thorough and was reprinted in newspapers all over the world. In vivid Victorian prose, he captured the devastation and overwhelming scale of the event. It would turn out to be the biggest loss of life in a transatlantic steamship disaster up to that point in time and would continue to be until the *Titanic*.

Within a year he would become the managing director of the newspaper, where he remained for ten years before entering politics and being elected premier of Nova Scotia. He then made the jump to federal politics and in 1896 he became the federal minister of finance in the government of Sir Wilfrid Laurier. He later served as finance minister in William Lyon Mackenzie King's government.

When the *Delta* left the wharf at 3:00 A.M. on April 2, Fielding was aboard, snatching a couple of hours' sleep before embarking on a long day of electrifying activity and overwhelming sadness, all of which, with only a pencil and notebook, he had to take in, put into context, and communicate while working on an impossible deadline without any communication with the paper. He brought the colossal tragedy of the situation into the parlours of Halifax and the world: "Man, woman and child had been alike swallowed up by the greedy deep that strove hard to keep its human prey, and fought for it with angry breaker and sullen roar of surf."[5]

Half the distance the three vessels travelled to the wreck site was within Halifax Harbour itself. Then, once they reached Chebucto Head, which marks the outer limit of the harbour and the beginning of the open sea, there it was: the "elusive" Sambro light, welcoming them and guiding them all the way to their destination. It was just twenty-four hours since the six lookouts had managed to miss the light. Without it, the way was fraught with opportunities to "come to grief," in the parlance of shipping disasters. It enabled vessels to avoid the rocks, reefs, and shoals along the coast: The Sisters, Blind Sister, Black Rock, Broad Breaker, Pollock Shoal, Mad Rock, and many, many more that lay along the route. To avoid all of that granite in the darkness, they would have run offshore and turned back again in a wide semi-circle, keeping the light as the epicentre of the route.

One of the most famous pieces of coastline in Canada is at Peggys Cove, a short boat ride or drive (today) from where the *Delta*, *Lady Head*, and *Goliah* were heading. These days, hundreds of thousands of tourists from all over the world visit there annually. Adults and children walk, run, sit, take pictures, and play hide-and-seek on the grey–white granite—the same granite that ground the bottom out of the *Atlantic*. Summer or winter, it is, as the *Acadian Recorder* described it, "a scene of wild beauty and terrible grandeur." On a summer's day, hundreds of people can be seen wandering up and down the undulating rock formations. Long fingers of these formations run offshore, rising here and there to form low reefs and islands, lurking just below the surface at high tide and sticking up clearly when the tide is low. Shallow water and vigorous currents make for productive fishing, and generations of families have lived a healthy, if challenging, life in the picturesque villages of the area.

The three vessels passed Marrs Head on the southern tip of Meaghers Island, staying offshore to avoid an area of shallow water called The Grampus that extended out from the island. They did a slow turn to the right, and travelled along the western side of the island towards the wreck. Those aboard must have been aghast at the sight that met them a few minutes later.

Boats were everywhere, arriving from all along the coast: flats, dories, rodneys, punts, seine boats, ketches, squids, and schooners, carrying the curious and the avaricious, some to gasp and groan; others to grasp and filch. Wreckage strewed the shoreline, interspersed with bodies, cargo, and scavengers. The port side of the wreck was forty-one feet down, wedged among the crevices and upon the boulders and ledges below; the starboard side was at surface level with a few show-offs walking about on it. On April 10, the *Halifax Evening Express* reported:

> At low water, the ill-fated ship can be walked over from where she parted, near the bow, to within a few feet of the stern, and yesterday the visitors to the place were gathered on her side to a number of a hundred or more.

Meaghers Island (also known as Marrs Island), where the *Atlantic* ran aground, is the outer of four small islands that continue out to sea at the end of a peninsula, where lies Lower Prospect. The outer tip of Meaghers Island is labelled on nautical charts as Marrs Head. When he reported the loss to White Star Line in Liverpool, Williams said that it had occurred on Marrs Head, and the event has been associated with that place ever since. But the remains of the *Atlantic* do not lie there. They are along the shore at the other end of the island.

Because of the shallow water, the two rescue ships could not go in to pick up the survivors; they had to anchor offshore. The tug could get in closer but still not all the way. The tug's captain had to send a boat ashore, or the local boats came out. They had to row or sail from far and wide to deliver their unexpected houseguests.

As the *Atlantic* had neared the land, the lookouts had seen breakers off to the right, the last thing they expected. They'd expected to see the Sambro light on their left, and as the ship pointed into the great maw of Halifax Harbour they would eventually have seen land on their left. The first breakers they saw off the starboard bow were most likely offshore as the waves rolled over the shallow area of the Grampus. Survivors said the ship struck several times and some said they heard a rumble and thought they were in Halifax and the anchor

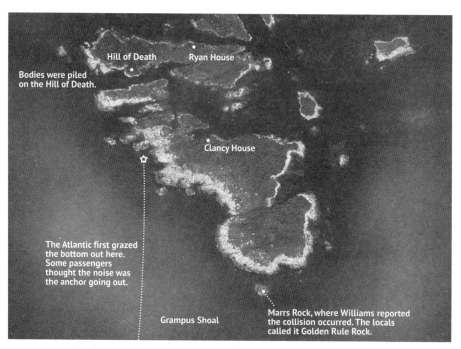

The *Atlantic* struck rocks offshore that tore open the bottom of the ship and caused the stern to sink within minutes of the grounding.

was going out.[6] That was the sound of the *Atlantic* grazing over the reefs before striking the shore. As if to confirm that, Second Steward Samuel May observed, "She first struck some way out from where she finally settled, and then ran over the other rocks, which must have torn her bottom all to pieces."[7] That would explain why the ship sank so quickly after coming to rest. It is also in line with testimony given by William Ancient when he described the ship at noon on April 1 as "lying almost broadside to the shore."[8] That would orient it precisely in line with the Grampus.

An aside: to test this hypothesis, I went out with experienced navigator Gary Fisher and, with Williams's navigation data in hand, we simulated the final ten minutes of the *Atlantic*'s last voyage. With Meaghers Island on our starboard bow and the point of final impact less than a mile away, the depth sounder indicated widely varying depths, ranging from more than one hundred feet up to within striking distance of the *Atlantic*'s bottom.

After the three rescue vessels got anchored, they began ferrying the survivors, a mournful and bedraggled consignment of mostly young men. The majority were dressed in whatever mismatched garments the people of the three communities didn't have on their own backs, along with what had been scrounged from bodies the previous morning by desperately cold, woefully underdressed men, many of whom had arrived on shore barefoot, straight from their beds. Many were badly bruised and beaten, others had broken bones, and most had frostbite.

Aboard the *Lady Head* were several customs officials, including Preventative Officer James Kerr, sent by Collector of Customs Edmund McDonald. They would remain on site, ensuring that cargo and personal possessions were not pilfered. They had their hands full. Edmund Ryan, as Justice of the Peace for the area, had already started documenting the bodies. Along with George Longard, the Justice of the Peace from Upper Prospect, he had spent the previous day examining each one for possessions, especially anything that would identify the person by name or at least by nationality or religion. If they could not identify the bodies by name, they could, at a minimum, ensure that each was accorded a funeral in the correct cemetery by a minister of their chosen faith.

Even at this early stage, the burial of the bodies was uppermost in Edmund Ryan's mind. They were strewn everywhere. He asked Kerr what was to be done but Kerr only had authority in customs matters, so he went to James Morrow, the S. Cunard and Company managing partner and agent for the White Star Line. Morrow replied that at that point he had no guidance from the owners of the steamship. The best he could do was send down coffins from Halifax.[9]

William S. Fielding and his colleagues from the other papers got down to business, surveying the scene and talking to people to gather as much information as they could in the limited time available. With so many papers pursuing the story, it was a competitive environment. Everything they reported was important, but people on both sides of the Atlantic wanted the names of the survivors. When news of the disaster reached Europe and the United States, thousands of people descended on White Star Line offices to learn if their loved ones were among the living or the dead.

The reporters convinced Captain Shaw of the *Delta* to station two men at the gangway of the ship, and as each survivor came aboard, they got his name and nationality.

The information they collected was later used to compile a list of survivors, which was sent over the wires to papers in the US and Europe. There are many disagreements and inconsistencies among the many passenger lists published after the disaster. The number of foreign names led to spelling errors by those taking the names, transcription errors by those copying them from Victorian handwriting, and typesetting errors at the newspapers. There were stowaways who did not get documented and births that occurred during the voyage—and now, 150 years later, it is difficult to read those papers, which are stained, wrinkled, faded, and often out of focus, having been copied to microfilm. Many people nowadays like to compile their genealogies and the passenger lists of immigrant ships are a fertile source of information. With so much interest in the *Atlantic*, many lists of victims and survivors got published and are now on the internet, creating headaches for researchers as they try to untangle the inconsistencies among them.

The final words from Thomas Moffatt paint a picture of the scene the survivors left behind:

We wandered about in that place the remaining part of the day, some without hats and some without boots, walking through the snow....

Before we left that place we saw a very melancholy sight. It was of a boat or two which came to the shore laden with the dead bodies of those that were taken from the ship. Their persons were then searched by an official, one reason perhaps being to produce an identification, and after this they were laid side by side on the grassy sward, finding their long and silent home on a foreign and secluded shore.

In the afternoon of the same day, about the hour of three or four, two small steamboats hove in sight, which soon bore us off to our long looked-for destination. As we were leaving the shore and getting farther out on the ocean's wave, we looked behind us and saw in the distance the ill-fated ship, of which we took a long and last look.[10]

It was actually around noon that nearly all the survivors, except the few who had walked, were aboard the ships and headed to Halifax, with 330 people on the SS *Delta* and 77 on the SS *Lady Head*. A few were unable to make the trip. Dr. Cuppage was still recovering in bed at Dennis Ryan's house[11] and Michael Carmody was at Clancy's along with Charles Flanly from the mizzen-mast rigging. There were others, as well. Overnight guests on the verge of death were a major inconvenience to the already traumatized households. After getting to Halifax, Michael Carmody spent a week in hospital; he left for the United States aboard the SS *Carlotta* of the New England and Nova Scotia Steamship Company on April 9.

Fielding's story on the morning of April 3 began with a few words about the trip back to Halifax:

Among the passengers coming up in the Delta there were ringing high praises for the gallantry of the three boats' crews, of Rev. Mr. Ancient,... of Third Officer Brady and Quartermasters Speakman and Owens, who first established communication with the shore. The kindness of the Prospect people was also universally acknowledged and praised.[12]

CHAPTER 12

THE HILL OF DEATH

Owing to the sudden influx of visitors the residences scattered on this point of the Nova Scotian coast were crowded to suffocation and scarcely afforded room for the new arrivals.

Halifax Morning Chronicle
April 3, 1873

In the mid-afternoon of April 2, 1873, two plumes of black smoke appeared off Chebucto Head. Since noon, people had been watching the harbour entrance for the two steamships. All eyes followed them as they glided past the downtown and started to tie up at Cunard's Wharf just past where the casino is today. The larger ship, SS *Delta*, tied up at 3:00 P.M. *Lady Head* docked an hour later. Slowly, ever so slowly, the passengers eased themselves down the gangway. Dressed in bits and pieces of clothing, they looked like hoboes. There were no women coming off; only men, most of them young. As they looked around, they saw lumber stacked on the dock and heard the sound of hammers pounding nails into the boards. The newly completed coffins were grim reminders of so many people who were no longer present. A few coffins were already aboard the schooner *Amateur* tied alongside, ready for transporting to the wreck site.

Survivors arriving in Halifax aboard the *Delta*. They wore whatever bits and pieces of mismatched clothing the local people could spare. (SKETCH BY JOSEPH BECKER, *FRANK LESLIE'S ILLUSTRATED NEWSPAPER*)

The ships docked in the shadow of the house in which local steamship pioneer Samuel Cunard had lived. He had founded the British and North America Royal Mail Steam Packet Company, by then known simply as Cunard's. It was the White Star Line's rival, from whom Ismay was trying to win market share. Because no White Star Line ships called at Halifax, they did not keep an office in the port and were represented by Cunard. It was ironic that local manager James Morrow was tasked with—and burdened by the life-altering stress of dealing with—this enormous and complex disaster, given Cunard's penchant for safety above all else, and the enviable record the company had achieved. The job would occupy at least some of Morrow's time for months to come.

In another irony, the two lines that would become the dominant British steamship companies shared something in common: they each experienced their first wreck on the rocks of Nova Scotia. Samuel Cunard had started by having four ships built: *Britannia*,

With five docks and extensive onshore properties near where the Halifax Casino is located today, S. Cunard and Company was the Halifax agent for Cunard steamships. It ran cruises to the West Indies using the *Delta* and other ships and was the agent for the Allan Line of steamers out of Montreal, which kept hundreds of employees busy in Halifax. Samuel Cunard's son William had been the head of the Halifax firm until 1868, when he moved to England, leaving Morrow as the sole manager until additional partners George Francklyn and Thomas Peters, grandsons of Samuel Cunard, joined in 1873.

The company owned a general merchandise trade and a large coaling business that fuelled steamers calling at Halifax and heated Halifax homes and businesses. Had the *Atlantic* made it to Halifax, the owners would have purchased coal from this company. It also represented Lloyd's and one or two other insurance companies.

With oil replacing coal as a fuel and with the arrival of jet travel, S. Cunard and Company declined. The city expropriated the property for new development in the 1970s. All that remains in the area first occupied by Abraham Cunard, Samuel's father, is an apartment tower called Cunard Court. The S. Cunard and Company name was last seen on trucks delivering fuel oil to Halifax homes. It was absorbed into Irving Oil in the early part of the twenty-first century.

Acadia, Caledonia, and *Columbia.* The *Columbia* was commissioned in 1841, thirty years before the *Atlantic,* and was lost off the southwest coast of Nova Scotia in 1843. The *Atlantic* was also one of four inaugural ships—*Oceanic, Atlantic, Baltic,* and *Republic*—for the White Star Line, commissioned in 1871, thirty years after the *Columbia*'s commissioning, and lost in 1873, thirty years after the *Columbia*'s loss. What the disasters did not share in common was that all aboard the Cunard ship were saved.[1]

Having seen almost all the survivors come aboard, and being able to account for the others, Captain Williams now had his first opportunity to make an estimate of the survivors—and from that to calculate the number of deaths. Although the number was record-breaking, it was not as large as had first been reported. The earliest reports had said there were around 750 dead. According to the captain, the *Atlantic* had on board 33 cabin passengers, with 800 in the steerage, and a crew (including officers) of 143 persons; making a total of 976 people. That made for 546 deaths.[2]

Fielding, who was the first person to report the numbers in a newspaper, added prudently, "This may not be precisely correct, but is nearly so."[3] He was already showing the instincts of a successful finance minister. He was also prescient in that determining the exact numbers has since turned out to be impossible.

With the disaster over, the rescue completed, and the survivors in Halifax, life should have been returning to normal for the people living near the wreck site. They should at least have been getting their beds back. But nothing would get back to normal for a long time. The area was inundated with visitors. For $2, the curious could board a tug in Halifax and cruise to the site. Relatives from communities far and wide were dropping by for a night or two to see what the fuss was about—and perhaps do a little scrounging. The salvagers were trying to start recovering the cargo. With between five and six hundred dead, there were a lot of corpses in need of immediate attention. Relatives of victims started arriving. Out-of-town reporters were showing up.

The *Evening Reporter* stated:

> *Including the number who went down by the road from the city, and which was being constantly added to from every little hamlet and vil-lage within a radius of 10 miles [there would] not have been less than six or seven hundred people cruising around the island in the vicinity of the wreck.*[4]

And where were all these visitors to stay? Anybody in a vessel with living quarters could stay aboard. For everybody else—and that included at least 95 percent of those who showed up—there was only one place: in somebody's house. The words of a reporter for the *Acadian Recorder* have much to tell us.

> *On landing at Ryans Island I was fortunate enough to meet with [Edmund] Ryan, of whom much has already been said in praise. I applied to him for lodgings for a few days, and he very kindly took me to his mother's comfortable house, where I am writing this moment.*[5]

This was incredible kindness and hospitality from a well-trauma-tized seventy-year-old widow.[6] From this writer, we get a first-hand account of how the people's otherwise quiet and uneventful lives had been turned upside down.

> *I find all the people about here deeply impressed with the scenes of the past few days. They speak of them in a subdued tone and their faces*

have not yet lost the traces of the terror which the circumstances of the disaster have evidently impressed on them. The women, particularly, are deeply affected.

The old lady, Mrs. Ryan, with whom I am stopping, never tires of telling of the many scenes—how scores of the poor wretches came to the house in the morning—half naked, half frozen, stupefied, and threw themselves on the floor by the stove, and were for a long time apparently unconscious and more dead than alive. And often as she tells her stories, she will burst out weeping as if telling of the death of a favorable child.[7]

The boat that took me to the island landed me at one of the most distressing spots I ever gazed upon....I stepped upon the land and worked my way through lanes of coffins, strewn about in every place...a field of sepulchres, scattered around like boxes and barrels....

I came to a body unconfined, lying on the ground....They told me it was the stewardess. She was...probably a ladylike and good-natured woman. But the agony depicted in her face! It will haunt me for years. She had made desperate struggles for life but they were made in vain. Her eyes were rolled entirely round and strained nearly out of their sockets, her teeth were clenched, and every feature was distorted with the most unendurable agony.

I turned away from the place sick and sad. My head was aching and I wished I could go somewhere or do something to banish forever from my mind the horrible scenes I had witnessed.[8]

The body referred to may have been that of Fanny McNally.

The reporter could return to Halifax but these people, the rescuers of the living and salvagers of the dead, and now the custodians of their bodies, had nowhere to go. They were at home, in shock, with more to endure, for the retrieval and examination of bodies would continue for weeks. When a body was found, it was taken to a place that came to be called the Hill of Death, on Ryans Island, not far from Mrs. Ryan's house, as the report above noted. That was where the *Acadian Recorder* reporter ended up, and what Edmund and Dennis

Ryan's mother had to contend with. It is on a scenic and peaceful little lagoon between Ryans Island and Norris Island. From the wreck site, it is the nearest access to quiet water and the logical place for dories and other boats to take newly recovered bodies. To this day, scuba divers report seeing leather shoes and boots on the bottom of the lagoon.

Bronze religious medallion recovered from the "Hill of Death." Side one reads: St. Louis De Gonzague; side two reads: O. S. Ange Soyez Mon Guide. (COURTESY SS *ATLANTIC* HERITAGE PARK)

The bodies laid out on the Hill of Death would have been accessible to anybody, including the local children, who must have had nightmares about it for the rest of their lives. Nowadays, grief counsellors are a standard part of the response for even minor events involving children and teens. These families were on their own and had to deal with the impact of what they experienced as well as they could. In a time and place where superstition was common, many stories were born—of ghost ships, of women in long white dresses walking the shores searching for their lost children—and these stories have lived on. Thirty-six-year-old William Hardiman, of Upper Prospect, was admitted to the Nova Scotia Hospital for the Insane, as it was then known, in August of 1875 after suffering for a year with delusions that involved both the *Atlantic* and being haunted by the devil.[9] Michael Duggan speaks of his great-granduncle Patrick Duggan, who served in the boat that rescued Chief Officer Firth, being haunted for the rest of his life by the image of Rosa Bateman hanging dead in the mizzen-mast rigging.[10]

On the other hand, life goes on, especially for kids. The distressed *Acadian Recorder* reporter mused,

> Is it not strange how we get accustomed to the most terrible scenes? It is said that the children on the island were very much agitated at first by the presence of so many dead bodies; this morning I heard them playing

hide and go seek in a building containing confined corpses. It is becoming an old story now.[11]

The building was an unused house owned by Robert Slaunwhite that was being prepared to be floated off the island and relocated to the mainland.[12]

VALUABLES RECOVERED FROM THE BODIES WERE TURNED OVER TO EDMUND Ryan and George Longard, who delivered them to James Kerr, the customs official. The records show that on one occasion John Keilly, James Landry, Hugh White, John D. Christian, and William B. Christian delivered money, jewellery, banking documents, photographs, and other valuables to the justices.

The bodies and what they held were documented only to the extent that it was possible. Given the quick exit they were forced to make from the ship, most did not bear any identification. Typical reports read like so:

Lot 11. Male body; about 45 years old, dark brown hair, red whiskers, with a little girl with her arms around him, about 4 years old, with earrings—45 sovereigns in purse found in his pocket.

Lot 57. Female body; supposed to be Mrs. Murphy from papers found on her person—two finger rings and photograph.[13]

The way the local magistrates took control of the scene and required people to hand over any valuables recovered from bodies raised a few eyebrows. Who did they think they were?

Edmund Ryan, as the magistrate for Lower Prospect, had been the first to let people know there was not to be a free-for-all. He conferred with Nicholas Christian, a fellow magistrate, to ensure he was on solid ground. After all, this was rural Nova Scotia and neither of them had ever had to deal with anything remotely similar to what they were dealing with now. Christian agreed that as the only representatives of the authorities, they had to make sure order was maintained.[14] But there was much muttering, and when the *Morning Chronicle* wondered in its pages on what authority the magistrates were acting, an obviously frazzled Edmund Ryan was quick to respond, with a letter to the *Express*:

> *Edmund Ryan, Esq., J.P. whose untiring labors at and about the wreck since that dreadful April morn, has been the theme of general praise, has requested us to insert the following note:*
>
> *Prospect, April 9*
>
> *To the editor of the Express*
>
> *Sir:*
> *Will you allow me to ask the "Chronicle" in reply to its question—"Under whose authority are the Magistrates of Prospect acting?" Who should have acted if not the Magistrates? We did not seek the work, and will willingly resign it to any authorized person; but had we not assumed the responsibility of looking after the valuables, it is likely there would not have been many left for "authorized" persons to look after.*
>
> *Yours truly.*
> *Edmund Ryan J.P.[15]*

Among the items that John Christian delivered were a Canadian two-dollar bill and a fifty-cent Canadian silver coin, indicating that the owner might have been a Canadian. Unfortunately, we do not have his name.

In the meantime, relatives and friends of passengers all over the world were anxiously awaiting the names of the survivors and the dead. On April 2, concerned relatives and friends swamped New York's Castle Garden, the immigration processing centre that preceded Ellis Island, looking for information that was not yet available. They were referred to the offices of the White Star Line, at No. 10 Broadway, which was also packed with people, all asking the same questions, and

There are several other known Canadians connections to the *Atlantic*. The first was David Boswell. He was originally reported to have died, having escaped the wreck wearing only his nightclothes, but he was alive, and arrived in Halifax a day later.[16] His late arrival indicates that he was unable to be moved as part of the pickup by the *Lady Head* and *Delta*. He was a master furniture maker, and as the family story goes, while he recovered onshore his toolbox washed up from the wreck. He took this as a sign that he wasn't meant to go to Boston as planned. In Halifax, he was clothed and fed not only by the Cunard representatives but also by what the newspaper describes as the "Scottish societies," probably the North British Society. Mr. Boswell was a Scot, having been born on May 5, 1849, in Edinburgh. He eventually travelled to the Canadian west instead. Signing up to join the Red River Expedition to Manitoba, he walked from Port Arthur, Ontario, to Winnipeg, Manitoba, with Indigenous guides. He befriended many Indigenous peoples and even learned their languages, counting them as his friends for life. He always said he'd survived the wreck because he was a strong swimmer and, of course, because he was a young man. He and his wife, Mary Leask, had three sons and a daughter. Boswell died in Winnipeg on March 25, 1925.[17]

The other Canadian was Irving Azariah Stuttaford, the steward from Kingston, Ontario. In Halifax, he and eleven others from the crew were accommodated at the Elm House on Water Street. They took out a newspaper ad expressing their gratitude to the proprietor, Mr. Fleming.[18]

Steerage passenger William Hoy, who has been credited with hauling many men up onto Golden Rule Rock once they arrived via the rope, is supposed to have saved a seventeen-year-old named William McAllister. Family tradition states that Hoy, who was on his way to settle in Canada, ended up going to Australia and being visited later in life by McAllister, who wanted to meet the man who had saved him. Unfortunately, Hoy had already died after living a full life.[19]

all getting the same unsatisfying answers from the company's agents. All the company's representatives could say was that they hoped at some point in the evening to obtain a list of the saved, which would be the list that the newspapermen had made as the survivors had come aboard the *Delta* one by one that morning. As soon as the *Delta* had landed, the news was taken to the telegraph office and the message was composed and sent.

Most of those inquiring of the White Star Line in New York were working-class people and nearly all had paid their $33 to the company to bring over a sister, brother, parent, or near relative from the old country. Among them was Patrick Hanley of Newark, New Jersey, inquiring about his uncle and aunt, Patrick and Mary Hanley, and their two sons, Michael and John, aged seventeen and twelve years. They would be devastated to learn that only twelve-year-old John had survived.

John and his brother had been sleeping in the bow with the single men while their parents were in the married quarters amidships. When the ship sank by the stern and rolled over, his parents were drowned. John had no recollection of what happened to his older brother but he followed the crowd, eventually ending up with six men in the upper steerage accommodations. Somebody broke a porthole and the men started going up through it and out onto the sloping side of the ship. It was a tight squeeze for a fully grown man. Passenger Richard Reynolds had reached down as a man below had passed John up.

When John Hanley got to Halifax it was noted that, unlike most of his grown-up companions, he was wearing sufficient clothing to protect him from the cold, ill-fitting though it might have been. William Neal, a haberdasher, took him to his store, Neal, White, and Company, at 94 Granville Street, and fitted him out from head to toe. Photographers Wellington Chase and William O'Donnell had him pose for a portrait in their studios. On April 4, Chase's photo was advertised for sale, with the proceeds going to John.[20]

The photos were a popular item, as was John. He was showered with attention and a dozen families even offered to adopt him, but he still had a family in New Jersey, albeit reduced significantly. Several newspapers reported that he did not seem to be overly affected by the loss of his family. The trauma had probably put him into a state of shock, as his later life would indicate.

CHAPTER 13

FAREWELL TO NOVA SCOTIA, YOUR SEA-BOUND COAST

All the survivors arrived in Liverpool concur in extolling the bravery and humanity of the people of Prospect Island, and of the family of Ryan, on Ryan's Island, as well as of the prompt kindness of the Halifax people and the agent of the Cunard Company, Mr. J. C. Morrison.

Bradford Observer
April 22, 1873

The citizens of Halifax came out in force to welcome the survivors, stopping them in the streets with offers of food and clothing, always curious to hear about their experiences. They had left Europe with such high hopes and now there was none among them who had not suffered a life-changing loss—whole families gone in a flash of time, with no chance to even say goodbye; property gone; savings vanished. Most may have boarded the ship poor, but now they were penniless. The newspapers were filled with their stories. There was such a demand for information that the *Acadian Recorder* printed a second edition on April 2 and the *Halifax Evening Reporter* offered to buy papers back from subscribers so they could resell them the same day.[1]

As a result of the *Atlantic* loss, on the afternoon of April 2, 1873, James Morrow's staff at Cunard's Halifax office had a lot to deal with. Morrow had been called out of bed before dawn to approve the use of the *Delta* and to start making arrangements for the surviving passengers. He had assigned John Hoyt, John Milsom, Charles Francklyn, and J. C. Morrison to arrange accommodation and transportation. The immediate need was to get them properly clothed.

That meant serving, at a minimum, survivors who spoke German, Dutch, Norwegian, Swedish, and French as well as those from the British Isles who spoke English, Irish, Scots, and Welsh. Many of them spoke only their native tongue. In cases where there were similar ethnic populations in Halifax, the immigrants were received by committees of the various national societies, who attended to their needs, located them in boarding houses, and furnished them with food, clothing, and so on.

They were mostly men from twenty to twenty-five years of age. Many were in a pitiable condition—without shoes, feet swollen and bruised, clothes torn and drenched, some with bits of carpet, matting, and blankets around them, and all distressed and weakened from their long exposure to the elements.

The Cunard men did such a good job that their efforts were mentioned in several newspapers. They got each man a suit of clothing and a room at a hotel or a bed at the hospital. They helped get letters off to loved ones and found a berth on the steamships *Chase* and *Falmouth*, en route to the US. One group was billeted at the British Hotel in Halifax and they were so pleased with their stay that forty-six of them, including Thomas Moffatt and Charles Flanly, took out an ad in the paper on April 3 to thank the proprietors, Charles and Mrs. Ramsay, for their kindness and hospitality. "Indeed," they added, "we were not only treated with the greatest hospitality, but we had all the clothes, boots, and other necessaries we wished for, which the boarders in the hotel and outside gentlemen brought in abundance."[2]

Captain Williams booked into the Halifax Hotel, the leading hotel on the east coast, in the company of at least eight saloon-class passengers. He would remain in Halifax for more than a month. In the Acadian Hotel, farther down the scale, Chief Engineer John Foxley was rooming with the engineers who had walked to Halifax. Passengers and crew were billeted in rooming houses and hotels all over town, including at the Mansion House where Thomas Chapman and others were placed.[3] In the days following their departures, notices appeared in various papers thanking their hosts for their kindness.

After getting everybody clothed, fed, and rested, on Thursday, April 3, 1873, S. Cunard and Company sent a telegram to the White Star Line office in New York, advising them that two hundred passengers were expected to leave Halifax aboard the steamer *Chase* that morning for New York via Portland, Maine, with others to follow on the steamer *Falmouth* in the evening. They were expected to be in New York on Saturday.[4]

The *New York Tribune* reported on April 8 that 316 had arrived in New York. Some survivors were delayed in Halifax because of injuries, and a few others like Freeman Marckwald and David Boswell went by other routes and at other times, bringing the number of survivors to approximately four hundred.

The ships departed from the Dominion Wharf where George P. Black, the agents of the New England and Nova Scotia Steamship Company, had its premises. With all they had been through, the men were glad to be getting on their way. To make the trip more pleasant for his former countrymen, one German citizen of Halifax distributed a hundred or so briar pipes, along with a pound of tobacco per person. Before long, the air on the wharf was blue from a multitude of Germans puffing contentedly. Some others had provided rum, and a few had become intoxicated but, before long, all were on their way to the United States.

From Portland, they continued to Boston by rail, arriving on the morning of Saturday, April 5, just as the Halifax inquiry into the cause of the disaster was getting started, and were met at the station by Mr. Murdoch of the White Star Line, accompanied by Hamilton Perry, who had once served as captain of the *Atlantic*. Present was steward Henry Roberts, also from the *Atlantic*.[5] In the meantime, another steward, Thomas Dunn, was en route from Halifax with injured saloon passengers Samuel Vick and Simon Comachio.[6]

The short visit to Boston began with a reception at Faneuil Hall in Boston National Historical Park and a breakfast hosted by the mayor, Henry Pierce. Curious Bostonians streamed into the hall to see the survivors—and especially John Hanley, who left $100 richer after a collection was taken among the onlookers.[7] They also had lunch before travelling on to New York, taking the short train ride on the Old Colony and Newport Railroad to Fall River and then boarding the SS *Newport* for the trip to New York.

Absent from those boarding the railcars was twenty-two-year-old James Pym, a passenger from Plymouth. He remained in Boston and got a job with the *Boston Traveler*, where he worked for at least fifty-seven years. His story appeared in the *Linotype News* in 1930. At that time he was eighty years old and still going strong, having worked as a compositor, makeup man, copy-cutter, and proofreader. He had two sons.

John Hanley wearing an outfit provided by Halifax clothier and City Alderman William Neal. The photo was taken by William O'Donnell at his studio.

They arrived at 7:00 A.M. on Sunday. The *Newport* had its regular passengers disembark at their pier at the foot of Murray Street. With that done, the emigrants were put aboard the towboat *William Fletcher* under the care of the White Star Line agent Mr. Gardiner and conveyed to Castle Garden, where a huge and very emotional crowd had been waiting since before dawn.

John Hanley was finally reunited with his two sisters, Brigid and Mary. Like many of the reunions, it was bittersweet. The *New York Tribune* commented,

He was conveyed to the reception room and was convulsively clasped to his sister's bosom in a paroxysm of mingled grief and joy, after which he was seized by her husband and similarly embraced, the scene affecting the bystanders to tears.[8]

Brigid and Mary had immigrated to the US years before. They lived and worked in Newark, New Jersey, likely in a textile mill. Brigid married Hugh Towey in Newark, and at the time of the wreck she had one young son, also named John. She and her husband eventually had a total of seven children—six sons and one daughter. Her little brother, John, not surprisingly, moved in with his sisters. Mary, called "Aunt Marie" by her nieces and nephews, was unmarried and also lived with Brigid and Hugh.

Those not staying in New York spent the day at Castle Garden chatting, smoking, and napping. To add insult to injury, William Hoy was robbed, having his pockets picked while he slept on the floor at Castle Garden. The thief made off with $50—all the money Hoy possessed.[9]

They were served another substantial dinner at 4:00 P.M., and at five o'clock they boarded the SS *Virginia Seymour* and were taken to the Erie Railroad depot. There they boarded two first-class railway cars and at 7:00 P.M. they left Jersey City on the Western Express. Chicago was the primary destination, with thirty survivors headed there. Twenty went to Cleveland, four to Duluth, and three to other points in Minnesota; two went to Youngstown, Ohio, two to Detroit, and one to Saginaw, Michigan. The White Star Line provided emigrant-class transportation, but the Erie Railroad Company upgraded everybody to first class and put them on an express train, as did the Pennsylvania Central Railroad with its share of the passengers.[10]

At this time, James H. Sparks, the White Star Line agent in New York, released details about the numbers of steerage passengers lost and saved. He provided a list, stating that 585 had perished and 311 had survived, for a total of 896 steerage passengers. That's about 100 too many as compared to other reports. He declared that the list would prove to be in excess of the actual loss because of the difficulty in reading the names on the message from England—an understatement, to be sure.

CHAPTER 14

LEAD US
NOT INTO
TEMPTATION

I saw one man, who passed from the main to the fore rigging,
snatch the watch out of the pocket of Mr. Price, who was lying dead
in the rigging.[1]

John Gilbert
Steward

For those outside the three communities involved in the rescue, the only way for anybody without access to a newspaper to find out about the wreck would have been through personal contact. The few families in the tiny farming community of Brookside, NS, got the word from one of the two groups that walked to Halifax in the afternoon of April 1. Along the shore, the news spread from Prospect to Shad Bay, East and West Dover, McGraths Cove, and Peggys Cove, and in the other direction to Pennant and the largest community on the coast, Sambro, and then farther along to Ketch Harbour, Portuguese Cove, and Herring Cove, where the remains of HMS *Tribune*, a Royal Navy frigate that had sunk in 1797 after striking a shoal, lay.[2]

An armada descended on the site to discover a prize of indescribable proportions. This was no schooner or even a barque or coastal steamer. The *Atlantic* was in a league of its own, a big, fat, rich ship with a thousand people and their belongings, along with a valuable cargo.

This is the earliest known photograph of the wrecked *Atlantic*, with the bow broken off and pushed by the waves. (SOURCE UNKNOWN)

For people along the coast living a basic existence, the opportunities were mind-boggling.

The unwritten law along most seacoasts is that if a ship comes to grief, anybody who can is expected to help rescue and comfort the living, but once that job is over, the ship and anything aboard is fair game. That, of course, is not the law of the sea. As long as the ship is not abandoned by those entrusted with its care, then the ship and its contents remain the property of the owners. To reinforce that, Captain Williams posted reliable members of the crew as sentries under the direction of an officer or quartermaster.

When the *Martin van Buren*, a large supply ship travelling from New York to Europe in January 1945, was discovered abandoned across the bay from where the *Atlantic* wrecked, it was said that it fed the community of Sambro for two years, despite the best efforts of the Royal Canadian Mounted Police. Some folks from those parts will still give you a big smile at the mention of the *Martin van Buren*. As author Jack Zinck observes, "Those who can still recall that day clearly in their minds may chuckle at the antics that took place so close to their homes, and at how the attitudes of people will change when opportunity presents itself."[3]

Captain Williams had given diving master John Sheridan and salvager Alfred Larder provisional authority to salvage the cargo,[4] but anything else was impossible to police, and that was not their responsibility. There was plenty of flotsam floating around—useful things like lumber that were of little value to the White Star Line, so why not take it home? That wasn't stealing, was it? And if it was floating around, well, nobody owned it, right?

Wrong! As it turns out, the insurance company owned it. Anybody who picked up anything from the ship was committing not one, but two, crimes. They would be stealing from the insurance company, and if they took the item home they could be charged with smuggling because goods coming into Canada were subject to customs duties. Authority over the site was immediately in the hands of the customs men like Edmund McDonald and James Kerr.

Especially troubling, though, was that many bodies were also floating around and they could be readily divested of any valuables. The majority of the people living along the coast were God-fearing folk, but temptation was in the air and there was much to be tempted by. Many immigrants carried on their persons the value of all their worldly possessions, which had been converted to gold coins which were often sewn into a piece of clothing, such as the lining of a vest, and worn throughout the trip.

The crew and stowaways were accused of grievous offenses to the bodies—even of cutting off fingers to get rings. That has led to a story, still told today, about one man so greedy he didn't stop to remove the rings, but instead cut off the fingers and threw them into a jar of brine to preserve them until he had time to remove the jewellery. The story has great shock value but it sounds unlikely.

But it wasn't only the crew that was accused, as the *Acadian Recorder* noted on April 12:

Painful rumors have been in circulation of plundering by the fishermen, but we have it on the best authority that these statements are in nearly every case totally untrue.

The captain was quoted in the *Chicago Tribune*:

He said that the people at Prospect did all they could for the living and the dead, but among the crowds who flocked to the place from the surrounding country, there were some who robbed the bodies when they could get a chance.[5]

Many papers reported how the fishermen watched over the bodies and protected them from looters. They were likely driven not just by normal decency, but also because they felt a certain bond with the people they had been unable to save, given the massive effort they had expended rescuing the people they did manage to get ashore, many of whom would have been relatives of the dead. Nicholas Christian reported,

I saw one of the crew quarrel with Edmund Ryan who insisted upon his delivering up some jewellery which he had taken from the dead body of a woman. Ryan asked me should he not take charge of the articles as a Justice of the Peace. I said "yes" and he succeeded in getting them. One of the passengers having run away to the woods with a valuable image, Ryan followed him, recovered it and gave it into my charge. I afterwards delivered it to Mr. Kerr, the customs officer.[6]

Other papers ran articles and editorials that took a broad-brush approach and swept up a lot of innocent crew members. There had been some thirty-five stewards and stewardesses on board, of whom twenty survived, and the surviving stewards were sufficiently piqued to send a delegation to the newspapers asking that they be spared the reproach being directed at the crew as a whole. One contended:

The sailors are changed every voyage, and consequently often bad characters get on board. The stewards are permanently in the company's service, and unless their characters are good, will not be employed. The papers have put us all down among the crew and thus we have been unjustly condemned for the offence of others.

"We admit to the justice of the stewards' statements and have pleasure in publishing them," wrote the *Morning Chronicle* on April 5, 1873.

The stewards had a point. Many within the crew required little by way of skill. For example, the firemen needed only to be able to shovel coal and tolerate the heat of the boiler room, which they called the stoke hole. They were not retained by the company as employees but were released after each voyage and a new batch rounded up before departure.

However, they must have liked the White Star Line because the crew documents indicate that almost half of the crew on the *Atlantic*'s nineteenth voyage had sailed on the previous trip, and nearly two-thirds stated that their previous trip had been on a White Star Line ship. During later testimony at the inquiry, most of the officers were asked about the crew and the responses were similar. They were no better nor worse than most other crews. When asked, the captain replied, "The seamen we had were as good as the average....If we obtain ten seamen out of a crew of forty we consider ourselves fortunate."[7]

Under the circumstances of the moment, it would be fair to conclude that some, both crew members and locals, were at their best—and some were at their worst.

James Kerr was adamant that anything recovered was to be turned over to him and he made a point of being seen around the site. Edmund Ryan and George Longard, as Justices of the Peace, collected watches, coins, jewellery, documents, and other personal possessions from friends, relatives, and strangers on behalf of Mr. Kerr. By April 10, $6,000 in cash and jewellery had been collected and turned over to Kerr[8] but it was impossible to police everything and a lot got carted away. For example, the SS *Atlantic* Heritage Park has in its artifact collection a large bronze clock believed to be the clock from the chart room of the *Atlantic*. It was donated by a local retiree in his mid-seventies, who remembered it being kept in his mother's dresser drawer when he was a child. Included is the key to wind it, as the clock still works; it runs for eight days between rewinds. To recover that clock would have required somebody to board the wreck before it sank, make his way to the chart room, and take it from the wall, and have the presence of mind to take the key, which would have been inserted in the winding hole.

Peter Christian and the clock that was in his family from the day the *Atlantic* wrecked. He donated it to the SS *Atlantic* Heritage Park. (CHRIS DEVANNEY)

Not everybody was trying to steal something. On April 12, the *Evening Express* told of three fishermen from Sambro who had recovered a bale of silk, which they turned over to the customs authorities. "The salvage on the bale will be a respectable sum for the honest fishermen," the paper reported approvingly.

At the other extreme, nobody had a kind word for the stowaways. We only know the names of two, and those are from police records. So many accusations were levelled against them that they deemed it wise to leave the area, so they took a train to Digby and sailed across the Bay of Fundy to Saint John, New Brunswick. By April 15, one man was in custody for stealing while on the steamer bound for Saint John and another had twice been before the court for drunkenness.[9]

Chapter 15

Dust to Dust

Even though the most important part of the response to the *Atlantic* calamity—safeguarding the survivors—was in hand, there was much more to be done. City Council and the mayor had already met, as had the provincial legislature. Telegrams were flying back and forth between Halifax and Ottawa, the capital of the newly confederated Canada, as yet consisting of only six provinces. (Today, of course, there are ten provinces and three territories.)

The immediate issue was taking care of the dead. Many bodies were still inside the wreck; how many was anybody's guess. There was also an urgent need to salvage the cargo. On the evening of April 2, Captain Israel J. Merritt of the Coast Wrecking Company dispatched an agent and four divers from New York by train to Halifax.[1] On the same train was J. J. Pennell of New York, representing the White Star Line, along with relatives of several saloon-class passengers whose bodies they were hoping to acquire. As they neared Halifax, their Saint John, NB, express train of the Intercolonial Railway collided with a derailed coal train from Pictou, NS, killing the engineer and baggage master—two more deaths that week associated with coal. They booked into the Halifax Hotel on Hollis Street, where Captain Williams was staying.

On April 5, the Mutual Marine Insurance Company announced that it would be sending an additional eight divers to the scene to help with the work.[2] It was a sizeable investment for the insurers but they had a lot at stake. The more cargo recovered, the less they would have to pay. Halifax wrecker John Sheridan and his ten divers had not been able to get inside the wreck, but he was confident they would be able to get the bodies. Then, he discovered that White Star Line had made no allowance for divers to bring up the bodies; they were expected only to recover cargo. Sheridan and Alfred Larder already had a crew of sixty-five men ready to go to work when the weather settled down. They finally got into the water on April 5 and complained about the bodies getting in the way of the job. The idea that the remains of loved ones were considered just a nuisance riled the newspapers and thus the relatives.

White Star Line was finally embarrassed into paying to have the bodies recovered—$50 for cabin class and $20 for steerage. No, the steerage passengers were not worth less, but having a diver go down long corridors into cabins was more complex, time consuming, and dangerous and, therefore, justified a higher fee. The task of retrieving bodies went to Sheridan's divers, while the Coast Wrecking Company's men worked on the cargo.

With the initial commotion past and the survivors gone, another small but influential group descended upon the area. No-holds-barred editorializing had already hit the streets of New York. The papers there had plenty to say about the White Star Line and Captain Williams. Having reprinted the work of the Halifax papers, they decided this disaster was so big that their own correspondents should be on site. April 5 saw the arrival of Thomas Maguire from the *New York Herald*, Samuel J. Barrows from Horace Greeley's *New York Tribune*, and Joseph Becker, an artist from *Frank Leslie's Illustrated Newspaper*.[3] His job was to create visuals from the site for display in the paper.

Although photography had been around since the 1840s, the technology did not exist to reproduce photographs in newspapers. *Frank Leslie's Illustrated Newspaper*, the *Daily Graphic*, *Harper's Weekly*, all from New York; the *Canadian Illustrated News*, founded in 1869 in Montreal; and the *Illustrated London News* all gave the *Atlantic* disaster extensive coverage, and their sketches constitute an important historical source of information.

They hired the *Herbert Hoover* and headed to the wreck site the next morning. There was so much traffic going back and forth to Lower Prospect that on April 7, a daily shuttle service began to the site. Passengers could depart from Cronan's Wharf, below Cogswell Street, on the *Unicorn* at 10:00 A.M. and return the same day.[4]

Saloon-class passenger Freeman Marckwald sent a dispatch to the Associated Press for printing in American newspapers:

Say to friends of the cabin class passengers of the steamer Atlantic that I will remain with the wreck until I have secured all the lost cabin passengers. I have boxes going to the wreck this morning to receive the bodies. The bodies of Mrs. Fisher and Miss Merritt we have. The bodies of Mr. and Mrs. Merritt, Miss Scrymser, and John H. Price I have great hopes of securing.[5]

Unbeknown to Marckwald, William Christian, a shopkeeper from Upper Prospect, had recovered the body of Mr. Merritt that day. Working from a small boat, he had grappled two bodies from the bottom, one of which was Merritt's. When he learned that Merritt's brother-in-law was at the Halifax Hotel, he went to Halifax, registered at the International Hotel, and called on W. P. Scrymser, who had also lost his sister, Annie. He returned to Scrymser a watch and chain, two rings, a pocket knife, money, and some keys.[6] Mr. Christian refused to accept a cash reward, but later he was presented with a personalized silver medal from the appreciative relatives.

Mr. And Mrs. William Merritt had been married the previous July, and were returning from a European bridal tour. Miss Merritt, sister of the groom, and Miss Scrymser, sister of the bride, had joined them in Europe and were returning with them.

Twenty-one saloon-class passengers had died. It was expected that all those bodies would be shipped to the United States. Marckwald finished his work and on April 10, with nearly all the crew and passengers gone, he departed for Portland aboard the *Falmouth*.[7]

There were still the more than five hundred bodies that would not be claimed. Many had no family in North America, and relatives in Europe could not afford the trip to Halifax, nor could they afford to ship the remains of their loved ones home. They would have to be buried in Nova Scotia.

As the *Delta* had steamed into Halifax Harbour with its load of survivors on April 2, the provincial legislature was meeting in a special session to discuss funding to ensure the survivors were taken care of. Picking them up was just the beginning, and it was difficult to determine what amount would be needed. The resolution stated:

> *Resolved, that the government be authorized to expend such a sum out of the Provincial Treasure as may be deemed necessary to render such support and to afford such abilities for their comfort as the distressing circumstances of their position may demand.*[8] *It passed with the support of all parties in the house.*

With that done, the provincial government contacted Halifax city officials, asking the Council to grant a parcel of land in Camp Hill Cemetery for the dead. Council convened a special meeting and passed a resolution to comply, subject to the supervision of the Committee of Cemetery and the City Medical Officer. At that point, no decision had been made to bring the bodies to Halifax for burial. Coffins were being built at Cunard's wharves and sent to Lower Prospect, while Edmund Ryan and George Longard were still trying to identify bodies, which were now lying on the Hill of Death on Ryans Island, awaiting burial.

Not being one to wait for others when he could act himself, William Ancient offered a solution. Burying the dead was the job of the church, so he would make space available behind his church in Terence Bay.[9] That would put the burial site three miles from the wreck site by boat, which was the only practical way to travel.

Meanwhile, the *Morning Chronicle*, assuming the bodies would be buried in Halifax, wrote grandly:

We cordially endorse the proposal to bring all the bodies to the city and inter them in the public cemetery at Camp Hill. Should that be done, the citizens of Halifax will, we are sure, promptly provide funds to erect over the great grave a monument that will point to future generations the resting place of the Atlantic's dead. It's not too much to expect that there will often come to Halifax some friend of one or more of the 550 human beings who perished at [Lower] Prospect on Tuesday morning. As citizens, will we not feel prouder if we can take those friends to Camp Hill—10 minutes walk from the city—and say "We did what we could for your dead. We buried them among our fathers and our friends, and we placed this monument here to mark their resting place." The people of Prospect will no doubt find graves for them, but we think Halifax should relieve them of that duty, and that it would be best to have the bodies interred in some place easy of access to the friends of the deceased, who whenever they chance to come this way will want to see the burial place.

American newspapers were sensitive to the burden that had been placed on the city and were fulsome in their confidence that the right thing would be done:

The President and other members of the government in Washington speak in grateful praise of the legislative and municipal liberality of Halifax, in the promptness of the action manifested on this memorable occasion. The proposition to bring the bodies to Halifax, even if it should not be accomplished, and have them decently interred in a cemetery, removes the last thought of neglect or indifference. You have done well by the poor unfortunates and their mourning relatives. "Halifax" for three days past, has been upon the lips of everybody, but only with feelings of gratitude for the assistance rendered the living, and the decent burial of the dead, on a strange coast, away from home and loving relatives and friends.[10]

With the federal, provincial, and municipal governments involved, much to-ing and fro-ing would occur before things got settled. The city wanted to have the dead buried on Lawlors Island in Halifax Harbour.[11] The commissioner of Public Works and Mines, Daniel McDonald, was expected to make the decision but he announced in the legislature that graves had been dug already and some bodies had been buried near the scene of the wreck. Reverend Ancient, it seemed, had made space available in his cemetery. No, another member insisted; he had spoken to Third Officer Brady and no graves had been dug. But all Brady actually knew was that no bodies had been buried near the wreck site.

Oh, for a telephone! It was patented just three years later.

After more discussion, it was decided to await the return of the chief clerk of the Board of Works, Henry Reid, who was at the site. In the meantime, James Morrow, on behalf of the White Star Line, was complaining that the whole business of cleaning up after the wreck was costing a lot of money and he petitioned the government to pay the cost of the burials. This was a reversal of what he had communicated just a day earlier. The government had contacted S. Cunard and Company to see if they needed help. James Morrow replied that he had been directed by White Star Line in both Liverpool and New York to supply the survivors with all they required. Assistance from the government would not be required—for the survivors. They would help the living, but the dead were somebody else's problem.

Therefore, the job had fallen to the customs department of the Dominion Government in Ottawa. The day after the wreck, they had telegraphed Edmund M. McDonald, the collector of customs, to arrange for the burials. He turned to James Kerr, his man on-site, to deal with it. (Recall that when Edmund Ryan asked him what to do with the bodies, Kerr had put him off.)

The fact that there were hundreds to be buried did not deter William Ancient from doing what he saw as his duty. He suggested to James Morrow that he would make space available for the Protestants near the cemetery beside St. Paul's church in Terence Bay. Morrow thought that was reasonable. And so it was settled. Despite all the discussion by the various levels of governmental authority, a Halifax businessman decided where they would be buried. Rev. Martin Maas, the Roman Catholic priest at Upper Prospect, was anxious to give the dead of his faith a proper Catholic burial, so the Roman Catholics assumed that was the course to be taken.

Those not identified as Catholic or Protestant—Jews, Muslims, atheists, and everyone else—were buried by Ancient. Tradition in the communities required that the Catholics be buried *alongside* the Catholic cemetery and the Protestants alongside the Protestant cemetery, not *within* the cemeteries.

The provincial government then informed Ottawa by telegram to Joseph Howe, who at that time was the secretary of state for the provinces and slated to become the lieutenant-governor of Nova Scotia in a matter of weeks. He passed the telegram to the minister of marine and fisheries, New Brunswick's Peter Mitchell, who told the Commons that the decision had been made to bury the bodies in Prospect.

Actually, the wreck was at Lower Prospect. Up the road was Terence Bay. Nearly three miles across the water was Upper Prospect, but the whole area got referred to simply as Prospect. To this day, there is confusion about what's what, especially since what was called Upper Prospect in 1873 is known today as Prospect!

As far as we know, only four people—two officers and two saloon passengers—were buried in Halifax. Of all the victims buried in Nova Scotia, Second Officer Henry Metcalfe received the biggest funeral. The body, which was reported to be "very much bruised and the clothing almost torn from the body" was taken to Halifax on April 4 aboard the *Goliah*, along with the bodies of five saloon passengers slated for shipping to the United States. The bell of St. Paul's church, which is today the oldest Protestant church in Canada, tolled as Rev. Dr. Warren conducted the service. With ships' flags in the harbour flying at half-mast, Metcalfe was buried in Camp Hill Cemetery. In attendance were Captain Williams, remaining officers and crew of the *Atlantic*, some cabin and steerage passengers from the *Atlantic*, Cunard officials, officers of Allan Line and Anchor Line ships that were in port, and a number of citizens.[12]

The other officer was the purser, twenty-three-year-old Ambrose Worthington. His gravestone is easy to find in Camp Hill Cemetery;

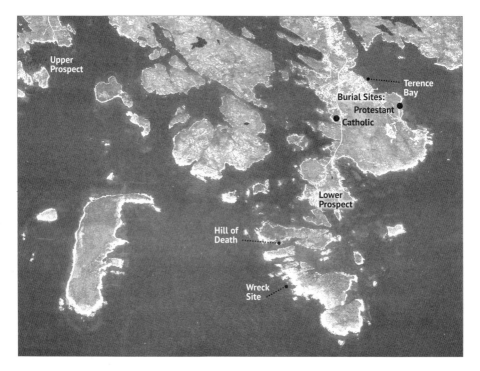

As bodies were recovered, they were taken to the Hill of Death on Ryans Island, where Edmund Ryan examined them for identification. They were then taken across the island and went by boat to one of the burial sites, which are adjacent to existing Roman Catholic and Anglican cemeteries on land that was acquired for the purpose of burying the bodies. The site labelled "Protestant" contains any bodies that could not be identified as Roman Catholic.

the others have disappeared. His body was recovered on May 7 and interred on May 9.[13] Even though the records show that Metcalfe is buried nearby, there is nothing to identify the grave. An Italian marble tombstone, ordered by Captain Williams and Third Officer Brady, was completed by the firm of Bishop & Evans near the end of April, inscribed: "In memory of Henry Ismay Metcalfe, 2nd officer S.S. Atlantic, died April 1st, 1873, aged 28 years. Deeply regretted by his family and brother officers." We don't know whether it was actually placed there, but it is not to be found today.[14]

Mrs. Lewiston (sometimes spelled Lauriston) Davidson, fifty-four, and her seventeen-year-old daughter Lillian were also reported to have been buried in Camp Hill on April 12.[15] Their last moments were described by passenger Samuel Vick:

> *By my side at the time were Mrs. Davidson and her daughter, both of them in the greatest distress, and while we were holding a hurried conversation the wave came on and in an instant both ladies were hurled over the vessel's side and instantly disappeared. I came very near going with them, but was grasped by a man above me who was hanging to the rigging, and who kept a firm hold on me until the effect of the wave had passed away.[16]*

In describing the slaphappy way the bodies were brought ashore, *New York Tribune* correspondent Samuel Barrows mentioned Mrs. Davidson's arrival: "And here is an elderly lady, stockingless, and with her dress thrown around her hastily....She proves to be Mrs. Davidson."[17]

Another reporter who was present picked up the story with even greater distaste:

> *She [Mrs. Davidson] is scarcely interred, when a boat arrives with still another body and stands a little piece from the shore. They fancy they have a prize, as one can plainly see by the greedy grin on their faces. They have another cabin passenger—a young woman, they say, and they "must have ten dollars for her." One of the magistrates agrees to the terms and she is dragged ashore. Oh, my God—can it be, can it be? She is recognized at once by some of the saved passengers who are near. "She was a beautiful sunny-eyed girl," they say. "Poor Miss Davidson," says another. I look upon her and am chained to the spot. I forget where I am. Her light flaxen ringlets hang down over her shoulders, long and beautiful. She has evidently realized the situation for she has thrown on a cloth sacque with bugled braid. Her delicate hands and white tapering fingers looked as natural as life. I felt as I looked upon her face, purple with the agony of death, that I was the most hard-hearted wretch in the universe, that I did not weep. They laid her in her rough coffin and wrote on the outside in red chalk, "Miss Davidson, London."[18]*

Photos of the headstone are extant but extensive searches in Camp Hill Cemetery have turned up nothing. On Lillian's person was a note, meant to be opened should her mother die on the voyage, instructing her daughter on how to find her uncle in California.[19] That would have been quite an undertaking for a grieving, unaccompanied seventeen-year-old girl in 1873.

The bodies of the other saloon passengers were shipped to relatives, or friends came for them, but these two must not have had anybody to claim their bodies.

On October 22, 1852, the Bishop Of Nova Scotia, Hibbert Binney, had paid Charles Lordly of Chester five shillings for a parcel of land to be used as a cemetery. Over the next few years, a church had been erected nearby, where Reverend Ancient was serving.[20] Now, for $140, Lordly sold a second parcel of land to the government for the burial of the SS *Atlantic* bodies in Terence Bay.

Alongside the road between Terence Bay and Lower Prospect, Rev. Martin Maas, the Roman Catholic priest from Upper Prospect, buried about 250 Roman Catholic bodies. He had to come nearly three miles by boat from Upper Prospect to what today is called the Star of the Sea Cemetery. At the beginning, burials took place daily as bodies were recovered. As time went on, they were sporadic. As the weeks passed, a few were laid to rest on beaches miles from the wreck site, near where they were found by fishermen or other sailors. Rev. Maas buried the last bodies recovered from the ship, those of a man, woman, and child brought up on July 11.[21]

The *Acadian Recorder* provides a remarkable account of work at what sounds like the Roman Catholic site:

> *Truly this is a terrible business that is going on here. To watch the disposal of the hundreds of bodies would suggest the idea of a flourishing business in fish or apples. You may see the first of the bodies brought to shore and thrown down on the ground in the peat and mud. I myself saw this morning as many as fifteen or twenty, including men, women and children, scarcely any of them capable of recognition, lying side by side—a most horrible and sickening sight. Next the magistrate and some whom he has employed, commence searching the bodies. They*

sometimes find money and generally some paper or other, giving the name or nationality. After diligent search has been made, and all the valuables secured, a cargo of coffins comes in. Then the men go briskly to work, put the bodies in and then nail them up. A boat arrives and takes a cargo of the bodies to a cove on the mainland. There they are landed by scores. Then come carts and oxen and men who carry them to a piece of ground nearby in a most dismal looking wilderness. Great trenches are here dug by a brigade of diggers, who are ever going ominously about with long shovels on their shoulders. These trenches ordinarily hold about two dozen coffins. Then the shovellers bury them over with the upturned soil. Thus are they disposed of. No weeping friends gather around. No pall is thrown over to indicate the grief of the mourners; no hearse; nothing to indicate care or respect. Could there be a sadder sight?[22]

Meanwhile, boatload after boatload of Protestant and other corpses slowly wound their way along the narrow channel called Ryans Gut, past the village of Lower Prospect, and along the coast to Tennant Point, where a lighthouse stands today. From there, they went into Terence Bay up to the high bluff where Reverend Ancient's little church stood looking out to sea, a navigation point for vessels in local waters. On many trips, Ancient was aboard the boat, quietly relieving the authorities of their duty as he moved bodies, superintended the digging of the graves, read the burial service of the church, and made sure the coffins were properly covered.

On April 6, the diggers began the first long trench behind St. Paul's church, into which plain, newly made coffins were placed, three and even four atop one another. Ancient buried sixty-five bodies, and three days later another ninety-one were interred. For almost three months it continued until, by June 20, 276 had been laid to rest. The last one buried there was a headless body found ten days later.

More of the dead were yet to be found. The *Acadian Recorder* reported on October 6 that salvage divers had found four men and one woman partially buried beneath one of the iron plates from the hull. By then, nobody was paying to have bodies recovered so they were left there.

One of the iconic photographs of the disaster, taken by Halifax photographer Wellington Chase, shows Ancient, his robes buffeted by the relentless winds, standing above a large grave containing many rough coffins, and reading the burial service in the presence of a couple of dozen locals, mostly women, with a few men leaning on their shovels—a doleful scene indeed.

An excerpt from the *New York Herald* on April 9 provides additional detail:

> *The graves or trenches where they are consigned are about 12 feet wide, thirty or 40 feet long and four or five feet deep. The rude coffins containing the unfortunate victims are placed in these four abreast and two deep and are then covered over with 12 or 15 inches of earth. Such has been the rude ceremonies over the hundreds of human beings who went down in the ill-fated Atlantic. There have been no obsequies, no friends near to shed a parting tear over their graves and the only requiem which will be heard will be the dashing surf along the coast where they met their untimely fate.*

Rev. William Ancient presiding, at St. Paul's Church in Terence Bay, over the April 1873 burial service for some of the Protestant victims of the wreck of SS *Atlantic*. (W. Chase, Public domain, via Wikimedia Commons)

Table 1. Protestant and other bodies buried near St. Paul's church in Terence Bay.

Date	Quantity	Date	Quantity
April 6	65	May 8	8
April 9	91	May 9	3
April 12	15	May 15	1
April 15	3	June 1	2
April 22	55	June 8	2
April 28	2	June 20	2
May 1	8	July	1
May 7	19	Total	277

(*Source: Halifax Herald, December 8, 1905*)

Of the upwards of five hundred people who were buried in Lower Prospect and Terence Bay, there is not a single headstone that recalls a name or a birthplace. In both cemeteries, there is a simple granite post with a bronze plaque marking the common graves. These came many years after the wooden markers erected at the time of the burial had gone back to the earth.

The only steerage passenger's monument of which I am aware is in Tigeaghna graveyard, Parish of Lisdowney, County Kilkenny, Ireland. It is included on a family upright memorial to which names have been added, starting in 1815. One line reads, "Also here lies Bridget Brown, who was lost on her way to America, aged 22 in the ill fated Atlantic April 1, 1873." In keeping with so many parts of the *Atlantic* story, this one sadly contains two errors. First of all, there is very little likelihood that Bridget is in that grave. Records show she died in the wreck but there is no way the family of a single female steerage passenger could have afforded to bring her body back to Ireland for burial. Second, all other records show that Bridget was thirty-two years old. Her older brother, John, probably had the information put on the headstone. He was illiterate and somehow things went awry in getting the inscription placed on the stone. Such was the way for many of the steerage folk on the *Atlantic*. Requiescant in pace. Amen.[23]

Bridget's brother, John, and his wife, Ellen Cantwell, had a little girl whom they baptized Bridget on December 17, 1873, eight months after the loss of the *Atlantic*.

It was said at the time that the burial sites would become a city of the dead to which a melancholy interest would attach for years and years to come.[24] That did not happen. Instead, the sites were overgrown by the forest—and succeeding generations forgot they existed at all. Some newspapers claimed they were within a short distance of the scene of the wreck, but that was not so. For those most likely to pay their respects—the people of Lower Prospect and Upper Prospect, who were directly involved in the rescue—it was a sizeable walk or boat ride that could not be undertaken on the spur of the moment, particularly for people whose waking hours were taken up with ensuring the survival of their own loved ones. And it was out of the question for all the people in Halifax who had been involved in the days following the wreck. Most of them, living in the time before inexpensive transportation, never saw the graves at all.

Although nobody would have believed it at the time, the story of the *Atlantic* disaster was destined to be forgotten. William Ancient's offer to James Morrow to bury the bodies where they were, and to relieve everybody else of the responsibility, was probably the biggest factor in the forgetting as the years slipped by.

CHAPTER 16

THE FIVE HUNDRED-POUND PROMISE

Those who reached the shore in safety were most kindly treated by the
good people of the place and supplied with shelter, food and clothing,
and every comfort a poor but hospitable fishing village could afford.
But for the assistance rendered by the hardy fishermen scarcely any
would have survived to tell the story of the disaster.

Harper's Weekly
April 19, 1873

O n April 2, just over twenty-four hours after the captain made the promise to pay $500 (or perhaps £500) for every boatload of passengers landed from the ship, Edmund Ryan met at his house with James Morrow, the White Star agent, and asked what the people could expect by way of remuneration. He later told the Vice Admiralty Court during a hearing into remuneration for salvage services that Morrow replied, "Those who performed salvage services will be paid and well paid for all that they have done. They might not receive the money for a month or more but the money will be sure to come."[1]

The newspapers were busy recommending their favourite heroes for medals. Rev. William Ancient was at the top for the Albert Medal, named for Prince Albert, the husband of Queen Victoria. They also suggested Royal Humane Society medals for Ancient, Chief Officer

Firth, Third Officer Brady, the "three quartermasters" (presumably Robert Thomas, Edward Owens, and John Speakman, who were being vocal about the lives they had saved), and, bringing up the rear, the crews of the boats that had carried out the rescue.

On April 4, the Halifax *Daily Reporter and Times* newspaper began a subscription for Ancient, naming three locations in Halifax where money could be dropped off. F. H. Baker, a Halifax lobster merchant and publisher of a literary journal called the *Mayflower*, kicked it off with a letter, saying,

> *I am off for the wreck early tomorrow, but you can put my name down on list subscribers for one hundred dollars.*[2]

Between April 4 and May 15, around eighty-five subscribers donated $1,098.30, or about $21,000 in today's funds, with donations ranging from 25 cents from John Hogan to Mr. Baker's $100. To donate, there was no GoFundMe, nobody knocked on doors, subscribers could not mail contributions in. They had to walk to one of the three downtown locations and walk back again, so those who donated meant business. Even so, the newspaper had to print a barrage of reminders for subscribers to fulfill their promises and get their money in.

There was nothing ambiguous about who the money was meant to reward. It was called The Ancient Testimonial Fund, and to nail home the point, the *Daily Reporter* noted:

> *Our contemporary, the Chronicle, asks "What about the boat's crew?" We have proposed to all the subscribers we have met, that a public meeting be called at Temperance Hall at an early date, and an admission fee be charged—the proceeds of which will go the boat's crew.*[3]

Temperance Hall, built in 1850 and owned by the Halifax Temperance Hall Company, was the main public meeting place in the city. The "boat's crew" mentioned refers to the boat that took Ancient out to the wreck, not the crews of the three rescue boats. To the *Daily Reporter*, they did not seem to exist.

Other groups near and far started collecting money to help support the survivors. For Americans, the survivors quickly became the centre of everybody's attention.

Unfortunately the rescuers were out of sight in the two Prospects and Terence Bay, and they quickly became an afterthought—always lumped together as the "poor fishermen." What interest there was in the rescue became focused on the effort by William Ancient to save John Firth. This was a time when the Irish were not held in particularly high esteem. The idea of a young English clergyman who had served in the Royal Navy, rightly and properly leading a group of simple Irish in the rescue of survivors, had a ring of heroism for the newspapers. They ran with it and within days Ancient was being credited with doing far more than he had done. It was later concluded that 417 had survived, and the captain estimated that 370 had been rescued by the locals. Of that, Ancient had rescued just one and assisted with one other, but the legend now had legs. To this day, there are accounts of his being among the first on site and leading the rescue.

He was lionized everywhere. The day after the wreck, the Union Protection Company of Halifax, a private fire protection service, at a meeting of members, resolved that the company:

> Highly appreciating the gallant conduct of the Rev. W. J. Ancient and the boat's crew who accompanied him in saving the life of Mr. J. W. Firth...that a subscription list be opened amongst the members...for the purpose of subscribing towards a testimonial to the parties above named, as a recognition of the esteem in which they are held by this Company.[4]

They had rescued two people!

The members gave generously and two and a half months later Captain George Yates, along with several company members, presented Ancient with a cheque for $155, and another for $78 to be divided among the boat's crew. There was nothing for those who had rescued the other 368 survivors.

On May 5, the *Halifax Novascotian* reprinted a letter that ran in the *New York World* from John T. Metcalfe with the injunction,

Will you kindly let the enclosed $25 go toward the sum for the benefit of that brave Mr. Ancient who showed such pluck and Christian muscularity in the Atlantic wreck?

It was one of a host of letters and comments encouraging readers to send money to Ancient.

Those saved by the men in the boats had a different attitude. Some, like Oswald Jugla, a rescued saloon-class passenger who subscribed $100 to a fund opened in New York for the benefit of the fishermen, knew to whom they owed their lives, and donated accordingly if they had the means.[5]

In a letter to the *New York Herald*, he wrote:

They gave us all their provisions, parted with all their clothes. No people ever proved themselves more true Christians. Many of the saved passengers would have died from hunger and a protracted exposure if it had not been for the kindness of those poor people.[6]

On April 15, Mayor Duggan announced that he had received $50 from John Baldwin and $5 from Nicholas Wirell specifically for the fishermen. By the 17th he had another $50 from the lieutenant-governor, Sir Hastings Doyle (who couldn't resist throwing in $20 for Ancient), plus $25 from John Bates of Boston and $5 from Harry Moody.[7]

A man in New York sent a telegram to the Archbishop of Halifax saying, "Draw upon me for £100 and expend the same among the survivors of the Atlantic." (Signed) T. A. Vyse Jr., No. 531 Broadway.

In the city of Chicago, four businessmen, H. F. Jennison, Franz Henckel, Fred L. Fake, and Augustus Johnson, were so moved by the *Atlantic* story that they started a collection for the relief of passengers and others. They at first intended to raise money to reward Brady and the fishermen, but upon hearing of the destitute condition of the passengers, it was decided the money would be better spent on them. Calling themselves the Chicago Relief Commission, their first report noted that they had received 123 donations totalling $965.00. On April 11, the White Star Line agent in Chicago announced that $2,000 had been raised.[8]

But they did not forget the people to whom the living owed their lives. Sarah Jane O'Reilly received a gold locket and chain with £20 sterling, as did Kate and Agatha O'Brien, with lockets and £10 each, but the pièce de résistance went to Ancient—a lavish gold pocket watch with an inscription and engraving of the *Atlantic,* along with $500. The inscription read:

Presented to the Rev. W. J. Ancient by the citizens of Chicago for heroic conduct in rescuing passengers from steamer Atlantic April 1st 1873.[9]

Edward Owens, the quartermaster who was the first man to attempt the swim to the rock shortly after the *Atlantic* struck, got wind of the Chicago fund. He wrote to the White Star Office in New York seeking recognition for his part in the rescue. J. H. Sparks sent him a reply dated October 29, 1873, stating the committee had allocated all the money they had, but comforted him with "the satisfaction of knowing that your duty was well performed on the trying occasion, and this reflection is reward of more value than what was your due from the Chicago Fund."[10]

Perhaps Owens would have preferred to decide that for himself. What he did not tell Sparks was that he had already received a reward from the Chicago group. On July 30 the *Liverpool Mercury* reported that the three who had gotten the first rope to the rock—Brady, Speakman, and Owens—had all received gold watches, as had Fourth Officer Brown. The paper observed,

The presentation takes the form of a costly gold watch, the value of which varies according to the rank of the recipients. Mr. Brady's watch cost $500 and is a rich specimen of American work, being double cased and most expensively jewelled and chased.

The value of the watches varied "according to the rank of the recipients," not, it seems, according to the courage displayed by each.

I had the privilege of corresponding with John Brown's great-great-grandson regarding the watch. Not surprisingly, he was very proud of his ancestor. Family tradition had Brown as the first on the rock with the line and playing a central role in the rescue. There was no knowledge of the loss of the certificate for three months, but it is gratifying to know that he had his courage recognized despite the way events transpired. To this day, the watch survives in the possession of the family, in the case that it arrived in, and is itself in pristine condition, indicators that Brown probably put it away out of sight. The words of Williams, Firth, and Brady are throughout the newspaper accounts of the time, but I have not seen anything about or from John Brown, except this comment by Samuel Barrows in the *New York Tribune*:

> *The conduct of the fourth officer in refusing to give to the press any statement of his connection to the affair until it is dragged out of him at Court, is pressing prudence too far and naturally excites disfavour.*[11]

It sounds like "No comment" was all the papers were getting out of Brown, and they were not pleased.

The Liverpool Shipwreck and Humane Society awarded Ancient the Society's silver medal, along with £10 to be divided among the fishermen who conveyed passengers from Meaghers Island to the mainland. This became a common trend, to pass money to the fishermen through Ancient, on the assumption that he had led the rescue. They also awarded £10 to the Clancy family and £5 to Sarah Jane.[12]

But there were no medals or gushing declarations for Edmund or Dennis Ryan, or Thomas Twohig, or the O'Brien boys, or James Coolen, or the Blackburns. The Lower Prospect folk were easy to forget—especially for the White Star Line, faced with the loss of a profitable ship in her prime earning years and a valuable cargo.[13] Then there were the costs associated with the care and forwarding of the passengers.[14] And lawsuits were in the works. The family of deceased saloon passenger Herman Kruger was preparing one[15] and saloon passenger Freeman Marckwald also brought one.[16]

Of course, the White Star Line's competition saw opportunity in all this misfortune. The mail contracts were especially tantalizing. By the beginning of June, managers of the Inman Line (also known as the Liverpool, New York, and Philadelphia Steamship Company) were making the case to American postal officials that the White Star Line was an unreliable partner.[17] White Star's contract was to carry the Saturday mail from New York, and that required six ships to maintain the weekly service. Now, they were down to five and were forced to admit that they did not have a vessel to meet a scheduled sailing on June 21.[18] Cunard had three weekly crossings—two to New York and one to Boston—with sixteen ships allocated to the service. Inman had two crossings with ten ships; the Guion Line out of Liverpool (also known as the Liverpool and Great Western Steamship Company) had one with six ships. National had one and they could put any of their twelve ships on the run.[19] (For details about the various British-registered passenger steamship companies serving the North Atlantic out of Liverpool in 1873, see Appendix G, page 252.)

Despite all of that, the US Postal Service stuck with the White Star Line. Inman already carried the mail from Liverpool on Thursdays[20] and it was to the benefit of the post office to spread the business around to ensure there was competition.

With the survival of the line at stake, the minds of Thomas Ismay and his partners were off the *Atlantic* and on to other things. Less than six months later, the company was obliged to sell two freighters to raise cash. The *Tropic* went to the J. Serra y Font company of Bilbao, Spain, and was renamed *Federico*.[21] Her sister ship, *Asiatic*, was sold to the African Steamship Company and renamed *Ambriz*.[22]

And, so, the message from the White Star Line to the rescue men changed from one of great goodwill to one of mean-spiritedness and stinginess, from "you will be generously rewarded" to "the lives of the passengers & crew...were saved chiefly by the exertions of the officers and...crew of the steamship."[23]

How had it come to this? When the light from Michael Clancy's lantern appeared to Thomas Moffatt as he clung to life in the mizzen rigging, there was no doubt that his fervent prayers had been answered. And Michael Clancy had no doubt about what the Almighty expected of him and his neighbours. Money was the last thing on anybody's mind.

Of the whole effort put forth by the people and government of Nova Scotia, reporter William Fielding had written in the *Chronicle*:

The courage of the fishermen of Prospect, who hurried to the scene of
the wreck in their boats, and risked their lives to save the men of the
Atlantic, their hospitality displayed in opening their houses to the dis-
tressed, and sharing out their scanty wardrobe among the naked,
and all this generously; the action of the Legislature on behalf of the
Province, and of the Mayor on behalf of the city—in at once offering
shelter and food to the sufferers—but evinced effectively the sympa-
thy for the living and the sorrow for the dead felt in every section of the
country upon whose rocks the Atlantic was cast away.[24]

Nobody asked the captain for money. He offered it! And now, with
cupboards bare, clothing given away, houses dishevelled, fuel supplies
diminished, boats crying out for repair and even replacement, it was
badly needed.

Even one of the magistrates, George Longard, after inquiring about
having his expenses paid, had shown a reluctance to hand over some
of the valuables that had been entrusted to him after he received a
reply that he didn't like from James Kerr. It reached the point where
Edmund McDonald had to travel to the wreck site to resolve the situation. The solution was to post Halifax merchant and past mayor
Samuel Caldwell on site. All items recovered from bodies were to be
passed to him and he would decide on their disposition.[25]

It is true that Ancient had laboured mightily after the event was over,
but so did Edmund Ryan, who had gone through the pockets of close
to five hundred corpses as they came out of the water, identified them
if he could, gathered up their belongings while trying to keep pilferers
at bay, and then piled the bodies literally in his own backyard. So did
Sarah Jane O'Reilly, who had over three hundred barely living souls
go through her house, with some still recuperating there a week later.

In the meantime, the *Halifax Novascotian* newspaper had taken up
their cause, writing in an April 14 editorial:

What of the fishermen of Prospect, of those who were suddenly come
down upon by crowds of exhausted, semi-frozen, wholly famished
waifs? Who gave up their all for those who had lost their all? Who clad
and fed and warmed and did honour to the Nova Scotian name, and

added lustre to the crown of the province? Have they been rewarded?
Truly, this press has spoken well of them, private eulogy has not failed,
but where is the public recognition of the people?

Shall merit go by unrewarded? We trust not and we appeal to every
class—to every individual, to unite in testifying, in a solid, substan-
tial and pecuniary manner, their appreciation of the conduct of the
Prospect fishermen.

The challenge brought a response from the *Mayflower Amateurs,*
an amateur dramatic group across the harbour in Dartmouth. They
suggested that the two dramatic clubs in Halifax join them for an
evening fundraiser.

A seriously patronizing reader of the *Evening Reporter* observed
that:

We should not forget the labour and toil of the fishermen's wives and
daughters who, no doubt, will be deprived of many a little article of
dress if father has to refill the flour barrel at his own expense.

He suggested a public meeting at Temperance Hall, presided over
by Mayor Duggan.

Then, let the Rev. Mr. Ancient and some representative men from
Prospect, say one or two from each crew, be notified to attend that they
may be presented to the audience....Let his worship present them to the
assembled citizens, whose applauding will be done in their own style.

It sounds like a cross between a cattle auction and *America's*
Funniest Home Videos. A military band would play and a resolution
taken to recommend them to the Royal Humane Society for medals,
with the accumulated take at the door of twenty-five cents a head
being divided among the rescuers and—who else but?—Mr. Ancient.

In the same issue, the *Evening Reporter* reminded its readers to
get their contributions in towards the testimonial for the Rev. Mr.
Ancient, making no mention of anybody else.[26]

A newspaper ad selling photos of John Hanley.

Meanwhile, as John Hanley was being courted by P. T. Barnum to join the circus, two Halifax photographers, like modern-day social media adversaries, were engaged in a public spat over his image. William O'Donnell had photographed several people, including Hanley and Rev. Ancient. Another photographer, R. R McLellan, had photographed those photographs, which, of course, rankled O'Donnell. He took out ads in the *Evening Reporter* and *Acadian Recorder* accusing McLellan of unprofessionalism. McLellan, denying nothing, simply pointed out that a woman had purchased the photos from O'Donnell, who was on the street "hawking them as he would blueberries and smelts" and brought them to him to be improved. "The photos to be copied were very bad, indeed," McLellan declared, "but by a few skillful touches bringing up parts and obliterating defects on the copy, I made the negatives passable, and they are now on free exhibition at my gallery for all who do not wish to buy."

O'Donnell reminded readers of his ads that they could get the real thing from him for twenty-five cents instead of paying McLellan forty-five cents for "trashy copies."[27]

A reader of the *Morning Chronicle* was more focused in his thinking. Even though the wreck was underwater, the *Atlantic* still represented a lot of value that could go to the rescue crews. In a letter to the paper on April 18, the nameless subscriber wrote:

> The law, I believe, provides that the vessel and cargo are liable to pay salvage to parties saving the lives of the passengers and crew on board....If the law permits such a course why are steps not being taken to make the property of the White Star Line—that is, the portion of the Atlantic still existing—contribute its quota to swell the reward these good and brave people merit? All things considered it would be far more equitable and just that the property of the company should pay a liberal proportion than that our citizens should subscribe it unaided.

Chapter 17

The Lawsuit

*To these men chiefly belongs the credit of having at the risk of their own
lives rescued from death over 400 souls. They, as well as several others
of whose bravery I have heard, should certainly receive some reward
for their noble conduct.*[1]

Freeman Marckwald
Saloon passenger

As the days turned into weeks, the main activity at the wreck
site centred around the salvage of cargo as the men from the
three rescue boats watched one schooner-load after another depart.
They knew that, for each load, the Coast Wrecking Company got paid,
the diving company represented by Larder and Sheridan got paid, the
divers got paid, and the captains and crew were paid. But had the fishermen not done far more valuable salvage work, with the exception that
the recovery was of human lives? The inanimate cargo was recovered
one working day at a time when the weather was cooperating. Their
salvage had been completed under onerous conditions, with the clock
ticking as they struggled to get people out of the elements alive.

Convinced that they had been dealt an injustice they decided to
take action—action remarkably in line with the anonymous letter-
writer's thoughts in his note to the *Morning Chronicle*.

Because their grievance centred around a maritime event, they went to the Vice Admiralty Court at Halifax. This special naval court existed in parts of the British Empire to adjudicate disputes dealing with maritime matters such as prize cargoes in times of war. When a British-registered ship captured an enemy vessel, the Vice Admiralty Court decided the share that members of the warship's company should receive. It had expanded its jurisdiction to deal with issues pertaining to shipwrecks as well. Being associated with the organization had its downside, as one marshal of the court found out. One evening, while discharging his duties, he was shot at from a vessel at a south-end wharf because somebody didn't like a ruling.[2]

Lawrence G. Power represented the "promovents," as the claimants were called. He petitioned the court to place a lien on what remained of the *Atlantic*, to seize the wreck and the cargo. Under the terms of the salvage contract, the Coast Wrecking Company and others involved in the recovery of the cargo were to be paid 40 percent of its value by the insurance underwriters, so the court case became a tug-of-war between the promovents and, not the White Star Line, but the Atlantic Insurance Company of New York, represented by Joseph Ritchie, more commonly known as J. Norman Ritchie. He represented Captain Williams at the Halifax inquiry and was appointed a justice of the Supreme Court of Nova Scotia in September 1885.

On May 21, 1873, Dennis Ryan and James Coolen journeyed to Halifax and appeared before the court on behalf of Francis Ryan, Patrick Dollard, John Blackburn, Michael O'Brien, James O'Brien, William Benjamin Blackburn, William Lacey, Samuel Blackburn the younger, Stephen Ryan, Alexander Brophy, Edmund Ryan, and Michael Clancy of Lower Prospect; Thomas Twohig of Pennant; and Samuel White, James Power the younger, John Purcell, and William Coolen of Upper Prospect.

They swore to the facts of the rescue before L. W. DesBarres, the registrar of the court, that on April 1 they had gone to the wreck site before dawn and were instrumental in saving the lives of 370 passengers and crew "or thereabouts." They further swore that they had applied, on behalf of themselves and others, to James B. Morrow of S. Cunard and Company, the Halifax agents of the *Atlantic*'s owners, for remuneration, but that he had refused to pay an adequate sum, and therefore the aid and process of the court were now required to enforce their demand.

On May 28, on behalf of the Atlantic Insurance Company and other underwriters of the cargo, J. Norman Ritchie shot back, appearing before a surrogate of Sir William Young, judge of the Vice Admiralty Court, praying the worshipful court to judge against the promovents.

Now that both sides had squared off, there followed a series of affidavits, in which the parties laid out their cases.

Ritchie presented his case on June 27, to whit:

1. *The lives of the passengers and crew were saved chiefly by the efforts of the officers and part of the crew of the Atlantic and by persons other than the promovents, whose salvage services were inefficient and of little avail and rendered without risk on their part.*

(This strange assertion contradicted the telegram sent by the third officer to the *Atlantic*'s owners on April 1 and the one sent by them to the Board of Trade on April 2. It also contradicted the letter sent by the captain to Ismay, Imrie, and Company giving the details of the disaster and presented—by Ritchie—at the Halifax inquiry.)

2. *Communication from the ship to the shore was effected by the officers and crew of the ship at great personal risk and a large portion of the passengers and crew were landed before the promovents came on the scene. All they did was save a few men off the ship and the rock after daylight, which they did without any risk to themselves or their boats because they would not take them near the ship or rocks "and obliged each person to throw himself into the water towards the boat and run the chance of being picked up by them or drowned."*

3. *The captain did not promise to pay $500 for each load rescued from the ship.*

4. *While they were landing the passengers and crew, the wind was from the west and moderate and the sea comparatively smooth and conditions were what they as fishermen were used to. The wind and sea did not increase until the middle of the day when the promovents stopped*

providing their services even though there were still persons in the rigging in extreme peril, some of whom were lost and those saved had to be saved by other persons.

5. *Even though the ship was wrecked on April 1 and the crews and passengers were around for some time, with the captain, one officer and others around until May 1 or later, no claims for salvage were made until everybody from the ship had left the province and it became impossible to obtain their evidence.*

6. *On top of that, the promovents were guilty of plundering the wreck and cargo.*

7. *The government of Canada had already granted $3,000 to be distributed among those persons living in the neighbourhood of the wreck who assisted in saving the lives of passengers and crew and the promovents' share would fully compensate them for their services.*[3]

Things then dragged on until the end of the year, with a few of the fishermen going to Halifax to make a deposition. These are valuable documents among these records that enable the details of the rescue to be pieced together. The documents are not narratives describing events presented in the words of the witnesses, as might occur in a modern courtroom. In the days before even manual typewriters were widespread, the only way to document something was to write it longhand with a pencil or pen. This was a laborious process of dipping the nib of the pen into the inkwell and writing a few words before dipping again, all the while trying to capture what the deponent was saying. For the sake of efficiency, only the answers to questions were written down, meaning that the deposition is a series of answers to unknown questions, following one another without being separated into paragraphs or even new lines.

A deposition was a page or several pages of text, paraphrased and written in the language, not of the speaker, but of the scrivener as he understood it. In some cases, parts are crossed off and corrected where he read a portion back to the witness, who then clarified some points. There are separate affidavits sworn and then signed by each deponent who chose to do so.

The promovents' case was based on a principle called "life salvage." It stated that the saving of a life carried with it a financial value that could be paid from the value of the cargo or the vessel. The court had impounded a shipment of cargo valued at $9,733.33 aboard the schooner *Annie Brown* and ordered the combatants to present their cases. To avoid having the contested cargo held up, thus causing inconvenience and cost to the consignees, Archibald Sutherland, acting marshal of the Vice Admiralty Court, allowed a bond to be posted so that the cargo could be sent on its way. Enter J. B. Morrow, again, and another Halifax merchant, William Harrington, whose company, Lawson, Harrington, and Company owned the steam tugs *Goliah* and *Henry Hoover*.[4] Between them, they put up £2,000 as security to enable the case to proceed.

Some of the rescuers were not comfortable with the idea that they should be paid for such services. In a letter to the *Halifax Herald* in 1906, Sarah Jane O'Reilly let it be known that she and her family had acted out of simple Christian charity, without thought that they should receive any compensation. Her father, Michael Clancy, even though his name appeared on the legal documents, withdrew his name from the suit soon after it was launched.[5]

Those who went forward argued that they, of course, had acted out of the same sentiments as Clancy, but the captain had made a promise that was heard by many witnesses, and they had now been taken advantage of. They were seeking only to recoup their expenses and receive a fair recompense for the time and effort expended. They argued that they had carried the greatest part of the burden. Michael Clancy, even though he was the first local person on site, did not go in the rescue boats. He was in his sixties. And the men from Upper Prospect arrived well after the rescue got going and had been there less than half as long as most of the others from Lower Prospect.

The depositions clearly refuted the hollow claims levelled by Norman Ritchie, as follows:

To the first two charges, it was true that the crew had brought the ropes to the rock and some had been saved through those efforts, but only the most robust and the most fortunate. Many passenger accounts unrelated to the lawsuit gave heartbreaking details of their toil to save themselves and the hopeless situation they found themselves in when they got to the rock—and of the vast numbers who consequently lost their lives.

With equal passion, the promovents' lawyer credited the fishermen with saving people through courage, determination, and skilful boat handling. Considering that Ismay himself had reported to the Board of Trade that the fishermen had saved the survivors, it was a bit much that the White Star Line was now doing an about-face on that point.

Nicholas Christian, a respected businessman and Justice of the Peace testified:

> *The men who went in the boats to the rock and the ship ran much risk of losing their lives owing to the high wind and heavy sea. This was the opinion of all the men who were on the shore. Numbers of hardy able fishermen could not be induced to go in the boats at all. Some gave up after one trip and others after two. Had it not been for the fishermen one-fourth of the whole number rescued would have been saved.*

To the third item, the $500 promise that was heard by the crew of the first boat, there was no way to prove or disprove it. That they cooked it up seems unlikely, considering the lengths to which they took their claim. The fact that one of the ship's crew, Quartermaster Charles Roylance, claimed to have heard it, and that passenger William Hogan also heard it lends credence to the fishermen's claim.

Five hundred dollars would be $10,000 in today's money. Per load! It's hard to believe that anybody would take such an offer seriously. Williams was probably surprised that they did.

Item four is not much of an argument. It should have been part of number one. To say that the wind was from the west, implying that this lessened the risk, shows a lack of understanding of the wreck site. In that area, a westerly or southwest wind comes straight off the horizon, so their argument was wrong. If they wanted to play down the power of the wind they should have said it was coming from the north or northeast, off the land. As for the power of the wind, each promovent stated that the wind was increasing. On that one, nobody could prove anything. The fishermen provided other neutral parties to testify that the wind had been increasing.

That they had waited until the captain and officers had left the province was answered with the argument that they had been given what they considered to be a solid promise to pay and they did not feel the need to call on anybody to support their case. James Morrow made the point that he had tried to track Brady down because he was the person most familiar with the early hours of the event, and most involved in the days after the wreck occurred—and would have known what was promised—but he was unable to find him.

The sixth charge, that the fishermen were guilty of plundering the wreck and cargo, was simply meant to discredit them. Plundering or not plundering the wreck after the fact had nothing to do with the issue the court was asked to decide on. All the fishermen vehemently denied it. The customs man, James Kerr, was called to testify. He noted that many of them were often seen around the site in the days following the event but nobody delivered any cargo to him, implying, of course, that they must have been picking stuff up and taking it home. The fishermen's lawyer, Lawrence Power, asked him flatly if he was aware of their taking anything from the site and he had to admit that he was not. "I don't know if the promovents got anything at the wreck or not. I did not discover any of them plundering. I was in the neighbourhood of the wreck for two months."[6]

And, finally, the argument that the Canadian government had allocated money to pay expenses and rewards was simply an attempt to weasel out of their obligations.

The final deposition came on the last day of 1873, consisting of Rev. William Ancient's description of the rescue of John Firth. Two weeks later, James B. Morrow and his son James departed for England. The senior Morrow, the nephew of Samuel Cunard's wife, Susan, was at the breaking point over the events of the past nine months. Described as being completely worn out, he had decided that a change of scene would help him recover. His wife, Matilda, is quoted as saying that his health gave way completely. "Fears were entertained," she said, "that he would never physically be fit for much again."[7]

Morrow died from a heart attack on September 10, 1880, at age forty-nine. It was felt that his early death was a result of the stress of dealing with the wreck and its aftermath.

On March 14, 1874, Sir William Young brought down his verdict.

CHAPTER 18

MEDALS, MONEY, AND WATCHES

The Relief Committee of Boston report that the amount received was $1050.43. The surplus, if any, will be sent to the poor fishermen of Nova Scotia, who stripped the clothes from their backs and exhausted their scanty supplies of provisions to warm and feed the shipwrecked men.

Halifax Morning Chronicle
April 1873

O n May 23, 1873, the Canadian Parliament budgeted the sum of $3,000 for expenses in connection with the burial of bodies, the provision of coffins, and the conferring of rewards on deserving individuals. On December 29, Henry W. Johnston, the Nova Scotia manager for the Department of Marine and Fisheries, told the court that

in accordance with the said grant in and about the month of September last the sum of $1,560 was distributed among the inhabitants of Prospect and its vicinity for their services in rescuing and providing for the passengers and crew of the Atlantic.

Johnston provided the amounts paid to the promovents (see Table 2 on page 138), which came to a total of $736.60, which would imply that the remainder, coming to $823.40, was paid to others in Lower Prospect, Upper Prospect, and Terence Bay, who presented accounts for expenses.

The $1,560 appears in the "Statement of Expenditures on account of rewards for saving Life" in the annual report of the Department of Marine and Fisheries of the Government of Canada for 1874. The single line item is labelled, "Dennis Ryan & 48 others for assisting to save lives and administering to the wants of the rescued."[1]

When the Vice Admiralty Court ruled in March of 1874, it awarded most of the rescue-boat crew members $100 ($2,000 in today's money). Thus were twelve of the group paid, including the four Ryans, consisting of Edmund and his brother Dennis and cousins Stephen and Francis. The Blackburns—John, William and Samuel the younger— received the same, as did the O'Brien brothers, Michael and James the younger. The bulk of the effort to get the survivors ashore had relied on just four families: the Ryans, Blackburns, O'Briens, and Coolens! Patrick Dollard, Thomas Twohig, and William Lacey were the other recipients of $100. William Coolen and John Purcell received $60 each and Alexander Brophy was paid $30.

One person, James Coolen, received $150. His boat was the first one launched and he was one of only two men (Dennis Ryan was the other) who would risk the first trip to the rock. Of his effort, Nicholas Christian told the court that Coolen was "continually at work in the boats from the time of my arrival until the work stopped. He exerted himself I think more than anyone I saw there."[2]

Thirteen men from Lower Prospect were rewarded, as were five from Upper Prospect, one from Terence Bay, and one from Pennant.

On behalf of the group, Edmund Ryan received the payment on April 20, 1874, more than a year after the event.

In addition, James Morrow had testified that he paid all the expense claims made by those billeting survivors, so there was an as-of-yet undefined amount in addition to those above. It is likely that many who were farther from the wreck, in Upper Prospect and Terence Bay, and who billeted survivors for the night, would not have submitted expenses to Morrow, considering what they did to be normal Christian hospitality.

To convert these amounts to today's funds, multiply by twenty. For example, those receiving $100 would receive $2,000 today.

Table 2. Awards and reimbursements paid to local rescuers.

Vice Admiralty Court:		Government of Canada:		Total
Rewards	Amount	For Expenses	Amount	
James Coolen	$150	James Coolen	$61.10	$211.10
Edmund Ryan	$100	Elizabeth Ryan	$34.50	$134.50
Stephen Ryan	$100	Stephen Ryan	$61.10	$161.10
Dennis Ryan	$100	Dennis Ryan	$65.20	$165.20
Francis Ryan	$100	Francis Ryan	$55.25	$155.25
William B. Blackburn	$100	W. B. Blackburn	$58.20	$158.20
Samuel Blackburn	$100	Samuel Blackburn	$59.00	$159.00
John Blackburn	$100	John Blackburn	$43.00	$143.00
Michael O'Brien	$100	Michael O'Brien	$43.00	$143.00
James O'Brien	$100	James O'Brien	$43.00	$143.00
William Lacey	$100	William Lacey	$62.75	$162.75
Patrick Dollard	$100	Patrick Dollard	$43.00	$143.00
Thomas Twohig	$100	Thomas Twohig	$43.00	$143.00
William Coolen	$60	William Coolen	$21.50	$81.50
John Purcell	$60	John Purcell	$21.50	$81.50
Alexander Brophy	$30	Alexander Brophy	$21.50	$51.50

(Source: Greg Cochkanoff and Bob Chaulk, *SS Atlantic: The White Star Line's First Disaster at Sea*)

Missing from this list are the names of Michael Clancy and his daughter, Sarah Jane O'Reilly. His name had been automatically included in the list of people involved in the action at the Vice Admiralty Court, but he had made a point of removing it as the action smacked to him of an attempt to profit from other people's misfortune. James Morrow took up Clancy's case and went directly to Ismay, Imrie, and Company, who paid him £200, making him the highest-paid of everybody, and rightly so. That would come to perhaps $12,000 today.

Most payers treated the efforts of women as part of the efforts of the family, but the Chicago Relief Commission took a more forward-thinking view. They conferred both gifts and money on Sarah Jane and the two O'Brien sisters, Agatha and Kate—the only women to be singled out for special recognition. While Elizabeth Ryan did not receive anything by way of gifts, she was the only woman to receive a payment from the government for expenses. Others would have had expenses covered by James Morrow on behalf of the White Star Line.

Table 3. Gifts conferred upon rescuers and family members.

Recipient	Organization	Item/Amount
William Ancient	Royal Humane Society	Medal
William Ancient	Liverpool Shipwreck and Humane Society	Silver medal
William Ancient	Government of Canada	Gold watch
William Ancient	Government of Canada	$500
William Ancient	City of Chicago	Gold watch
William Ancient	Union Protection Company	$155
William Ancient	John T. Metcalfe, New York	$25
William Ancient	Humane Society of Massachusetts	Certificate
Michael Clancy	White Star Line	£200
Michael Clancy	Liverpool Shipwreck and Humane Society	£10
Sarah Jane O'Reilly	Liverpool Shipwreck and Humane Society	£5
Sarah Jane O'Reilly	City of Chicago	£20
Sarah Jane O'Reilly	City of Chicago	Gold locket
Kate O'Brien	City of Chicago	£10
Kate O'Brien	City of Chicago	Gold locket
Agatha O'Brien	City of Chicago	£10
Agatha O'Brien	City of Chicago	Gold locket
Cornelius Brady	City of Chicago	Gold watch
John Brown	City of Chicago	Gold watch
John Speakman	City of Chicago	Gold watch
Edward Owens	City of Chicago	Gold watch
Edmund Ryan	Government of Canada	Gold watch

Recipient	Organization	Item/Amount
William B. Christian	Relatives of Mr. W. H. Merritt	Medal
Fishermen	Cabin Passenger Oswald Jugla, New York	$100 total
Samuel White, James Power, Patrick Duggan, John Slaunwhite	Union Protection Company	Equal shares from $78
Fishermen	Liverpool Shipwreck and Humane Society	£10 total

The Relief Committee of Boston reported collecting $1,050.43, principally for the survivors when they arrived in the city. The surplus, if any, was to be sent to the fishermen of Nova Scotia.[3] On June 17, William Ancient also received $557.37 from the Committee of the Boston Atlantic Relief Fund—half for him and the remainder to be distributed to those whom he deemed worthy.[4]

While travelling on the *Celtic* on his return to England, Brady's fellow passengers decided to recognize his efforts and bravery and

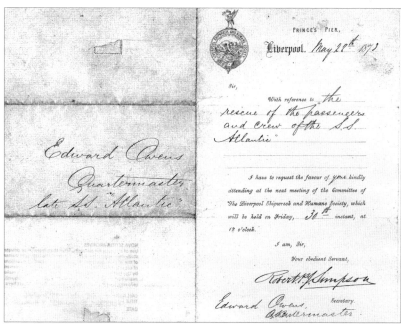

Not long after getting back to Liverpool, Edward Owens, John Speakman, and Robert Thomas were invited to tell their stories to the Liverpool Shipwreck and Humane Society to determine if they deserved medals. It was determined that they did not.

presented him with a purse of gold sovereigns. (When the wealthy decide to be generous, it is clearly good to be in the room.)

The three quartermasters who were active in the rescue, Robert Thomas, Edward Owens, and John Speakman, were considered for medals by the Liverpool Shipwreck and Humane Society but they were unable to present a consistent testimony when they were invited to visit on May 30. Their stories were so conflicting that they were sent on their way with £2 apiece for expenses, but no medals.

It is hard to know what to make of that decision but, on the surface, it appears to be the reverse of how William Ancient was treated.

In addition to the amounts above, the federal government paid the following expenses related to the burial of bodies[5] and the inquiry:[6]

Table 4. Burial expenses paid by the federal government.

Land for burial of Roman Catholic bodies	H. Crosskill	$71.50
Enclosing the Roman Catholic burial site with a fence	Rev. Martin Maas	$100.00
Labour interring Protestant bodies	Rev. W. J. Ancient	$274.25
Labour of persons working at the wreck site	Edmund Ryan	$912.00

Table 5. Halifax Inquiry expenses paid by the federal government.

Inquiry into loss of *Atlantic*	E. M. McDonald	$210.60
Inquiry into loss of *Atlantic*	Captain Peter A. Scott	$40.00
Inquiry into loss of *Atlantic*	G. A. McKenzie	$48.00
Counsel fee investigating *Atlantic*	Samuel L. Shannon	$155.00
Counsel fee investigating *Atlantic*	Hiram Blanchard	$150.00

Edmund M. McDonald, the collector of customs for Nova Scotia, conducted the inquiry, assisted by expert witnesses Scott and McKenzie. Samuel L. Shannon and Hiram Blanchard, legal counsel, represented the Crown at the inquiry.

Chapter 19

Cargo and Artifacts

Three schooners—the J. W. Falt, Nimble and Thistle—were at
Prospect, loaded, last night, with goods saved from the wreck of the
Atlantic, and were ready to sail for Halifax. Four others are loading at
the scene.

Halifax Daily Acadian Recorder
April 10, 1873

With the survivors, crew, and other key players in the drama
gone, the big thing remaining was the recovery of cargo
and any bodies still in the wreck.

On April 12, the *Chronicle* reported that the schooners *Nimble* and
Napier were at Cunard's wharf discharging goods where, less than two
weeks earlier, survivors had arrived.

These small schooners could anchor above the wreck and take
goods aboard as they came to the surface.

If a salvaged item was water-damaged, the packing was compro-
mised, or the ownership could not be established, it was taken to
Halifax and auctioned. The *Nimble, Napier, Daisy, Thistle,* and *J. W. Falt*
were kept busy during the spring and summer, carrying cases, crates,
casks, and kegs, as well as bales, bundles, and barrels to auction at
Halifax. Cargo recovered intact in original shipping containers was

Two steamers, three schooners, and a host of smaller craft involved in salvage at the wreck site. The small boat ashore in the foreground is a dory like the one used in the first rescue attempt. (W.R. MacAskill, Nova Scotia Archives, 1987-453 no. 3249)

considered to be of full value and was taken to New York for forwarding to consignees. It went aboard bigger vessels like the *Meta*, *Florence B. Towers*, and the brigantine *D. W. Hennesey*, chartered from Port Hawkesbury.

While the *Atlantic* was a dark cloud for many, it also had a silver lining for some. Marine operators, divers, rooming houses, and hotels were already increasing their business. The benefits from the slightly damaged cargo would be shared widely among the citizenry. On April 15, Halifax Mayor James Duggan, who happened to be an auctioneer as well as a merchant, held his first of many auctions. Not long after that, local merchants like McInnis and Tupper, W. H. Bauld, A. L. Woods, and others were advertising deals on items like black silk, black lustres, *real* Balbriggan hose (!), and other useful items.

The men employed in salvaging the cargo discovered that the *Atlantic* had not been exempted from the time-honoured practice of smuggling. They found within the centre of several crockery crates some tin cases containing valuable silks, the evident intention being to evade the payment of duties in New York.

And there were bigger items. The *Morning Chronicle* reported on April 15:

> *The Atlantic did not break up in Sunday's storm, as it was feared she would. The only effect the storm had was to carry away her mainmast about noon. Immediately after the mast went, a large case containing a fine carriage was washed out, and was saved almost undamaged.*

This carriage, called a phaeton, survives in the collection of Sherbrooke Village, a historic tourist community located on the eastern shore of Nova Scotia. There were two aboard that were saved and sold at auction in Halifax. Patrick Power, a leading dry goods merchant of Halifax and a Member of Parliament, purchased one of them. After Mr. Power's death in 1881, the phaeton became the property of Mary, one of his three daughters. Following Mary's marriage ten years later to Angus MacIsaac of Antigonish, it was taken there and used for several years as the family conveyance. At the time, carriages of such fine workmanship were rare in Nova Scotia. A 1934 article in the *Halifax Herald* about the rediscovery of the carriage noted that at that time, when it was almost seventy years old, it was in "a remarkable state of preservation, with the exception of the upholstery."[1]

April 23 was a busy day for the salvage effort, with two large vessels arriving from New York. The wrecking schooner *Meteor* and the steamer *Lackawana*, belonging to the Coast Wrecking Company, arrived in Halifax and sailed to the wreck

Even though Patrick Power was affected by the *Atlantic* only in an incidental way, another steamship disaster had had a lasting effect on his family. Two years previously, in January 1871, the *City of Boston* left Halifax bound for Liverpool and was never heard from again. One of the passengers was his twenty-one-year-old son Patrick Jr. who was making his first business trip to England on behalf of the family firm.

There was another family connection, as well. Lawrence G. Power, the lawyer who represented the promovents in the lawsuit before the Vice Admiralty Court, was another of Patrick Power's five sons. Born in Halifax in 1841, he attended Harvard Law School and was called to the bar in 1866. He was the author of several books including a biography of Richard John Uniacke. He became a senator in 1877 and died on September 12, 1921.

the next day. Also on the 23rd, the *Perit* sailed from Prospect to New York with a cargo of salvaged goods, having been on site since April 18.

Despite that activity, progress throughout April had been slow because of the way the wreck was lying. To improve access, on April 29, the Coast Wrecking Company detonated three large explosive charges. The entire deck disconnected from the hull, setting the contents of the ship free. Debris floated everywhere, causing an overwhelming sense of grief for the people still waiting for the bodies of their loved ones. One man wept bitterly, having spent all he had to journey from the United States in search of his still-missing wife. Over the weeks, more than 140 coffins had been opened for his inspection. A Mr. Mott, from Halifax, pressed $13 into the man's hand to help him get by.[2]

The Coast Wrecking Company detonated three more blasts the next day, blowing the upper side of the wreck open, leaving nothing to be seen from the surface. Walking around on the exposed side of the ship had been a must-do for male visitors to the site, but now that was over. Cargo and bodies were now in abundance, but the bodies were unrecognizable after a month underwater and the shocks of the explosions. The body count officially increased to 391 recovered to that point. One schooner was directly loaded with cargo and another nearly so.[3]

Bad weather followed almost immediately, causing much of the cargo to float out to sea. The *Evening Reporter* noted,

> *It is thought that the blowing up of the ship was injudicious, and not much more property will be recovered. The Coast Wrecking Company will hardly be able to pay expenses.*[4]

WITH NOTHING LEFT TO SEE, THE LAST PART OF THE DRAMA—GOING TO Lower Prospect to ogle the wreck—was over and the daily newspaper coverage of the *Atlantic* story began to thin out. By the end of May, they were down to periodic one- or two-sentence updates on the progress of the salvage, short descriptions of body recoveries and burials, and news about what Reverend Ancient was up to. He had become a celebrity, and anything he did was considered newsworthy—moving to Halifax to lead a bigger church, being guest preacher at another church, appearing on the stage at Temperance Hall, having his wife and family return from England, and receiving the money raised for him as the *Atlantic* hero.[5]

Maintaining vessels, divers, and support crews on-site required a steady flow of valuable salvage. That flow inevitably slowed, and on September 12, 1873, D. H. Pitts, a brother-in-law and partner to Daniel Cronan, one of the richest men in Halifax, purchased what remained of the *Atlantic* and cargo for $4,400, or approximately $88,000 in today's currency. Daniel Pitts's crew continued salvaging the wreck until November 1876, using the fifty-ton schooner *Leander* with a crew of six men under command of Israel Daniels. Diver Leonard Lyons earned his keep, going underwater some days at one o'clock and staying down until sunset, while weighted down by a sixty-two- pound helmet, twenty pounds of lead on each foot, and three forty-five-pound weights—one over each shoulder and one around his middle.[6]

Over the years, the wreck site of the *Atlantic* has yielded a large number of artifacts compared to other wrecks of the period. The *Atlantic* was a big ship for the time, carrying an unusually large number of people and a lot of cargo, and was lost in relatively shallow water close to shore, making it easy to access in fine weather. The remains lie in a very dynamic area, strewn on a slope in water from twenty to eighty feet deep and pounded by winter storms that churn things up. Scuba divers still find small items such as coins, bottles, and bits of jewellery. Typical shipwreck debris like portholes or deadeyes are very scarce, having been picked up over the decades by salvagers and souvenir hunters.

In addition to the carriage, there are some significant artifacts from the *Atlantic* in Nova Scotia homes and museums, including ornaments, dishes, cutlery, bottles of wine, champagne, soda pop, jewellery and other personal items, and some larger objects. The SS *Atlantic* Heritage Park holds one of the quarter boards, an eleven-foot–long elaborately carved and brightly painted wooden sign with the ship's name that would have hung on the topmost house that contained the wheelhouse and chartroom. On October 14, 1874, a year and a half after the wreck,

Captain Patrick Pottie was conning his schooner along the Eastern Shore of Nova Scotia, twelve miles offshore from the Liscomb Light, when he came alongside the unusual piece of wood. He was more than 125 miles from the wreck site. He fished it out and took it home and eventually gave it to his granddaughter, Emmeline McPhee of River Bourgeois. It was in her possession in 1927 when the local newspaper featured the story.

It found its way to Halifax, and when Barb Corbin and her husband were looking for something to hang above the fireplace in their new cottage in Indian Harbour, NS, Ethel Connors went out to her barn in Kline Heights near Halifax and produced the quarter board, which had been there for years. It hung above Mrs. Corbin's fireplace until 2016, when she was preparing to sell her house and donated it to the museum.

The Heritage Centre also has what is purported to be the flag from the ship. It was donated to the Centre by Andrew Thomas, the great-grandson of Captain Williams. The flag has been across Canada and the United States as part of various exhibits. Mr. Thomas purchased it from a private collector. It has been dated to the 1870s and is made from finely woven wool. The star is made from three panels sewn onto the red background.[7]

Also on display is one of the seven anchors that were aboard the ship. It is the smallest, a kedge anchor that weighed 541 pounds when the *Atlantic* was surveyed. The ship's main bower anchors were almost ten times that weight. This anchor was retrieved from the site by William (Billy) Slaunwhite of Terence Bay, who discovered it while diving for sea urchins. There is a record of an anchor being uncovered by a diver in the 1960s, while diving from Harry Blackburn's boat, but it is unclear if it was brought up at that time or if this is the same anchor.[8] Harry Blackburn was a descendant of William Blackburn, one of the first on-site and a key member of the rescue team.

Another diver also saw it and decided that he would like to have it to display on his lawn. Mr. Slaunwhite was determined that it should stay in the community, so he quickly rigged up a homemade floatation device using a two hundred–gallon furnace-oil tank, to which he attached a winch. He took it to the wreck site and positioned it above the anchor. He winched the anchor off the bottom but it was too heavy to get into his boat, so he towed the tank with the anchor hanging below to the wharf in Terence Bay, three miles away, and soon the anchor was on display next to the burial site of the victims, where it sat for twenty years. It was recently moved indoors at the Heritage Park to prevent further deterioration.

CHAPTER 20

THE HALIFAX INQUIRY

Whether all proceedings in connection with the inquiry in Halifax were regular or not I am not able positively to say; I must, at the same time, say, according to our experience, that Canadian inquiries of this kind are generally well looked after. [1]

Chichester Parkinson-Fortescue, M.P.
President of the British Board of Trade

With the striking events of the wreck now in the past and the survivors' dramatic stories becoming scarcer, people were waiting eagerly for the judgement of the Halifax inquiry. In the British Isles a stiff upper lip was in evidence. In Belfast, where the *Atlantic* had been built, the *Weekly Telegraph* reported optimistically:

With the testimony of the captain supporting the assertions of the owners, every confidence is felt that the forthcoming inquiry into the loss of the splendid steamer will establish the fact that her loss was not in any way owing to her construction or equipment.[2]

English papers were equally upbeat:

General satisfaction has been expressed in Liverpool at the publica-tion of Messrs. Ismay and Co.'s letter, denying the imputations of the

Atlantic having been insufficiently supplied with coal. The disaster,
as far as can be judged at present, will not damage the prestige of the
White Star Company. The Adriatic, which sailed yesterday, took out 95
saloon and 834 steerage passengers, there being no withdrawal.[3]

Everybody was wondering how this modern, relatively new ship, in perfect working order, with up-to-date Admiralty charts aboard, commanded by well-qualified officers belonging to the world's leading seafaring nation, approaching a well-known harbour marked by four lighthouses—the outermost of which could be seen for twenty-one miles in reasonable weather—ended up on the rocks woefully off course.

Who was to blame and what was to be done to them? There were already calls in England to charge Captain Williams with murder. It was imperative that the questions get answered while the people responsible were all together. Only the dead would be staying in Nova Scotia. The living wanted to get far away from the place as quickly as they could.

Despite Ismay's instructions to James Sparks, the White Star Line agent in New York, to send the officers to Liverpool post-haste, they were under orders from Canadian authorities to stay put in Halifax. They got their subpoenas early. A few wily crew members tried to skip out by paying their own way on a ship but they were found out.[4] Some passengers were also detained.

At 11:00 A.M. on the first day that the divers were able to get into the water—April 5—Edmund M. McDonald, the collector of customs for Nova Scotia, convened the inquiry. He was assisted by Captain George A. McKenzie, a retired master mariner, and Captain Peter A. Scott, RN, chairman of the Board of Examiners of Masters and Mates for Canada. They questioned twenty-three people, including all of the surviving deck officers and some of the quartermasters, engineers, lookouts, and passengers, all of whom had been aboard the ship. Expert witnesses included an American captain experienced with Halifax Harbour and the coastline near the wreck, a Halifax Harbour pilot, and the keepers of three lighthouses. Nobody involved in the rescue was called.

The captain, of course, was found culpable. He ultimately lost his certificate for two years, which sounds light, but his attention to duty during the wrecking and rescue was deemed to be commendable and therefore he did not lose it permanently. Williams's whole demeanour during his time in Halifax was remarkable in that he was very open about his failures, and very contrite. There are several long interviews with him in the Halifax and New York newspapers in which he expresses deep remorse and talks in detail about how he could and should have done things differently. His letters to the White Star Line advising them of the loss of the ship also survive, containing technical details about that fateful morning and also his explanations of what must have happened.

Briefly, the inquiry learned that the ship got caught in a strong current that swept it off course to the west—or left of where they thought they were—causing them to miss the harbour entirely. That is a feat in itself, considering that Halifax Harbour is more than seven miles wide at its opening. They were searching for the Sambro light, which should have been at their eleven- and then ten-o'clock positions as it came into view and they drew up to it, but the ship's ongoing movement to the left caused the light to, in effect, travel through their twelve-, one-, and two-o'clock positions, and when they ran aground the light was directly off to their right at the three-o'clock position.

There were enough lookouts to have seen that happen, so the big question is—why did they not see the light? Even though the inquiry testimony varied regarding the weather that night, it was evident that there was no storm or widespread fog. The inquirers were left with no choice but to conclude that the lookouts were simply not paying attention, which is shocking if it is true.

Given that the ship was far off course, travelling faster than they realized, and they were unable to find the light—what was going through the heads of the officers standing the watch? We'll never know what Metcalfe was thinking, since he died in the aftermath of the crash. All we have are Quartermaster Robert Thomas's inconsistent comments and testimony that make Metcalfe seem indecisive; not a good thing for a person in his position. Was there anything he could have done? Metcalfe must have felt there was nothing, but the inquiry stated that he should have checked the depth—called sounding, or heaving the lead. Fourth Officer Brown felt differently: "We did not heave the lead on account of the clearness of the night and the certainty of seeing the light."[5]

The inquiry singled out this failure as the most costly error of all.

While the inquiry supposedly set out to get to the truth, the panel of inquirers and lawyers were constrained by what they probably considered common decency. Metcalfe was dead. What could he contribute now? When Williams responded to a question about Metcalfe's competence by saying he was a steady man whom he would not have put on the watch if he'd had any qualms, they left it at that. Whether Williams knew anything about Metcalfe's past we do not know.

All the officers should have been grilled about Metcalfe, because he was in command of the ship when the accident occurred. We don't even know what Williams thought of Metcalfe's losing the ship. That seems like a basic question to ask—to push the captain to give his take on Metcalfe. Quartermaster Thomas's testimony included a number of accusations about Metcalfe's performance in the last moments. That testimony should have been picked apart word by word. Instead, the attitude seems to have been that Thomas was only a quartermaster. Why would he provide anything of value?

Thomas Ismay, the managing director of the White Star Line, certainly knew Metcalfe. He owned the ship that had sent the *Bretagne* to the bottom with Metcalf as chief officer—and he was Metcalfe's first cousin. He must have rued the day he ever gave him a job after getting his certificate back. Clearly, nepotism in England played a role in Nova Scotia's worst shipwreck. And the class system kept the inquiry from getting at the truth.

ON APRIL 8, THREE DAYS AFTER THE COMMENCEMENT OF THE INQUIRY, the Allan Line steamer *North American* departed Halifax, arriving in Liverpool on the 21st. Aboard were eleven officers of the *Atlantic*, along with nine steerage passengers, eleven firemen, and twenty seamen. They included the first and fourth officers and chief engineer, as well as the other engineers who had testified at the inquiry.[6]

Even though the White Star Line was not legally bound to pay the crew after the date of the *Atlantic*'s wreck, it paid them for the full month until they arrived in England.[7] When survivors arrived in New York, the company also paid their expenses, such as meals while they waited at Castle Garden.[8]

In the middle of all the suffering and sadness, those who came back alive received a rousing welcome. The English village of Crowthorn gave a hero's welcome to John Speakman, the man who had swum the rope to the rock. The village was draped in flags and banners and a triumphal arch erected. There was a tea party, followed by music and dancing.[9]

There would be no opportunity to re-examine any testimony given at the inquiry. It cost money to have men hanging around in Halifax and the loss of the *Atlantic* had already cost the White Star Line enough. Of the officers, only the captain and Third Officer Brady remained. Everybody

Quartermaster John Speakman swam the first rope to the rock after Quartermaster Edward Owens's unsuccessful attempt. (NS ARCHIVES, NOTMAN STUDIO, NO. 1983-310 #90095)

else had to get back to work on the other ships that had to pick up the slack to enable the company to survive this huge blow. The pressure was on McDonald to get the inquiry completed. Letters full of questions were circulating in England among the government, the company, the Board of Trade, and the insurers, and the answer was always the same: nothing could happen until the Halifax inquiry was wrapped up and copies were received in England.

The inquirers brought down their judgement on April 18. Many in England were shocked to learn at this point that this was *the* inquiry and that it would be binding in Britain.

The inquiry criticized the White Star Line for putting Williams in the position of having to divert to Halifax for coal.

During the three preceding days the ship had been on a reduced consumption of coal and from the fact that after this reduced consumption she was found on the eleventh day of the passage with less than forty-eight hours' supply remaining, the inference seems inevitable, that she had not sufficient coal on board when sailing, for a ship of her class.[10]

Captain Williams was also severely criticized for leaving the bridge when approaching a strange coast at night. As noted earlier, his Extra Master's certificate was suspended for two years as a result of the inquiry, but it was not permanently revoked because of his outstanding conduct during the event. Fourth Officer Brown lost his certificate for three months for not calling the captain.

Those were predictable judgements, but the charge of having put the ship to sea with insufficient coal could spell disaster.

The White Star Line was at a critical point. The company was growing. New ships were being built. Given the loss of a profitable, well-regarded asset like the *Atlantic*, and the deaths of nearly six hundred people, Ismay had to act.

The wreck area. The boat is above the ledge where the ship's bow was located. The rocky area covering most of the image is part of Meaghers Island; the Clancys lived in the small cove at upper right. The narrow, treed island at the top is Ryans Island. Another smaller island (Hennesseys Island) is before Lower Prospect on the mainland. (CHRIS DEVANNEY)

Golden Rule Rock was halfway from the ship to the shore, but the gap shown in the middle of this picture was too rough, so men got stranded on the rock and had to be rescued. (GREG COCHKANOFF)

A 1:144 scale model of the *Atlantic*. The taper of the bottom below the bow—called the forefoot—enabled the ship to run up onto the rock, where it teetered until it slid left onto the ledge a few minutes after the grounding. (AUTHOR PHOTO)

Low tide at the place where the rescue boats brought the survivors ashore. Golden Rule Rock is right of centre, just below the horizon. The *Atlantic* was wrecked outside the rock. Much of what is seen in this image was progressively covered with water as the tide was rising throughout the rescue. The dark/light transition in the lower right corner indicates the limit of high tide. (AUTHOR PHOTO)

One of the two quarter boards from the *Atlantic* hung above a fireplace for fifty years before being donated to the Heritage Park. It is more than ten feet long. A schooner captain found it at sea six months after the wreck occurred. (AUTHOR PHOTO)

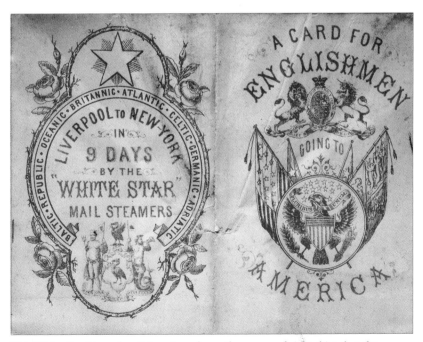

This White Star Line advertising piece shows the names of eight ships, but the *Germanic* entered service two years after the *Atlantic* was lost, and more than a month after the *Oceanic* had been taken off the Liverpool-to-New York service and transferred to the Pacific. It probably dates from the latter days of the *Atlantic*, when *Adriatic* and *Britannic* were being built. (AUTHOR'S COLLECTION)

The White Star Line flag that is believed to have flown on the *Atlantic*. It was donated by the captain's great-grandson. (Courtesy SS *Atlantic* Heritage Park Society)

ABOVE: A note from Eleanor Quigley to the SS *Atlantic* Heritage Park. Her great-uncle John Hanley is believed to be the only child to have survived the disaster. (Courtesy SS *Atlantic* Heritage Park Society and Eleanor Quigley)

AT LEFT: The clock from the *Atlantic*'s chart room, showing the time when the ship ran aground. The clock still works. (Courtesy SS *Atlantic* Heritage Park Society)

Coins from many nations have been recovered from the wreck site over the years. (Greg Cochkanoff)

The author near the remains of the *Atlantic*'s rapidly deteriorating boilers, eighty feet below the surface. This is the deepest part of the wreck. (Bob Semple)

Upper Prospect, with offshore fog hanging just above the water and obscuring a large island. This same effect probably hid the Sambro light, contributing to the *Atlantic*'s loss.
(Chris Devanney)

The rescue boats were dragged from the water on the lee side of the island and over the rocks, which were covered in snow and ice. Survivors went in the opposite direction. Clancy's house was behind the green hill on the right. Note the figure on the centre of the horizon. (Author photo)

Descendants of the great (from left): Vince Norris, great-grandson of Richard Norris, who was instrumental in the formation of the SS *Atlantic* Heritage Park Society; Travis Humphrey, of Blackburn descent; and Shirley Jollimore, a direct descendant of Michael Clancy through his daughter Sarah Jane O'Reilly. (Author photo)

Broken ice along the shore near the place where the Roman Catholic bodies were landed for burial. Ice covers the water in the background, as it would have that day. (AUTHOR PHOTO)

A team from the Saint Mary's University archaeology department using ground-penetrating radar to survey the site in Terence Bay where Reverend Ancient buried 277 bodies. There was some erosion but it was caught soon enough to keep the bodies from washing away. The Roman Catholic burial site is in Lower Prospect, about a kilometre away. (KATHY KAULBACH)

Protestant burial site, showing the reinforcing stones put in place in 1998 to curb erosion. The church was built after the one in which Reverend Ancient served was struck by lightning and burned in 1942. (KELLY CAMPBELL)

The granite monument at the burial site in Terence Bay, paid for by the White Star Line and installed in 1905 when Reverend A. F. Dentith was the pastor of the local church. It is about two miles from the wreck site, as the crow flies, above the gazebo at right. (AUTHOR PHOTO)

Chapter 21

Coal

The price of coal here is $6 a chaldron; in England it is $15. This accounts for the presumption, denied by the company and the officers, that the ship was coaled for Halifax instead of New York.

New York Tribune
April 8, 1873

On the west coast of Newfoundland, nestled among the mountains of Gros Morne National Park, is a tiny cove called Neddy Harbour, populated by a few fishermen and retirees. Before anybody lived there, it was a coaling station for ships of the Royal Navy. There is nothing to indicate that history, unless you don scuba gear and get into the water. Then you see stone ballast heaps from the original docks, wasted coal that fell into the water, and discarded beer bottles and other detritus from the ships that tied up there.

Before 1905, the west coast of Newfoundland was part of the French Shore, an area reserved for French fishermen. By treaty, nobody was allowed to settle there, but the French could catch all the codfish they wanted. The Royal Navy watched over them while they caught, gutted, salted, dried, and stowed their catch. Every spring, coal ships arrived in Neddy Harbour carrying the fuel supply for the season. The availability of coal, where and when needed, was an ever-complicating aspect of the age of steam. It was heavy, it took up a lot of space aboard, and a ship could run out of it—and be in big trouble. Some early steamers were known to have run out on the high seas and ended up burning furniture, masts, doors, and anything else they could spare to get to port.

On the other hand, when Prince Henry the Navigator sent his ships from Lisbon down the African coast in the fifteenth century in search of gold and slaves, the last thing on his mind was fuel. Dragons were an issue, as were currents, shoals, and fog, but the ships had an inexhaustible supply of wind—at least, most of the time. Steamships freed mariners from the vagaries of the wind, but placed a big new challenge in their lives—how to ensure a supply of readily available coal to keep their ships moving.

That was after they had solved the problem of where to keep the coal. The old salts shook their heads as they gazed in wonder at the first steamboats: belching smoke, clanging engines, salt-clogged pipes, lubricating oil everywhere, ash going overboard. Like all gainsayers, they could never visualize steam catching on. How could they ever afford, let alone carry, enough coal? The wind was free!

The challenges were overcome, one improvement at a time, but carrying the optimum amount of coal so as not to use up valuable space while ensuring there was enough to get to the destination was perhaps the biggest issue shipowners had to face. It certainly was for the emigrant ships going from Europe to North America, because coal took up space that could be used for paying passengers.

Humanity's relationship with coal has always been rocky. It is dirty, smoky, and troublesome. We have loved it and we have hated it. We love the heat but we hate the smell and the greasy smoke. We want the jobs but we despise the mines and the dust and the explosions, cave-ins, and diseases. We desire the electricity it generates but we don't want the scars on the landscape. We need the steel but we rue the smog. We adore the colourful aniline dyes it produces, but not the grime on the buildings.

An aging fuel oil salesman who started out in his career selling coal told me there were thirty-eight kinds of coal sold in Halifax. At one time, he worked for Cunard Fuels, which was started by Samuel Cunard when he was a Halifax merchant and his ships were propelled by the wind. Selling coal made him well-off, but using coal to drive his ships made him wealthy.

Different kinds of coal have different properties. Some burn hotter than others, some faster, some smokier. Some ignite more quickly; some burn longer. It all depends on the mine. For ships sailing out of Liverpool, the preferred mixture was three parts South Wales coal and one part Lancashire coal. Passing judgement on the coal quality was a standard pastime for engine-room crews and ships' officers during a voyage.

> We got here early this morning and have been getting coals all day, indeed they are not done yet and oh! the dirt; everything one touches seems to be black with coal dust so that we will be very glad when all gets washed down again.
>
> —Harriet Brown in a letter to her sister from aboard the SS *Hibernian*, 1889. Her husband, John Brown, was captain and had been fourth officer on the *Atlantic*.

However, for Ismay, the bigger question was not about the quality of the coal and how much was aboard the *Atlantic*. Everything rode on the answer to this question: Did the ship really have to bear up for Halifax? If it did not, then the ship had not been sent to sea with insufficient coal, and the White Star Line was not to blame. That would make it the captain's fault—a far more desirable outcome.

"The formidable personality of T. H. Ismay"[1] was brought to bear to save his company at this dire moment.

On April 9, four days into the deliberations, and long before the ruling of the Halifax inquiry, he telegraphed the Board of Trade:

> Our New York agent cables us that Halifax authorities state Inquiry re loss "Atlantic" is final. Please say if this is so, as we are most anxious for a full and searching official investigation on this side.[2]

The Board of Trade replied:

> The Inquiry into the loss of the "Atlantic" in Canada will be the only one held. The proposed Inquiry in this country was ordered before the Board of Trade knew that there would be one held in Canada; it has been countermanded, as they have no power to hold a second.[3]

The White Star Line replied immediately, making a strong case, which they summarized in just one—albeit long—sentence:

> The managers of the [Oceanic Steam Navigation Company] are very strongly of opinion that much evidence and important facts connected with this vessel and her equipment of coals, provisions, and otherwise, should be in the possession of any board of inquiry appointed to adjudicate on such a question as this, and seeing that witnesses competent to speak to those facts are in Liverpool, I venture to ask your assent to an arrangement whereby the present Inquiry at Halifax may be adjourned to Liverpool, where the supplementary and final part of the proceedings may take effect.[4]

Ismay was trying desperately to find a way to get what he perceived to be the important information heard, bearing in mind that this was more than a week before the ruling of the Halifax inquiry came out, with its damning conclusion that the ship had been sent to sea without enough coal. You might say it was prescient—if you did not remember that the newspapers were printing the proceedings, including the testimony, as they occurred—and Ismay may well have had somebody attending the inquiry and reporting to him by telegraph at the end of each day.

> We submit to you that this is a great hardship upon the Company which we represent, that it should be deprived of the opportunity of proving, by the testimony of unimpeachable witnesses, and by facts which cannot be gainsaid, how complete and thorough, in all respects, was the equipment of the steamer "Atlantic" as regards coals, provisions, stores, and all necessary outfit, and how excellent were the vessel's sea-going qualities, both as regards model and strength of construction. [5]

Meanwhile, to the assistant secretary of his marine department, he expressed his desperation:

> We owe it as a duty to ourselves and the public, that this terrible disaster should be traced home, and we trust no technical difficulties will

*be allowed to frustrate an impartial investigation on this side, if the
one already held proves to be (as we fear it will) ex parte, meagre and
incomplete.*[6]

Despite his desperate plea, Thomas Gray, the assistant secretary
of the marine department, responded for the Board of Trade that,

*The Inquiry at Halifax has been instituted by the Government of
Canada and not by the Board of Trade....It is not within the power of
the Board of Trade to comply with your request.*[7]

The owners of the *Atlantic* were not the only ones looking for a
deeper inquiry. James Brown, the father-in-law of saloon passenger
Herman Kruger, was looking for justice for the husband of his daughter Jane and father of his three grandchildren, James, Alfred, and
Herman. He wrote to the secretary of the Board, T. H. Farrar, in very
strong language, condemning the White Star Line and demanding an
additional inquiry in England. He ended his letter on a human note: "A
lady and three dear children, bereaved of husband and father through
this dire calamity, now around me, [are] more than cause enough for
my thus trespassing upon you."[8]

On May 6, 1873, James Brown's demands proved successful. The
reply from Thomas Gray informed him:

*An inquiry will shortly be held by this department as to the state of the
stores and coal of the ship on leaving England, and also to the conduct
of the officers of this department at the port of Liverpool."*[9]

Ismay was pleased with this news. It was not to be another inquiry;
rather, it was to be an "inspection" under the authority of the Merchant
Shipping Act of 1854. Retired Royal Navy Rear Admiral Charles F.
Schomberg, the Queen's Harbour Master at Holyhead, was appointed
to be the inspector, with the mandate to:

*Inquire and report whether the provisions of the Merchant Shipping
Acts and of the Passenger Acts have been complied with in the case of*

the survey and inspection of the steamship "Atlantic," and of her rigging and equipments, and of the stores, fuel, and provisions put on board of her.

The words of the mandate could have been in Ismay's own writing, they so perfectly matched what he had been campaigning for. In Thomas Gray's words, it was an investigation "into the circumstances connected with the dispatch of the vessel upon the voyage which terminated so disastrously."[10]

There was a third person dealing with the Board of Trade at that time. It was not a shipowner with connections, like Thomas Ismay, nor a wealthy businessman with a lawyer, like James Brown. It was the *Atlantic*'s Fourth Officer, John Brown. Because he was obliged to leave Halifax and return to England before the inquiry had completed, he had the shock and indignity of reading in the *Liverpool Mercury* newspaper that he had lost his certificate for three months.

Fourth Officer John Brown learned that he had been found to blame in the *Atlantic*'s loss when he read about it in a Liverpool newspaper. (COURTESY MICHAEL CLAYTON-BROWN)

Without an avenue of appeal, he had no option but to cast himself on the mercy of the licensing body, the Board of Trade. He made his case—a believable one—that he had lost his certificate unfairly. The captain's steward had arrived on the bridge at 2:40 A.M. with a mug of cocoa for the captain. He stopped the boy from calling the captain and told him to get permission from Second Officer Metcalfe, who was the senior officer of the watch. Metcalfe sent him away. The ruling of the inquiry, that he lose his certificate for three months, was for stopping the boy from calling the captain. He argued that he knew nothing about the cocoa. As junior officer of the watch, it was not his place to know, and he therefore had no authority to call the captain. Instead, he sent the boy to Metcalfe, who told him he would call the captain at 3:00 A.M. and to take the cocoa away. Brown felt, with some justification, that it was not his fault that things had turned out the way they did.

It was the ruling of the inquiry that if the captain had been called at that point, the calamity might have been avoided, so Brown was deemed culpable. To support his case, Brown presented a letter from Captain Williams saying he had done nothing to cause the wreck and had stood by his post throughout the disaster, saving lives and doing his duty.

Without his certificate, he was, of course, unable to sail as an officer. The certificate that had been suspended was a master's certificate. He had an offer to sail on a small vessel as a mate, a step down from where he had been, but at least it would enable him to support his widowed mother and her two children. He respectfully requested a subordinate certificate but was turned down. Even if he had a case, it was still a fact that he had been on watch when the *Atlantic* was lost, and the Board of Trade could not be seen allowing such a liberty.

Schomberg and his legal assistant, William Ravenhill, got down to business with their inspection on Saturday, May 10, in the boardroom at the Sailors' Home in Liverpool. They brought nineteen witnesses forward, starting with Captain J. F. C. Mackenzie, the Chief Emigration Officer for Liverpool, and ending on May 14 with Edward Bozlen, a coal stevedore. The question was whether or not the *Atlantic* had been properly provisioned for the voyage and if the ship was sound and ready for the trip.

Testimony came from the men of the Board of Trade who had been tasked with ensuring that the ship and its contents complied with the regulations of the two acts in their various versions up to the time. Before every passenger ship departed, these men had to be satisfied that there was sufficient food for all aboard, along with water, clean places to sleep, clean toilets, and washing facilities and a refuge for the sick. They checked the engines, boilers, furnaces, and coal bunkers. They also checked the certificates of the compasses and chronometers. They got aboard the lifeboats and examined the supplies and counted the oars. They counted the life preservers and made sure they were up to standard.

When testimony was finished, Schomberg was satisfied with everything except the coal. He sided with the Halifax inquiry on that issue.

Ismay was flabbergasted, but he persisted, contending that he had new information that should be heard. He convinced the Board and, two weeks after it had supposedly finished, Schomberg was back from Holyhead and the investigation continued for another week.

This time there was just one subject—coal. Ismay, Imrie, and Company amassed a phalanx of expert witnesses, including other shipowners, past captains of the *Atlantic*, and past chief engineers of the *Atlantic*. Consulting engineers were engaged. The senior partner of the ship's builders, Edward Harland, came over from Belfast to testify. He had already travelled to Halifax to see the wreck for himself.

There was much debate about the fact that such a long ship was so narrow. With a width of forty-one feet, the *Atlantic* was eleven times as long as it was wide; the length-to-beam ratio was eleven to one. A sailing ship of the day would have been probably six to one. As soon as news of the *Atlantic* wreck had come out, the critics had declared that a wider ship would not have rolled over with such devastating results. On May 2, Harland visited the site of the *Atlantic* wreck to determine if they had a point. He concluded that they did not, and he and other ship designers continued for decades to design narrow hulls for speed and efficiency.

Schomberg even dragged in the captains of the seven barges that had coaled the *Atlantic*. They were questioned on whether they saw the coal being weighed, and whether somebody was aboard their vessels at all times to ensure nobody sneaked aboard to steal some. They called the person who stowed the coal on the ship, subordinate engineers from the *Atlantic*, and firemen from the *Atlantic*. They grilled Foxley, Williams, Firth, and Brady about what was said and when, on the subject of coal during the voyage.

They pored over logs of previous voyages and examined consumption rates of White Star Line sister ships. They weighed the coal baskets empty and again when they were full. They drilled into the most minute details about how the consumption was calculated, how consumption reports were prepared, and where things might have been missed.

On June 7, when nobody had anything else to say on the subject of coal on the *Atlantic*, Schomberg retired to prepare his report on the expanded investigation. It came down on June 11. The judgement:

> *No passenger ship of her class should be short of coals on the 11th day of her voyage to New York, as the Atlantic, in our opinion, undoubtedly was.*[11]

CHAPTER 22

THE FINAL VERDICT

I have no hesitation in saying that, with the means of economizing coal on the White Star Line, I should have proceeded, with 127 tons of coal on board, at 460 miles from New York, even with a gale ahead, and even with 900 people on board.[1]

George Herriott
Former Chief Engineer, SS Atlantic

Even though the inquiry, and parts one and two of the inspection, had all come to the same conclusion, the senior partners of the White Star Line were more convinced than ever that the *Atlantic* had not gone to sea short of coal. Their conviction was based on the testimony. G. Hamilton Fletcher, in a letter of appeal on June 24, commented that, "The conclusion at which the Inspector has arrived with respect to the supply of coal is directly contrary to the evidence given before him."[2] He asked that the conclusion not be released and asked for a second opinion.

The testimony showed that when Schomberg asked Digby Murray, the *Atlantic*'s first captain and now a marine expert at the Board of Trade, "How do you account for the *Atlantic* being short on her last voyage?" Captain Murray had replied,

I do not believe she was short. I do not think they expended the coal
they said they did. If I were 460 miles from New York, with a strong
gale ahead and 120 tons on board, I should have proceeded on.[3]

Schomberg had asked the same question of Edward Harland: "How
do you account for the Atlantic putting into Halifax eleven days out?"
Harland had replied,

From my experience of the report of engineers, I should say he would
almost invariably report less coal than he had. They do this in order
that they may have a greater reserve at the end of the voyage.

Mr. Foxley's statement as to seventy tons a day being used is very
improbable; it might happen if the quality was bad, but not such coal
as is put on board these vessels. Bad management of the fires would
increase the consumption materially.

The engineer always prefers to keep a margin of coals that he may have
a reserve of power. They have under-estimated, in my experience, to
the extent of 5 to 10 per cent. We arrive at this information by examin-
ing the logs of many of these vessels for the purpose of constructing the
bunkers of other ships.[4]

George Herriott, who had been the chief engineer on the *Atlantic*
before Foxley, had introduced another possibility. Schomberg said to
him, "It was stated by Mr. Foxley, the Chief Engineer of the Atlantic,
that on her last voyage the average consumption was seventy tons
per day."

"If it was so," Herriott replied, "it was through reckless driving,
and general indiscretion on his part."[5]

Because of these opinions, and others from equally distinguished
experts, Fletcher accused Schomberg of misapprehending his assign-
ment, adding that he had exceeded the legal authority of his mandate.
Fletcher slyly threw in for good measure:

It has come to our knowledge, that whilst the inquiry was pending the inspec-
tor was in communication with one of our competitors in the New York trade;

and although we do not for one moment suppose that a gentleman of Admiral Schomberg's position would knowingly permit his judgement to be influenced by communications received, we cannot help fearing that his mind has unconsciously received the bias which is apparent in the tenor of the report...[6]

He concluded by suggesting the evidence be given to somebody else capable of interpreting it, or they would reserve the right to elevate the issue to a higher authority. There was also the implied charge that if the *Atlantic* had gone to sea without sufficient coal, then what were the people who certified her as being fit for sea doing? In the final analysis, the Board of Trade would be as much at fault as the White Star Line.

Thomas Gray, the assistant secretary of the marine department of the Board of Trade, decided to seek the opinion of his own engineering department and asked Thomas W. Traill, the chief ship surveyor, and J. McFarlane Gray, surveyor for the Port of London and the inventor of the steam steering engine, to consider the evidence presented. They meticulously sifted through the testimony, made some astute observations, and came to a different conclusion, which they presented on December 6.

Not only did they deduce that the *Atlantic* diverted to Halifax without good reason, thereby exonerating the White Star Line on the matter of coal, but they also provided insight into the interactions between Williams and Foxley—and ultimately into why the *Atlantic* was lost.

From the start, they found inconsistencies in what Foxley had testified, and concluded:

The statements of Foxley, the chief engineer, with respect to quantities, are utterly worthless, and cannot be depended upon for any purpose. Even since the wreck, he seems to have several sets of figures; he gave one to the captain, that the consumption on the last two days had been sixty-five tons, and he kept another for himself, according to which that consumption was only sixty tons; and they each swore accordingly.

It is only on the statement of that witness that the assessors at Halifax, and also those at Liverpool, have found an opinion that the "Atlantic"

*was short of fuel. The evidence of the captain and of the navigating offi-
cers of the ship can have no weight in this matter; they do not profess to
have known anything about it, except from Foxley's representations.*[7]

All the captain's information about coal quantity and quality had
come from Foxley, and as the inspection progressed, Williams was
confronted with the likelihood that Foxley had lied. He had told the
Halifax inquiry that at noon on March 31, when they were at their
nearest point to Halifax, he had advised Williams that there were 127
tons left. Williams, Chief Officer Firth, and Foxley met and all agreed
that to continue to New York was cutting it too fine and it might be
prudent to divert to Halifax while there was time. The 127 tons might
take them to their destination, they reasoned, but then again, it might
not. Just a few more tons and they would be comfortable in continuing
to New York. The inquiry had commended them for making a wise
decision. Ships did it all the time.

Table 6. Ships that put in to Halifax to replenish coal in 1872 and 1873.

Ship	Date	Line
Britannia	January 1872	Anchor
Cuba	March 1872	Cunard
Silesia	November 1872	Hamburg
The Queen	December 1872	National
Siberia	December 1872	Cunard
Cuba	December 1872	Cunard
Glamorgan	December 1872	Cardiff
Idaho	January 1873	Guion
Minnesota	January 1873	Guion
Cuba	February 1873	Cunard
America	February 1873	Bremen
City of Washington	January 1873	Inman

Among the firemen at lunch that day on the ship, there was surprise. They didn't think the coal situation was tight, but it was not

their place to second-guess the captain. After all, it was not like there was any risk in going to Halifax.

Now, six weeks later, Williams was sitting in the witness chair being asked why he diverted to Halifax when there had been sufficient coal to get to New York. He was stunned. Foxley had indeed changed his story. Well, yes—the written report he gave the captain said there were 127 tons left, but then he told Williams that that was enough for two days' steaming to get them to New York—140 tons at 70 tons per day. Williams hotly denied that Foxley had told him anything about 140 tons and Chief Officer Firth backed him up.

Traill and McFarlane Gray found more holes in Foxley's story. When he explained how they calculated consumption, he told of how the trimmers carried the coal from the bunkers to the furnace in baskets that held seventy-five pounds. Simple math at the end of the day gave the day's consumption—provided the baskets were all counted. The third engineer, John Hodgson, told about the same process but in his explanation the baskets held fifty-five pounds of coal. If that were true, then Foxley's calculations of consumption were high. It turned out they were both right. There were some of each! Then, Third Engineer Hodgson testified that for several days the baskets were not even used. There was no tally kept. Foxley had simply estimated the consumption.

After giving sworn testimony at Halifax—testimony that led the inquiry to conclude that the *Atlantic* had gone to sea short on coal— Foxley had done an about-face. He must have realized that statements like, "It was on account of the high price of coals in England that we put in a smaller quantity of coals on this last voyage than on the previous ones" would get him into trouble with his employer. While sailing back to England, he had time to reflect and came up with a very different set of facts. In this new reality, there was lots of coal aboard, the very best of coal—wonderful stuff. He decided to advertise his new thinking, so on May 6, he swore a Public Instrument of Protest, in which he essentially blamed everything on the captain. It was printed on May 14 in *Lloyd's List,* a trade journal of the shipping industry. Among the many corrections, he had told the Halifax inquiry that the *Atlantic* had burned eighty tons of coal while still in port but now, he decided, it was only six to eight tons! And on it went.

An experienced chief engineer was able to look into the bunkers and have a good idea of how much coal was there. It was a common practice—as a double check, to confirm what the tally reported. George Herriott of the *Republic* did it all the time. But he was fastidious about his tally reports and he had a captain who expected them every day, as the rulebook required.

It was different on the *Atlantic*.

Williams told the Halifax inquiry that they departed Queenstown, Ireland, at 10:30 A.M. on March 21 with 829 tons of coal aboard to take them the 2,811 miles to their destination. Just *seven days later*, Foxley informed him that they were down to 319 tons! Williams was appalled. What had happened to the coal? He immediately ordered a cutback in consumption, even turning off the steam heating and causing discomfort to passengers. He was so discombobulated that he had trouble sleeping. It wasn't a disaster, because Halifax lay ahead and he could always go there for fuel, but he knew he would be the first White Star Line captain to do so and it would play havoc with the strict schedule the ship was on.

WHY WAS WILLIAMS SO SHOCKED AT THE COAL SITUATION? THERE CAN BE only one reason. It seems he was not receiving daily reports on consumption—a shocking revelation. Foxley had been flouting the rules, and getting away with it.

The captain was not doing his job. In their report, Traill and McFarlane Gray took a swat at Williams as they noted sarcastically:

> *The first day's consumption entered is one-eleventh of the fuel on board, so that Captain Williams must either have considered it quite proper to start from Queenstown with only eleven days' consumption on board, or he must never have thought anything at all about what fuel he had for the voyage, until he learnt on the 28th that there was only 319 tons left.*[8]

Through lax dealing with a subordinate, Williams had lost control of an essential piece of information required to operate his ship. He told the Liverpool investigation:

> On the 28th I told the Chief Steward and Engineer to be as careful as he could of the coals....I **believe** those orders were carried out by the Chief Engineer and I **know** they were on the part of the Chief Steward [author's emphasis].[9]

Faint praise for Foxley, the chief engineer, but Williams only had himself to blame. Digby Murray, the *Atlantic*'s first captain, had made sure he got his daily reports on coal consumption. He always knew what the situation was. All indications are that Williams had a less-than-reliable chief engineer and he let it slide. That Foxley could get away with not providing the daily reports says as much about Williams as it says about Foxley.

CHAPTER 23

THE HERO OF OUR SONG

What more can I suffer? If it were not for my wife and three little children at home, I should never have been here; I'd have stuck to that vessel till the last and gone down with her.[1]

Captain James Williams

Whenever a disaster occurs with a serious loss of life, everyone is looking for answers. When it's a shipwreck, all eyes turn to the one with absolute authority over everybody and everything aboard—the captain. The same questions are on everybody's lips. How did he fail so badly? What awful things can we find in his past to help us understand? There had never been such loss of life in a transatlantic passenger ship disaster, so James Williams attracted a lot of interest. During the following weeks, dozens of newspapers got his story, or at least ran it on their pages, and he gave a lot of testimony.

As soon as the story got out, the torrent of condemnation began. Unlike most who find themselves in such a place, Williams took full responsibility and made no excuses, speaking candidly about his failures, showing great contrition, often being overtaken with emotion.

Unlike Captain Edward Smith of the *Titanic*, who faded into the background and left the mess to his officers to handle, Williams took control, ordering everybody forward when the stern sank, getting people into the rigging, and assisting individual passengers, even while having to contend with his own physical limitations. He had to be helped off the ship, exhausted, when there were fewer than twenty left aboard and all were assured of rescue.

Those who testified at the Halifax inquiry spoke in support of Williams, saying he was competent, temperate, always seeing to the best interests of ship and passengers. Chief Officer Firth said, "During the twenty-seven years that I have followed the sea, I have not seen a better captain."[2] That's quite a compliment; Firth had sailed with Williams on only one unfinished voyage.

When he was captain of the *Manhattan* in 1868, one of his passengers was so impressed with the twenty-eight-year-old skipper that he wrote a long poem extolling his virtues, ending with:

May your life be happy and long;
Captain Jas. A. Williams,
the hero of our song.[3]

The *New York Tribune* started digging for information on Williams's past. They discovered he had been let go under unexplained circumstances from the Guion Line, one of the White Star Line's competitors. The word on the street was that it was because of alcohol. In interviews with W. H. Guion, they learned that Williams had been employed for five years and commanded four vessels, including the *Manhattan*. He left in October 1871. Guion considered Williams to be a "thoroughly capable and reliable officer and a brave man," citing the story of how Williams was injured while serving as second officer of the *Republic*.

Captain Williams in uniform. The photograph was taken at George Gardn[e]r Rockwood's studio in New York. (COURTESY ANDREW THOMAS)

But—he had gone from captain of four ships with Guion to second officer with a competitive line? That sounded peculiar. Guion would only say that Williams was not let go but given the opportunity to resign after

> a difficulty with some of his passengers, in which he was found, upon investigation, to be to blame, the nature of which, however, Mr. Guion preferred not to disclose. Captain Williams thereupon resigned and entered the service of the White Star Line.[4]

In an April 4 opinion piece, the *New York Times* took a stab at explaining the whys and wherefores:

> It is stated without reserve among steam-ship folks that he was dis-charged from the Guion Line because he was in the habit of imbibing too freely, and that he was taken into the employ of the White Star Line with the understanding if he behaved himself he would be promoted. He was bright, active and was soon promoted rapidly, owing to the line increasing the number of its fleet....Captain Williams was a genial com-panion, and somewhat of a popular commander, but doubtless he has made his last voyage in command of an ocean steamer.

The event on the *Republic*, which had put him in hospital close to death and left him walking with a cane, must have had a profound effect on him. Being captain of a large steamer in 1873 was a demand-ing job. He had 150 people reporting to him and at any time could be responsible for the lives of 1,000 people or more. Most men would not be able to handle the physical challenges: irregular sleep, outdoors in all kinds of weather in summer and winter, constantly climbing up and down stairs, and on his feet for hours at a time on an unsteady and unreliable floor.

By age thirty-three, he was captain of his fifth ship, so he had obviously had the right stuff. The question is: did he still have it?

Men in physical occupations, whether sailing a ship or playing football, are men of power. American President Theodore Roosevelt's dictum to walk softly and carry a big stick well matches the bearing of an English sea captain—cool, confident, and unafraid. Certainly, that would have been Williams's demeanour, but now he was physically diminished. By his own admission, his accident made it difficult for him to go into dark places (like the bunkers of a ship, where the coal was stored) and he could not handle the cold like he once could. These were limiting factors for a man who was expected to set an example of physical stamina and vigour.

The Halifax inquiry said that Williams should have been on the bridge and that going to sleep gave the impression that all was well. The reality is, he was probably exhausted. His own words describe his condition at the time: "We had three hundred nineteen tons at noon on the 28th. I hardly slept from then until the 31st for thinking of it."[5]

The steward arrived with the cocoa at twenty minutes to three. Metcalfe told him that he would call the captain and then sent the steward away. Why did he do that? Because he saw the stress that Williams was under and thought he could use a little more sleep? Perhaps—but, of course, that was not his place. His place was to do what the captain had ordered. On the other hand, Williams may have only told the steward about the cocoa:

> I left orders with the relieving officers to be called at three o'clock, **previous to which** I had left orders with my servant to be called at forty minutes past two o'clock [author's emphasis].[6]

Fourth Officer Brown testified to the inquiry that he was caught by surprise when the steward arrived with the cocoa, intending to call Williams. Either Williams did not inform Metcalfe or Metcalfe did not inform Brown, who should have been made aware in case he was the only officer on the bridge when the steward arrived.

Williams was asleep because he needed to sleep, as we all do. He did not retire to his cabin but remained clothed and lay down on a cot in the chart room, within speaking distance of the man at the wheel, like he had probably done many times before. However, going to sleep turned out to be a poor decision that night because it gave the officers the impression that going into Halifax was routine. But this was not Liverpool or Queenstown or New York, places that the

An engraving of George Gardner Rockwood's photo of Captain Williams appeared in *Harper's Weekly*, April 19, 1873. The technology had not been invented that enabled a photo to be printed.

officers and lookouts were familiar with. It was a new place, and as events were to show, there were unusual currents that none of them knew anything about. In his orders to the officers on watch, Williams instructed them to watch for the Sambro light and to keep a sharp lookout for ice. He said nothing about currents. The attitude that all was routine led the second officer, a man apparently lacking in sound judgement, to conclude that they were farther out to sea than they were, and even to make the egregious error of not calling the captain when ordered.

Captain Williams lamented afterwards:

The papers that have charged me with intemperance have done me a great injustice. I promised Thomas Ismay that not a drop of liquor should cross my lips on that vessel and I never broke that promise. Gentlemen would sometimes come into my room and smoke and drink themselves, and I would sometimes bet with passengers on the day's run. If they won they would take a glass of porter; if I won I'd take a cigar, but no liquor. The one thing I regret is that I was too sure of my course.[7]

His promise to Ismay raises a question. Was that something Ismay got from all his captains or was Williams on probation, as the *New York Times* article implies? Regardless, Williams's claims of temperance were supported by the testimony at the Halifax inquiry:

I never saw the captain take anything stronger than lemonade. He refused to take wine at dinner. [Daniel Kinnane, saloon passenger][8]

While [I was] in the smoking room the captain came in. He was asked to have a glass of wine but refused. [J. Spencer Jones, saloon passenger][9]

Nicholas Brandt, a saloon passenger who left the wreck in the same boat with the captain, had this to say:

I feared that the captain would drop off from exhaustion and fatigue.[10]

Not everybody was supportive. On June 7, saloon passenger Charles W. Allen wrote to Admiral Schomberg, leading the Liverpool investigation:

Captain Williams should be questioned as to what influence the probability of his not reaching New York in time to leave the following Saturday had on his causing the ship to run at such a rate so near land. On Sunday, the 30th, he remarked to writer, "We must be in New York in time to leave Saturday next, or we shall have to pay the United States Government $5,000 for breach of contract." It is my belief that the possibility of his not making the time influenced him a good deal, and induced reckless running.

If they were late they would default on the mail contract, which was an important source of revenue for the company, especially during lean times of the year. The *Atlantic* was carrying the Saturday mail from New York—another stress point for the captain. Allen continued,

I would also wish to state that Captain Williams played cards for money daily in the smoke-room, and on some days in the saloon, and that his so doing was the subject of conversation between myself and other passengers. In the interest of Atlantic travellers, I believe it would be a good thing that such practices should be forbidden.[11]

Most of Charles Allen's testimony at the Halifax inquiry was critical in tone, especially regarding the crew, but he did say this: "I considered that the captain and officers were competent."

This letter gives us another insight into Williams's habits. Whether or not gambling was appropriate for the captain of a White Star passenger liner, one thing is for sure: discussing the mail contract with a passenger was not, especially when it had to do with the company defaulting on an obligation. A. C. Thomas, a passenger who had crossed on the *Atlantic's* previous and, as it turned out, final trip to New York, agreed that Williams was very temperate with alcohol but he found him to be a little too familiar in his dealings with the passengers.[12]

The situation with the mail contract was actually worse than Williams knew. While he was dealing with his fuel situation, across the Atlantic, the next ship in the rotation was experiencing engine failure.[13] The *Republic*, under Captain Benjamin Gleadell, scheduled to depart Liverpool a week after Williams, left a day late, limped back over two hundred miles to stop at Queenstown, Ireland, then continued at full speed, trying to make up for lost time. The White Star Line would be late with the US Mail two weeks in a row.

On top of everything else, several steerage passengers were miffed because he spent all his time kibitzing with the saloon passengers and ignoring them. "He was always in the cabin, amusing himself with the ladies and gentlemen there, and seemed to think more of his cigar than anything else," James White told the *New York Daily Graphic*.[14]

Why, after the *Atlantic* disaster, did Williams not lose his certificate permanently? With such carnage, you would expect them to throw the book at him, but with his ready admission of culpability, and with the sympathy garnered by limping along with the aid of his cane, he was not easy to tar and feather. What really saved him was that, despite suffering grievously, he had not left the ship until he had no choice. He did not redeem himself, but nobody could say he deserted those who were suffering and in need of leadership.

As the *Halifax Evening Express* stated, Williams "showed no want of courage in the hour of supreme peril—only want of forethought."[15]

Steward John Gilbert told the papers about Williams after the collision.

> *When I got on the saloon deck I heard Captain Williams giving orders for all hands to come and launch the boats. I heard him call down the companionway for the ladies to come by and get into the boats....I heard him ask if any of the quartermasters could get a line to go from the ship to the rock....He shouted to the people on the mizzen rigging to endeavour to get into the fore or the main rigging as there would be less danger of being washed off.*[16]

With all that was happening and all that was about to come down on him, Williams was—and remained—single-minded in his efforts to minimize the effects of the disaster.

"I went to the wreck to take the Captain off," Brady told the Halifax inquiry, "knowing that he could not stand out much longer, but he refused till I took more of the saloon and steerage passengers. He was much exhausted when taken off, and we had to support him in getting up the rock."

The *Express* may have hit on something. Williams was competent and brave, but he had a fatal flaw as a leader. It was perhaps in discipline that his great weakness lay—his tendency to let things go, like he did in not following up with Foxley when the daily fuel status reports stopped coming, and in too quickly accepting Foxley's comments that the coal was bad. He wasn't getting the facts from the chief engineer, and he couldn't see it, or he refused to; then he trusted an incompetent second officer with the ship while he went for a nap.

And there was the case of the stowaways practically running amok:

They were the instigators of all the rows that occurred on board, from the time the vessel left Queenstown till she struck. The regular crew had to give their valuables to passengers and petty officers to keep for them, lest these stowaways should steal them. As it was, the crew lost many things. If they put a knife out of their hands for a moment it was snapped up, and the band of desperadoes stuck to each other in preventing the article taken being successfully claimed, giving any claimant a kick if he attempted to claim anything belonging to him.[17]

Why didn't Williams put the fear of God into them, clapping them in irons if they didn't comply? It was reported that he locked up a couple of men on a charge of acting like madmen when they became obsessed that the ship was going to be lost with all aboard. When they would not desist, he locked them up, inadvertently sealing their fate.[18] He could have done the same thing to the stowaways, but did not.

The fiasco with the coal wasn't Foxley's only misdemeanour with the captain. Following the wrecking, with the ship on the rocks, three officers dead, the chief officer barely alive after ten hours in the rigging, the third officer sent to Halifax to report the calamity, and the most junior officer the only one remaining, with Williams himself barely able to stand, did Foxley, the most senior officer after the captain on the site, step in to help out? He did not. Instead, he took his crew and headed to Halifax, leaving Williams to protect what was still a very valuable asset (the cargo) against a growing number of vigilante wreckers, with more arriving by the hour.[19] With the third officer already on the way to Halifax, there was no reason for Foxley to leave. The energy consumed on the eight-hour walk could have been put to better use at the wreck site.

But Foxley may have had another reason for bailing on the captain. They had diverted to Halifax because he had under-reported the coal. He didn't put the ship on the rocks, but the ship was on the rocks at least in part because of his actions. It is likely that could not bear to remain in the captain's presence, or to see the results of his folly all around him. Based on his subsequent actions, it is also reasonable to assume that he was already plotting how he was going to weasel his way out of shouldering his share of the blame.

Even though Foxley deserted him at that moment, Williams told the Liverpool investigation, "I had no reason to think there was any neglect of duty in the engine-room. Mr. Foxley is a good officer." When the interviewer challenged him, he had to confess, "I have known him only since I have been in the *Atlantic*."[20]

Williams deserved better. He wanted to think only the best about his officers. When asked about Second Officer Metcalfe, he replied in a similar way: "I had every confidence in the second officer. I had no reason to doubt his efficiency. He was a sober and steady man"[21]

He may not have known about Metcalfe's past—sinking the *Bretagne*, losing his certificate, having his crew desert in San Francisco—but it's hard to believe that he didn't have doubts about him. He had not called Williams as ordered; he ran the ship onto the rocks; and the last words Williams spoke to him were to correct a serious error he was making with the lifeboat, which ended up costing him his life. And still Williams insisted to the inquiry that Metcalfe was a good officer!

On the other hand, he had to work with the people he was given, and he would, no doubt, have been aware of the family relationship between Ismay and Metcalfe. He could have laid the blame on Metcalfe's doorstep but he chose not to. Now was not the time to trash the owner's cousin, who had just lost his life, although he came close to doing so when he had to defend himself at the inquiry:

> I am of opinion that the men on the lookout and the officers on duty might have been able at that distance to have seen that something was ahead, and if the officer of the watch had promptly given the order to reverse the engines the calamity might have been averted.[22]

And, in a letter to the Board of Trade in June 1873, when he was desperate for work and begging the Board to provide him a certificate for a lower rank so he could earn some money to support his family, Williams alluded to the temptation to say a few things about Metcalfe: "I will not here enter into a defence of my conduct, as the second officer was unfortunately lost."[23]

It is a pity that he did not. Perhaps we could have gained a better understanding of Metcalfe.

And, then came the most bitter pill of all, when the ruling from Traill and McFarlane Gray came down on December 6, 1873:

> We state that we are satisfied that the steamship "Atlantic" on her last voyage was supplied with sufficient coal for a voyage to New York at that season of the year, and that at the time the vessel's course was altered for Halifax, there still remained sufficient coal on board to have taken her to New York and to leave 70 tons in the bunkers, even if the weather did not improve.[24]

Now there was a third officer to share the blame. First, Foxley gave the captain faulty information, which caused him to make the unnecessary diversion to Halifax. Then, the captain made an error in navigation that put the ship off course, and finally, the second officer botched the handling of the ship in the closing hours. If the consequences had not been so serious it could be considered a comedy of errors. No wonder it got covered up. If such a thing were to happen today, the lawsuits would spell the end of the White Star Line—and there would never have been a *Titanic*.

ON APRIL 22, HALF A DOZEN OF THE CREW WHO HAD BEEN DETAINED TO perform guard duty at the site departed for Liverpool aboard the *Nestorian*.[25] Williams stayed in Halifax for more than a month, departing for the United States on May 7.[26] Quartermaster Owens had gone home the day before, armed with a note in Williams's handwriting:

> *This is to certify that the bearer, Edward Owens, Quartermaster is a good reliable man and seaman and did his duty at the loss of the Atlantic, being the second man to establish communication with the shore by means of ropes.*
>
> J. A. Williams, Commander

Williams had nobody to speak for him. On June 14, 1873, he wrote the Board of Trade:

> *I beg to apply for a certificate of first mate, my own as extra master having been suspended. I have a wife and three children dependent on me, and have no way of supporting them, save in the exercise of my profession. I would also beg to bring before your notice the excessive severity of the sentence (two years' suspension) passed upon me, and I would beg to say that the trial at Halifax N.S. took place immediately after the lamentable accident, and while the public mind was abnormally excited. The Court tried to be dispassionate in their judgement, yet I claim that they must have been more than human not to have been biased by public clamour.*[27]

The Board turned him down five days later.[28]

James Williams portrays many of the characteristics of the tragic hero of Greek literature. Aristotle wrote that "a man doesn't become a hero until he can see the root of his own downfall." Williams could not have said it more plainly: "The one thing that rebukes me, which I cannot keep out of my mind, which will remain with me as long as I live, is that I was too confident—too confident."[29]

Look at his image and you see a man who knows what he is about. Barely out of his teens, he had qualified as an officer and by age twenty-six or twenty-seven he was at the pinnacle of his profession—captain of a passenger liner on the North Atlantic. Even after the self-examination that led to the statement above, he then replied, "Never, sir, never!" when asked if the accident would have occurred if he had been on deck.

As far as we know, James Agnew Williams only went to sea one more time after the disaster. On November 2, 1874, he signed on to a small ten-year-old cargo steamer named the *Calabar,* sailing out of London—not out of Liverpool, where he was known. He was the third officer on a round trip to India, departing October 26, 1874.[30] Interestingly, the two-year suspension of his Extra Master certificate had not expired. He must have used his Third Officer certification.

Afterward, he and his wife, Lizzie, bought the Shrewsbury Hotel in Trafford, outside Manchester, which they ran for many years. During that time their family grew to six children. His great-grandson, Andrew Thomas, wrote,

> *Actually, family lore has it that she did all the running and he sat around looking magnificent but not doing much. My grandmother was born in 1886, quite a while after the wreck. She did not want it talked about, so as a kid growing up I never heard about it, though I had a sense that there was some dark secret no one was sharing.*[31]

Everybody and everything had zeroed in on the fact that Williams was asleep when the *Atlantic* grounded, and that circumstance rose to importance above all others in a litany of bad decisions, poor judgement, and bad luck on the part of others. The fact that Williams had proved himself to be brave, reliable, conscientious, and competent fell away before the magnitude of the disaster that his lapse in judgement had facilitated.

May none of our flaws ever result in such a convergence of regrettable circumstances to bring about such a great misfortune.

CHAPTER 24

DRIVING THE ATLANTIC

The Liverpool Court were asking for what could not possibly be told them, either for the "Atlantic" or for any other passenger steamer that ever existed, for in no single instance have coal quantities remaining ever been taken to the "exact amount."

Thomas W. Traill and J. McFarlane Gray
Joint Report on the Coal Supply, Dec. 8, 1873

If we remove from the picture the navigation error by Captain Williams and the ship-handling errors by Second Officer Metcalfe, there were still other factors that helped doom the *Atlantic*.

Even though Metcalfe and, perhaps, Fourth Officer John Brown were guilty of incompetent handling and subsequent loss of the ship, it is easy to overlook just how hard their jobs were. An officer commanding the watch on a 437-foot ship today has a comprehensive array of dials, readouts, and screens to provide detailed information about anything he or she wants to know regarding the ship's systems. Everybody is together on a comfortable, climate-controlled bridge, and if anybody has to step out, staying in touch is a breeze with portable radios and phones.

It is difficult to imagine how spartan things were for the *Atlantic*'s deck officers. The men on watch spent their time on an unprotected outdoor bridge away from the man at the helm. If the officer wanted to address him face to face, he had to walk upwards of twenty-five feet to a set of stairs, descend to the deck below, walk to a deckhouse, open the door and go into the wheelhouse, where the quartermaster was at the wheel.

As the ship travelled through the darkness, everybody had, at best, only a general idea of where the ship was. They checked the speed every couple of hours on a crude device called a log, so they had an approximation of how fast they were going. They had no idea what lay ahead in the blackness, and they had no idea how much water was below them. As for the engines, there were a few rudimentary gauges that could be viewed only in the engine room. The crew checked the fuel situation by looking into the coal bunkers and guessing how much remained or, if they followed the prescribed procedures, counting the number of baskets of coal that were shovelled into the furnaces each day and doing the math to calculate what remained.

In 1873, a steamship like the *Atlantic* was the largest and most complex thing built anywhere in the world. It was cutting-edge technology, but was managed with no technology whatever. On the bridge and in the wheelhouse, there were no instruments to guide those responsible for the safe running of the ship.

Until the invention of radar during the Second World War, the only thing identifiable in front of a ship was what could be seen by the lookouts. Consequently, huge ships could easily collide in the fog. Icebergs were another big risk between Europe and North America, as those aboard the *Titanic* soon found out.

On the night of February 18, 1942, three American warships, USS *Wilkes*, *Pollux*, and *Truxtun*, en route from Portland, Maine, to the US Naval base at Argentia, Newfoundland, slammed into the cliffs of the Burin Peninsula on the south coast of Newfoundland, resulting in huge loss of life. In her book about the disaster, writer Cassie Brown notes menacingly, "All three ships were not only being blown northwestward toward land, but had been influenced by the current in that direction for the past sixteen hours."[1]

Not much had changed. Sixty-nine years after the *Atlantic* disaster, also caused by lack of attention to currents and speed, the same scenario played itself out on three state-of-the-art ships commanded by supposedly competent officers.

The machinery and drivetrain of an 1873 steamship had evolved over half a century with little advancement in monitoring anything. With a few exceptions, like the electric telegraph, electricity was merely a curiosity for gentlemen to play with while entertaining the ladies in upper-class drawing rooms. Using it to monitor the vitals of a steamship was still decades away. Ships morphed from being driven by sails—putting to sea when the tide was favourable and then contending with whatever Mother Nature cast their way, lumbering along in the general direction of a continent—to being driven by powerful propulsion systems that became ever more complex, faster, and bigger, while relying on crude, centuries-old methods to provide the information required to run them. These old methods, along with intuition, tradition, experience, and informed guesswork, were the tools on the bridge as they sailed from one place to another. Under the circumstances, they did amazingly well, especially with navigation.

The only information at their fingertips was the ship's bearing—the direction it was travelling, which was read from a compass. Everything else had to be worked out, using a sextant and the sun at noon or the stars at night to determine the latitude. Using the ship's speed and an accurate timepiece called a chronometer, they could work out the longitude. These things were not checked when it suited the officer; they were scheduled events. After calculating longitude, latitude, and speed, they had a fairly accurate idea of where the ship was. But that was just for a point in time. As time passed, they relied on dead reckoning—informed guesswork—until the next readings were taken, usually the next day. If it was overcast, they continued to rely on dead reckoning and their understanding of their position diminished. If the weather continued overcast they soon were lost, but they could find themselves again when the sun came out. All that had been tolerable during the days of sail, but the lack of precision became increasingly significant as ships got faster and bigger.

In the days of the *Atlantic,* a device called the log was used to give an idea of a ship's speed. Figuring out the speed was not a glance at a speedometer; it was a process, requiring an officer and two sailors. The log was a triangular-shaped piece of wood with a weight on one corner. A line was attached at the centre of the triangle. The other requirement was an hourglass that measured 28 seconds. The three men stood at the stern of the vessel and the officer gave the order to heave the log overboard. The weighted corner made the log float vertically, thus causing resistance to movement in the water. As the ship moved away from the log, the line would be drawn out behind the ship. When a mark on the line appeared, the officer gave the order to flip the hourglass. When the sand in the hourglass had run down, the line was stopped and reeled back in. Every 47 feet, 3 inches there was a knot in the line. They counted the knots that had gone out and this gave them the speed of the ship in nautical miles per hour, which they expressed in knots. (A nautical mile is 6,080 feet, which is one minute of distance measured at the equator. The earth is 21,600 nautical miles in circumference.)

Officers often did a quick estimate of speed based on the number of revolutions the engine was making. The assumption was that the higher the engine speed, the faster the ship was travelling. This could only be an estimate because the winds would affect the water conditions and there were always currents that could not be factored in. Calculating ship speed based on engine revolutions was also affected by the efficiency of the propeller.

Earlier in the nineteenth century, a new apparatus called a "patent log" had been developed by Edward Massey. It consisted of a torpedo-shaped brass device about a foot long, with fins at the back. When it was towed behind the ship, the fins caused the torpedo to spin. The faster the ship went, the faster the torpedo spun. When it was retrieved, the speed could be read from dials on the torpedo.

The main drawback of measuring speed by towing something is that it is unable to compensate for current. If the ship is being pushed by a current, the log cannot account for that. Testimony at the inquiry indicated that the *Atlantic* carried Massey's patent log, but for some unexplained reason they used the common log. One of the conclusions of the inquiry was that the officers did not know how fast the ship was travelling and that it must have been travelling faster than they had thought. When they finally struck the coast, it was on Meaghers Island, which lies at virtually the same distance from where they changed course for Halifax as is the Sambro light—so despite using the common log, their speed measurements appear to have been reasonably accurate.

To calculate water depth, a large piece of lead called a sounding lead was dropped overboard and immediately retrieved after striking the bottom. The amount of line that went out indicated the depth. When approaching the coast the depth decreased, so the lead had to be hove continuously. Testimony showed that as the night wore on and the light was not seen, the officers on the *Atlantic* concluded that they were still offshore and did not heave the lead, even as a precaution. This was the most damning piece of evidence at the inquiry.

On any vehicle driven by an engine, speed is constantly monitored to ensure the engine is not being stressed. The officers commanding the *Atlantic* and other steamers did not concern themselves with the welfare of the engines. There was a whole engine-room crew dedicated to that job, as there is on ships today. If there was a problem with the engine, the information was delivered to the captain or the officer of the watch. The attitude of the deck officers was that the less they heard from the engine room, the better.

The fuel situation was also entirely within the purview of the engine-room crew. The amount of coal remaining was delivered in a report to the bridge at specified times—usually. As with the other methods of keeping the bridge informed, the amount of coal remaining relied on a human being, not a gauge that acted consistently. That fact began the series of blunders that led to the loss of the *Atlantic*.

Bearing all this in mind, one could argue that the *Atlantic* disaster was really caused by a lack of information. It started with confusion over how much fuel was aboard. That caused the captain to feel obliged to make the diversion to Halifax. After midnight there was confusion about where the ship was, the officers concluding that it was farther offshore than it really was. If they had known the depth of the water, they would have realized this was not the case. In the final minutes, if they had known what was ahead of the ship, they would have been aware that they were too close to the land. On a modern ship, all of that information, and much more, is readily available with a glance at a screen or an instrument.

Most of the necessary information could have been made available to the *Atlantic*'s officers but human judgement and optimism bias made them feel it was unnecessary. To repeat the words of Fourth Officer

Brown: "We did not heave the lead on account of the clearness of the night and the certainty of seeing the light."[2]

On the subject of coal, Third Engineer John Hodgson testified to the Liverpool investigation that while Foxley had estimated the remaining coal at 127 tons, Second Engineer Robert Ewing was of the opinion that there were 156 tons remaining, enough to easily get to New York. They even disagreed on how much coal was contained in a basket, with the third engineer stating that a basket was 55 pounds, while the chief engineer stated it was 75 pounds.[3]

The *Atlantic* was lost because of the actions of three men:

- The chief engineer misled the captain regarding the amount of coal remaining.
- The captain did not stay apprised of the coal situation and then he made an error in his navigation. In addition, he was not on the bridge at a critical time.
- The second officer failed to properly manage the ship during the final watch. When the steward arrived with the cocoa, he should have realized there had been a mix-up with the orders. He should have called the captain—if not immediately, then certainly by 3:00 A.M. as ordered.

Ultimately, though, the *Atlantic* was lost for want of an easy and accurate way to calculate how much fuel remained.

In addition to not being able to monitor the ship's environment and her propulsion systems, they also did not receive weather forecasts like ships do today. That's why the *Republic* had ended up in a hurricane and Williams was injured. Those aboard the *Atlantic* also would have known what the newspapers learned after the fact:

> A late Boston paper states that the records and observations of the United States Signal office show that had Captain Williams kept on his course he would have been met by one of the severest storms of the season, the centre of it being right on the track he would have traversed that day on his course to New York.[4]

Not that it mattered anymore.

CHAPTER 25

THE ELUSIVE LIGHT

Had the vessel been in possession of madmen the result could not have been more disastrous.[1]

William Roche
Commissioner of Halifax Harbour Pilots

I f they had only seen the light, everything would have been different. Reading the testimony of the lightkeepers, captains, and harbour pilots familiar with the Nova Scotia coast, waters, and weather gives a chilling idea of how fraught with danger was the job of taking a ship into Halifax Harbour at night—the winds, the currents, the visibility, the rocks. Knowing precisely where the ship was at all times was more than important; it was everything. On a long drive, the inevitable question, "When will we get there?" depends on knowing where we are now. For the *Atlantic's* lookouts that morning, only one thing could answer that question: seeing the Sambro light. With that, any competent navigator could estimate how far away the light was, and by considering its location relative to the ship they would know where the ship was.

Under ideal conditions, the Sambro light could supposedly be seen from twenty-one miles away. There is every indication that the officers on the deck that night took those numbers literally. But were they true? It was just an educated estimate printed on the chart. There

The Sambro Light, one of five lighthouses that guided the way into Halifax, was one of the most important in the world. Satellite navigation systems and other tools have greatly decreased the need for lighthouses.

was no way to accurately measure it. Even a lighthouse keeper talking about his own light could not be precise. Benjamin Fulker, keeper from 1863 to 1886 of the Devils Island light at the northeast entrance to Halifax Harbour, told the Halifax inquiry that his light was visible for "nine or ten miles."[2]

"Sambro Light is a very treacherous light to depend upon as to distance," Edward Mulligan told the Halifax inquiry. He would have known, having made weekly trips through the same waters for four years as captain of the SS *Carlotta*. "Our deck is about eighteen or twenty feet high above the water. Sambro Light can be seen in fine weather about twelve miles. In going up to the masthead about thirty feet higher we could make it out probably three or four miles further."[3]

That would be so because of the earth's curvature.

Today, the nautical chart for the Halifax Harbour approaches says that the light is visible for twenty-three miles.

The Admiralty charts in 1873 said it was visible for twenty-one miles, but Captain Mulligan's testimony seems to say that at the best of times the light was not visible past sixteen miles, as least not from the *Carlotta*. That is borne out by an artifact in the Maritime Museum of the Atlantic in Halifax—the Fresnel lens that was installed in the Sambro light in 1906, *increasing* the light's visibility to seventeen miles. It seems that the chart everybody was using was a bit optimistic. However, that is irrelevant because the *Atlantic* struck land a shade over seven miles from the light.

At 2:00 A.M. Quartermaster Robert Thomas had asked Fourth Officer Brown if he could climb up to the main yard to see if he could make out the land. He was convinced that they were getting close. Brown told him to forget it; they were still out to sea. Brown was placing a lot of trust in a light he had never seen before. So was Metcalfe. Three months later, as the *City of Washington* barrelled along in a Nova Scotia fog, a nervous passenger asked an officer if he knew where the ship was. The officer replied, "Oh, we know certainly, within three or five miles or so." Shortly afterward, the ship struck bottom, less than a hundred miles away from where the *Atlantic* had wrecked. Fortunately, it was near a sandy beach, and the 576 passengers were saved.[4] Williams was not the only steamship officer to suffer from overconfidence.

Patchy fog is a common occurrence in Nova Scotia waters, especially in spring. Piecing together the testimony of three of the four lighthouse keepers and the lookouts aboard the *Atlantic*, one gets the impression that the night was anything but clear. At 9:00 P.M. Benjamin Fulker at the Devils Island light could see the Chebucto Head light seven miles away, and beyond that he could see the Sambro light, twelve miles away. By 11:00 P.M. it was foggy and raining. He could still see Chebucto Head, but not Sambro. By 3:00 A.M. the rain had stopped and he could see both of them again. The rain and fog had limited his visibility to about six or seven miles.

Meanwhile, at the Sambro light, keeper William Gilkey reported that at 10:00 P.M. it was so foggy that they fired two cannon shots, so the lookouts on any ships would not have to rely on the light alone. (There was a full-time Royal Artillery gunner stationed there to operate the cannon.) Gilkey could barely make out the beam from the Chebucto Head light, five miles away. Edward Johnson, the keeper at Chebucto Head, could not see the Sambro light at all.[5] The lookouts aboard the *Carlotta* that night had finally seen it when they had gotten within four miles.[6]

Two more cannon shots rang out from Sambro Lighthouse at 2:00 A.M., just at the time that the *Atlantic*'s lookouts were searching in vain for the light they would probably have seen in good conditions.

By 3:00 A.M. the fog had begun to clear and a few stars appeared—enabling Joseph Carroll, aboard the *Atlantic*, to see the dreaded breakers on Meaghers Island.[7]

The weather can vary over short distances around the Nova Scotia coast, especially in winter and spring. Peter Coffin, a retired harbour pilot, told the inquiry:

> *I think there was a mistake made as to the clearness of the horizon. The horizon is somewhat deceptive. On one occasion when I ran for Sambro Light intending to pass three miles south of it, the horizon appeared well defined. I saw nothing of Sambro Light until we first saw the island on which stands the lighthouse, square on the beam. And even when I saw the land I could not for some time see the light, owing to the fog settling down, until it had obscured the light.[8] I was at a distance of about two and a half to three miles from it.[9]*

The light had been enshrouded in a layer of fog that did not come all the way down to the surface of the water, but was low enough to obscure the light while leaving Sambro Island and part of the light tower visible. That is a plausible explanation. Mariners were known to complain that the top of the tower was often obscured by fog. In 1864, serious consideration had been given to lowering the height of the tower.[10]

"On two occasions," Coffin testified, "we saw the flash of the guns from Sambro although we could not see the light nor hear the guns. On those occasions the horizon was thick, the fog very low and the stars visible."[11] The flash was visible because the guns were close to sea level and below the fog.

There were many reasons why the lookouts did not see the light, but the inquiry investigators still ruled that they should have. Williams agreed with them, because when he ran out of the wheelhouse he could see the clearness of the night, not realizing that the wind had just changed and brought what modern meteorologists call a clearing trend. He went to his grave believing that if he had been called he would have seen the approaching shoreline and would have saved his ship, presumably because he would have stopped and taken a sounding.

One final thing. The lighthouse keepers reported very strong west–southwest winds all evening and into the night until the winds swung around to the northwest just before the grounding. Quartermaster Thomas told the inquiry that the winds were on the port quarter at midnight and at 2:00 A.M. they were on the stern. Those winds would have combined with the west-setting current and helped speed up the ship's progress. That additional speed would not have registered on the log because they were moving in moving water, which explains the more moderate speeds reported by the quartermasters who were measuring the ship's progress throughout the evening and night.

Chapter 26

The Ancient Story

*Like the lighthouse gleam out upon a black waste of wild waters shines
the devoted courage of the Reverend Mr. Ancient over the dark and
horrid story of the shipwrecked steamship Atlantic.*

New York World
Quoted in the Halifax Novascotian, *May 5, 1873*

On April 20, 1873, the high-profile social reformer and preacher Henry Ward Beecher preached a sermon in the Plymouth Church in New York City about William Ancient's heroism. It was just one example of the overwhelming outpouring of admiration and affection towards Ancient, not only by the newspapers but by government authorities—and so one-sided that it deserves special examination.

Even in the Canadian House of Commons, he was unreservedly extolled. One member raved:

Everyone knew that he risked his life in trying to save the unfortunate passengers. Everyone knew that having saved them, he clothed, fed and housed them. Everyone knew that with his own hands he dug graves for those who had perished; that with his own hands he put the bodies into the graves and, having interred them, he read over them the funeral services of his Church.[1]

This was an exaggeration of what Ancient had done but it was in keeping with the story that was circulating about his role in the disaster.

As a result, on September 24, 1873, the Canadian secretary of state, J. C. Aikins, wrote to the lieutenant-governor of Nova Scotia, Adams Archibald:

> *The Dominion Government, having been pleased to award, on the recommendation of the Department of Marine and Fisheries, to the Rev. Wm. J. Ancient, of Turn's Bay, Nova Scotia, a gold watch, together with $500 in money, in acknowledgement of the gallant and humane conduct he displayed in rescuing the Chief Officer of the steamship Atlantic wrecked on Marr's Rock, near Halifax, on the 1st of April last, I beg leave to transmit herewith the cheque drawn in favor of Mr. Ancient for the sum of $500, and to state at the same time that the watch referred to has been forwarded by express.*

On Oct 8, in the presence of about thirty "gentlemen" in the Legislative Council Chamber, the lieutenant-governor presented Ancient with what the *Acadian Recorder* called "a massive gold watch and check for $500."

The watch bore the following inscription:

> *Presented by the Government of the Dominion of Canada to the Reverend William J. Ancient of Turn's Bay, Nova Scotia in acknowledgement of the gallant and humane conduct he displayed in rescuing at imminent peril to his own life, the life of the Chief Officer of the ill fated steamship Atlantic, wrecked on Marr's Rock off Meagher's Island, County of Halifax, Nova Scotia, April 1st, 1873.*[2]

The Reverend William Johnson Ancient. (NS ARCHIVES, NOTMAN STUDIO, NO. 1983-310 #90088)

In receiving the awards, Ancient noted that the men of Prospect had shown bravery, endurance, and humanity in their effort to save lives. The fact that they had failed to rescue the chief officer without his assistance, he said, was solely because they were not familiar with getting around in large vessels; he had been able to overcome this because of his experience on a warship (HMS *Mars*).[3]

This raises a question: why was he talking about the fishermen during this auspicious moment? Was he feeling some guilt that he was being thus recognized while they were all but ignored? The Prospect men had spent a gruelling four or so hours getting some 370 men off the rock and the ship, and had received credit only from the men they'd saved and some newspapers—usually one isolated sentence or small paragraph at a time. There were no official declarations of heroism for them. To get any recompense, they had to go to the Vice Admiralty Court, where their efforts were trivialized and they had to hear themselves accused of stealing from the wreck.

In Ancient's words, they had "failed to rescue the chief officer." No, they hadn't failed, they insisted. But nobody was listening. They had realized that they could not get to Firth while the tide was high—it had been rising while they rescued the others. They knew the tide would have to fall before they tried again. And just as low tide was imminent, Ancient arrived, assumed they had given up, and took matters into his own hands. "I was astonished to see two men in the mizzen rigging waving their arms and shouting to be taken off and no attempt whatever being made to rescue them," he stated.[4]

If they had given up, then why had they not gone home after their exhausting efforts? Why were they still there, with the boats, waiting? James Coolen testified that he had gone home to put on dry clothes and returned with the intention of rescuing them when the tide fell, but when he got back, Ancient had already gone out with his boat![5]

So the assumption has forever been made that these men, who had done so much, had not been able to finish the job. Ancient had to do it and make excuses for them.

Superlatives were always used to describe William Ancient, and whenever there was a reference to the rescue, his name was always front and centre. Note another piece from the *Acadian Recorder* on May 17, 1873:

> *An item of $3,000 has been placed in the supplementary estimates for*
> *the expenses in connection with the burial of the bodies recovered from*
> *the wreck of the Atlantic [and] for conferring rewards on the Rev Mr.*
> *Ancient and other parties in the vicinity of Prospect, who assisted in the*
> *rescue and provided for persons saved from the wreck.*

Only one name is mentioned with regard to the rescue—"the Rev Mr. Ancient"—even though the money was intended for all who participated. Everybody else got bundled into "other parties...who assisted" in the rescue. It was this watering down of the central role played by the people of Lower Prospect that led Sarah Jane O'Reilly to write to the *Halifax Herald* in April 1906. In her opening words, it is easy to tell that she has something on her mind:

> *On the anniversary of the wreck of the steamer Atlantic, lost so many*
> *years ago, I take the occasion to write the true account of the wreck as*
> *seen by myself and as known by the people of Prospect and vicinity.*

It is very likely that Sarah Jane wrote her letter in response to comments Ancient had made while unveiling the granite monument at the gravesite in Terence Bay four months earlier, on December 7, 1905. On that occasion he gave a detailed description of his rescue of Chief Officer Firth and Charles Flanly from the mizzen-mast rigging. He started by saying,

> *As there appears to be considerable misunderstanding as to the facts*
> *respecting the wreck of the Atlantic and my connection with it, I think*
> *it well that I, speaking in the presence of several eyewitnesses, should*
> *say a few words by way of correction. In the first place, it has been*
> *stated in the papers recently...that I did not reach the scene of the disas-*
> *ter until one or two o'clock in the afternoon. The fact is that it could*
> *not have been later than ten in the forenoon.*

It was actually noon, according to his affidavit to the Vice Admiralty Court, to which he swore and signed on December 31, 1873.

On that point, Sarah Jane wrote, "Mr. Ancient, who is styled the hero of the wreck, did not reach the place until two o'clock, when all had been saved or drowned except two men."

More than thirty years had passed, so they can both be excused for not remembering the precise time, but Sarah Jane was clearly stinging over the attention that Ancient had received, especially at the expense of the people who had rescued 370 souls, while he had rescued two.

"In regard to some of the accounts published," she wrote, "I can say they are not true; one in particular giving the place of the wreck as Terrance [sic] Bay and consequently the rescue to Mr. Ancient." But nevertheless, that perception is still out there.

Ancient closed his comments with words about her efforts on that morning:

> *Wherever I went I found the women doing everything in their power to make the poor creatures comfortable by making up good fires in their stoves and preparing for them whatever food they could. And no one was more gratified than I, when some weeks later I had the pleasure of distributing something like $600 amongst them, money sent by sympathizers in the United States and elsewhere. And also handing to each of the two Misses O'Brien and Mrs. [O'Reilly], daughter of Mr. Clancy, a beautiful gold locket and chain from the citizens of Chicago as a mark of appreciation of their kindness to residents of that city.*[6]

Ancient was honoured by the federal government in front of an audience at the provincial legislature. Sarah Jane had her reward dropped off at her house by this same Ancient. It would always be thus, as the leadership role was placed upon him and he naturally assumed it.

It would be unfair to say that William Ancient knowingly tried to usurp the position of the Prospect people. His words on the occasion of the presentation of the watch were meant to be gracious and to indicate his desire to give them the credit they deserved, as he did on other occasions. People like Sarah Jane, Dennis Ryan, and James

Coolen were simply the victims of an old foe—the longstanding antipathy of the powerful English towards the Irish—and Ancient was their unwitting instrument. "Racial animosity was disastrously strengthened by religious enmity," was how author and historian Cecil Woodham-Smith described the historical attitude of the English towards the Irish.[7]

At that time, people everywhere were identified first and foremost by their national origins; people in the British Isles were noted as being English or Welsh, Irish or Scot. The Irish in the United States were subjected to the same attitudes, which can be seen in the caricatures of them in the illustrated newspapers from the time, or in job ads with the notation "Irish need not apply." It even found its way into the coverage of the salvage of the *Atlantic*, as evidenced in the wording in newspapers of the day, such as the *Daily Acadian Recorder*, which commented on "Patrick Leahy, a young Irishman whose brogue was very prominent."[8] When they arrived in New York, the *Tribune* said the survivors were "of average intelligence and some appeared to have received a good common school education."[9]

It would also be unfair to ascribe malice to the reporters and authorities who had trouble remembering the heroism of the Prospect people. They just did what came naturally, carrying on an institutionalized attitude that had found its way across the Atlantic from the old country. While they fell over themselves to interview as many survivors as they could find, including crew members and officers of the ship, there are no interviews with anybody from the three Nova Scotia communities. The closest we get is again from Fielding:

> The talk in the Blackburn's was all of the wreck, of the saved, of the lost....It was evident that every effort that could be put forth to save any of the living crowded on the rock and in the rigging had been cheerfully and energetically made, and nothing could be pleasanter that to hear stalwart sailor after stalwart sailor extol the conduct of some volunteer companion in danger, the name of one of the Ryans being, in particular, frequently mentioned.

Even in this instance, the first name of "the Ryan" was not deemed important enough to highlight. There were four Ryans in the rescue boats—Edmund, Dennis, Stephen, and Francis. It was probably a reference to Dennis, whose name is prominent throughout the rescue.

Just a month after the wreck occurred it was announced that, after six years in Terence Bay, Rev. Ancient would be moving to Halifax to work in the Trinity Church section of St. Paul's Parish. The papers assumed that this move was a reward for his work at the rescue. He was inducted into his new role on June 29, 1874. In 1880, he was appointed rector of the rural parish of Rawdon, NS, and in 1890 to Londonderry, NS, a busy iron-mining and smelting town of five thousand that today has a new name (Great Village) with a population of around two hundred. In 1895 he returned to Halifax when he was appointed clerical secretary-treasurer of the Anglican diocese of Nova Scotia.

He was described as having a genial face, a bright eye, a clear head, and a warm heart. Courageous, energetic, impatient; intolerant of rum, dancing, and fiddling, William Ancient died on July 20, 1908, at age seventy-two. He had not been well for a while. His obituary, perhaps meant to be warm, ended on an odd note: "For many months it had been painfully evident to those who met him on the broad thoroughfares that his frail body was but ripening for the tomb."[10]

Ancient lies buried in St. John's Cemetery in Halifax, not far from the graves of 121 *Titanic* victims. He was survived by his wife, Emma, and three daughters, one married and two at home. One of them became a teacher on Sable Island, teaching the children of the lighthouse keepers and rescue station personnel on this long and narrow sandbar 180 miles offshore from Halifax.[11]

In 2020, author and historian Frank Jastrzembski of Wisconsin, having read about Ancient's heroism, went looking for his grave. Upon locating it, he was touched to learn that it was unmarked. He commissioned a headstone to be placed at the grave and started a campaign to raise the more than three thousand dollars to have a headstone erected. At the time of writing, the campaign is closing in on its target.

CHAPTER 27

MYTHS, LIES, AND OTHER UNTRUTHS

There have been many misstatements published at various times in regards to this wreck, and more or less fiction introduced each time the story has been told.

Sarah Jane O'Reilly
Letter to Halifax Herald, *April 3, 1906*

O n April 12, 1873, the *Canadian Illustrated News* wrote:

A great many facts and a vast amount of fiction have been served up both typographically and pictorially, and the theme will not be worn out for some time. The sketches in this week's issue are from our special artist, who has carefully prepared them, and may be considered accurate.

If only that were true. They had already confused the name of the *Atlantic*'s owners and morphed White Star Line and Oceanic Steam Navigation Company into the White Star and Ocean Company. A century later, when the respected Halifax historian Phyllis Blakely wrote a piece for the *Nova Scotia Historical Quarterly*, she referenced the offending *Canadian Illustrated News* edition, the cover of which contained a misrepresentation of the rescue of Firth by Rev. Ancient.[1] Heroic though it appeared, it was entirely incorrect. Firth did not carry Rosa Bateman down to the deck; he lashed her body to the rigging, after which he fell into the water and Ancient had to reel him in.

The premise of Ms. Blakeley's article—that Ancient led the rescue—has now been entrenched in the records of the Nova Scotia Historical Society.

After a century and a half of telling and retelling the story, too many people filled the gaps with errors, guesses, lies, and assumptions, leaving the story of the SS *Atlantic* awash in a swill of untruth. Some of it has already been mentioned, such as the idea that the ship struck Marrs Rock as described in virtually every report, and the myth that Ancient led the rescue.

Captain Williams was often described in newspapers as having been asleep in his cabin when the ship struck. Not so. Some newspapers said he was drunk—also untrue.

Many writers have assumed the event happened during a big storm. Again, untrue.

The front page of *Canadian Illustrated News* erroneously depicting John Firth as though he has just climbed down from the rigging carrying Rosa Bateman's body in one arm. Reverent Ancient is shown in the water.

There were reports that the steerage passengers had been locked downstairs and were unable to get to the deck. This was denied by all who were asked about it during the inquiry and by passengers interviewed by the newspapers.

Other reports said that the crew abandoned the women and families. Anybody knowing anything about the rapidity of events after the *Atlantic* struck knows this is an empty accusation.

One author wrote about Captain Williams that, "within two years he was back on the bridge of a White Star liner."[2] It appears that this author assumed that the small cargo steamer named the *Calabar*, on which Williams embarked on November 2, 1874, was a White Star Line ship.

PERHAPS THE ASPECT THAT HAS GENERATED MORE CONFLICTING STORIES than any other is this: how many people were aboard and how many perished? Much of the problem stems from the fact that there were so many foreign names that got spelled differently by different newspapers. For example, Fisk Grimes in one paper became Fish Grime in another. The surname Johannes shows up as Johanne, Johans, Johan, John, Jos or just J. Are Elsa Pohradalta and Ellser Persdatler the same person? Or should it be Persdotter? Persdatter? Pehrsdeatter? They are all out there in the lists. English names also got confused. Michael Clancy became Thomas Clancy in one book, and John Speakman became George Speakman in another.

What are the chances that two Patrick Murphys boarded at Queenstown, Ireland? Very good, actually. Father and son often had the same first name—still do—and Mary the mother and Mary the daughter were common. There might even be Patrick the grandfather and Mary the aunt in the same family.

In my years of researching the *Atlantic* story, I have accumulated more than twenty-five totals for the people aboard and the people who perished. They range from a low of 790 aboard to a high of 1038. The numbers of deaths have been reported from a low of 414 to a high of 750.

Even Brady's first estimate of 750 deaths has seeped into the records and turns up from time to time. When Ismay, Imrie, and Company responded to the query from the Board of Trade, they dropped it to 700. Already, they were trying to make it sound a little less severe.

On April 2, in a letter to Ismay, Imrie, and Company, Williams reported that out of 949 people aboard, 414 had been lost and 535 saved.

Later the same day, after most of the living had boarded the *Delta* and the *Lady Head* for the trip to Halifax, Captain Williams estimated that there had been 976 aboard and 546 had been lost.

At the Halifax inquiry he said that, of 957 persons aboard, 535 had been lost.

The official report and ruling of the inquiry came on April 18. It concluded there were 952 on board. The lost numbered 535.

At the Liverpool investigation on June 2, 1873, Williams said:

I can't recollect exactly how many people were on board. The books, papers, etc. are lost; but I believe there were 936, including the crew, which was 146, and this included the 12 stowaways, I think. It may have been 957 persons, but I do not believe it was; not more than 943 at the outside.[3]

Why was he so unsure? He would have been given the numbers when they departed Queenstown, Ireland, but the two men whose job it was to know precisely had been lost. Hugh Christie, the chief steward, oversaw the people tasked with feeding and seeing to the passengers' comfort, while Ambrose Worthington, the purser, paid the bills. Knowing exactly how many people were aboard was central to the roles of these men.

The best we can do a century and a half later is to conclude that there were around 950 aboard, of which some 550 perished, leaving approximately 400 survivors.

WHEN THE UNITED STATES POSTMASTER GENERAL DECIDED NOT TO CANCEL the mail contract with White Star Line, his reasoning was that it would be unfair to do so, "on account of accidents which human skill and forethought could not wholly prevent."[4] That might be true in some circumstances but it was not the case with the *Atlantic*.

The passenger records were lost, so the confusion can be forgiven, but there are other not-so-innocent untruths that came about because of the effort made to hide the loss of such a big ship with so many lives. At a time when Britannia ruled the waves, a disaster like the *Atlantic*, caused by incompetence, was a huge embarrassment—not only to the White Star Line, but to the whole seafaring fraternity of the United Kingdom. Perhaps that is why some just chose to ignore it. Two incidents illustrate this fact.

First, when the respected *Nautical Magazine* did a profile of the White Star Line in 1876, three years after the loss of the *Atlantic*, they seem to have forgotten that the *Atlantic* had ever existed and that it was the second ship built for the company.

The article stated, "The pioneer ship of the line was the *Oceanic*.... The succeeding vessels of the line followed each other rapidly....The *Baltic* sailed from Liverpool in September, 1871, and was followed by the *Republic*." There is no mention of the *Atlantic*, which had been launched on November 26, 1870. A mere three years after the biggest steamship disaster up to that time, they simply pretended that the *Atlantic* had never existed. No historical writer could possibly have been that uninformed. The omission had to be intentional.

A week after the disaster, on April 7, 1873, the White Star Line ran an ad in the *Liverpool Mercury* extolling its weekly service to New York, and there in the list of eight ships was the *Atlantic*—a week after the *Atlantic* had been lost! Did they think nobody would notice?

The Nautical Magazine continues, with breathtaking hypocrisy, "Subsequent events have proved that the builders in designing these vessels have reached a high degree of perfection in speed, and what is more important, safety."

And on it goes: "...a fact most honourable to its officers, namely, that they have been enabled to save considerably over 100 lives, whom they rescued from watery graves, during the past four or five years." If it was only 100 lives, then the *Atlantic's* officers and survivors were left out of that count, as well.[5]

Families of victims of the *Atlantic* would never have read this magazine, but if they had, it would have been particularly maddening to see the way this appalling disaster was being blithely overlooked.

You would think that the loss of a ship resulting in some 550 deaths would be hard to forget—but to this day very little is known about it, even in the community where it occurred.

The second disappearance of an association with the *Atlantic* came when William Kidley retired. He joined the White Star Line in 1870 and sailed, according to newspaper articles at the time of his retirement, on the *Oceanic*, *Gaelic*, *Coptic*, *Ionic*, *Adriatic*, and *Gothic*. The *Atlantic* gets no mention but the crew documents indicate he was an officer on the *Atlantic*'s eighteenth voyage, the one before it was wrecked.

In an interview in 1906, Kidley was asked if he had ever been in a shipwreck. He replied, "In all my time at sea I have never had an accident—a serious accident, that is."[6] True, no doubt, but you would think he might mention how he had dodged a bullet in 1873 when he was reassigned at the last minute and missed the *Atlantic*'s final voyage.

Once something incorrect is committed to paper, we are stuck with it for as long as the document exists. The errors in books, magazines, and newspapers not only get read by the purchasers and perhaps others in the household, but for decades they have been acquired by libraries and archives, where the mistakes get institutionalized and continue to misinform long into the future.

The first reports printed contained many inaccuracies. It was such a big story that newspapers rushed to get information from anybody involved who had something to say. There were some four hundred survivors whose opinions, prejudices, falsehoods, and exaggerations are still out there, and many an unwary or careless researcher has become ensnared in them.

But some accounts do not even rank with the bad reports or the omissions. There are also outright fabrications. Within months of the disaster, the Old Franklin Publishing House of Philadelphia brought out a book entitled *Carrie Clancy: The Heroine of the Atlantic*. Touted as "A full account of the services which this noble young lady, who is a poor fisherman's daughter, rendered on the occasion of the wreck of the Atlantic," this book is a bizarre concoction of fact and fiction. It supposedly tells the thrilling story of Michael Clancy's daughter

Perhaps the most common image of the *Atlantic* on the rocks, this Currier and Ives print contains several errors. The ship is leaning the wrong way; the men on the rope seem to be going in the wrong direction and are not touching the water; and women and children are not only swimming around but do not appear to be coming from the ship. (PUBLIC DOMAIN)

Carrie being awakened and sending out the call, "Rouse up! Rouse up! Every man of you! Out with the boats!"

According to the book, "One after another of the hardy fishermen, leaping from their beds, answered the brave girl's summons."[7]

With Carrie diving into the water and rescuing women and babies, the accounts are comical and silly, but it has become part of the historical record. Even the highly respected Maritime Museum of the Atlantic—the oldest and largest Maritime Museum in Canada—portrays Carrie as Michael Clancy's daughter in its Marine Heritage Database, even though there was no such person. Clancy's real—and heroic—daughter was Sarah Jane O'Reilly.

In addition to the crew documents, there was another official document about the crew in the form of a report of a survey conducted by Emigration Officer W. C. Geary. He reported there were 143 crew members, including officers. The number of crew members in various trades is similar to the crew documents, but few agree as to the exact number. Significant is the number of ship's boys. That was the lowest rank aboard and consisted of young men ranging in age from teenagers to those in their early twenties. Geary reported there were none aboard, but the crew's papers show six, including the youngest crew member to die, thirteen-year-old John Davenport, who was on his first voyage. Three of the six boys died.

When asked about the crew on the *Atlantic*, the ship's officers tended to be grudgingly supportive, while the newspapers accused them of a litany of sins. According to the *New York Times*:

> The crew was one of the hardest that was ever gathered in any vessel. They were picked up about the Liverpool wharves and docks, and it was with the greatest difficulty that they were kept under control during the voyage.[8]

The crew documents do not bear that out. They indicate that two-thirds had, on their voyage previous to the disaster, sailed on a White Star Line ship, with half having been on the *Atlantic*. There are multiple cases of crew representatives complaining to the newspapers about their treatment, noting that the bad actors were the surviving stowaways, who had been a problem on the voyage and who continued to be, at the wreck site.[9]

Even some of the testimony by those who were there can be difficult to unravel. The testimony of three of the quartermasters is especially prickly. Robert Thomas was on the bridge at the moment of the grounding and gave a wealth of testimony about what happened before and after. Captain Williams dismissed his claims about the conversation in which he kept warning Metcalfe to slow down the ship because they were getting close to the land. Williams said that no officer would tolerate such impertinence from a quartermaster. Yet one of the passengers told the *New York Herald* that he had overheard the conversation.

Thomas also claimed to have saved several people but Third Officer Brady scoffed at him, accusing Thomas of being interested in saving only one life—his own. In his support, on April 12, twenty-six crew-men swore an affidavit before Halifax Mayor James Duggan and had it placed in the *Evening Express* of April 16, claiming that they owed their lives to Robert Thomas. And Michael Clancy, known to be an honourable and decent man, swore an affidavit that Thomas was the first ashore and worked bravely in saving lives.[10]

Whom are we to believe? C. H. Milsom, writing in 1975, says, "Thomas may have been protesting too much, but there is no doubt that he was a brave man." He cites an incident in 1865 when Thomas was awarded the Silver Medal by the Liverpool Shipwreck and Humane Society for helping to save survivors from the *Ibis*. Not long after the *Atlantic* disaster, Thomas was again recognized for jumping into the Mersey River to rescue a man who had fallen in. And, in 1875, Thomas himself was seriously injured while trying to rescue another man from the sea.[11]

Even the monument, erected at one of the burial sites in 1905, is a cause for confusion, right up to this day. The monument reads: "Near this spot was wrecked the SS Atlantic April 1st 1873." The monument is in the village of Terence Bay on the property of William Ancient's church, three miles from the wreck site. It is the main attraction for visitors who naturally assume that the wreck site is within view of where they are standing. It is not, nor can it be seen, even with binoculars, as the site is blocked by islands. The wreck site is not visible from anywhere along the shore.

As for the monument, there are numerous reports that it was not erected in 1905, but in 1915. It is well documented that it was erected in 1905.

A common assertion about the *Atlantic* tragedy was that all the married couples died, and all the children except one—John Hanley. Because it is an established fact that all the women died, and there are so many stories about men choosing to remain with their wives, it is often said that all the married men died, too. But there are stories that contradict all those claims.

We already know that James Bateman survived after his wife Rosa perished in the rigging next to Chief Officer Firth. In addition, twenty-six-year-old William Glenfield of Plymouth, who had returned to England from America to get married, lost his new wife, Annie. We don't know how they got separated; all we know is that he went ashore in the last boat, having spent seven hours in the rigging of the mizzen and main masts. With his money and belongings gone, Annie's trunk washed ashore and was pillaged, but he managed to save a pair of her slippers to remember her by.[12] What a contrast to William Booth, who survived and wrote home to his wife in Oswaldtwistle: "There was not a woman saved. It is a good job you did not come, or I should have lost you."[13]

As the days following the disaster turned into weeks, there were indications of bad blood within the communities. On April 5, some unnamed person wrote to the *Morning Chronicle* complaining that four men from Upper Prospect weren't getting credit for the part they played in the rescue and that all the attention was going to the men from Lower Prospect. When the *Chronicle* took their side, the *Evening Reporter* came out two days later with the names of five more who were displeased, saying diplomatically:

> *These men rendered valuable assistance in rescuing the passengers from the ship and conveying them to the shore. These men relieved the heroic men who were first at the wreck, and who performed deeds of valour that will long be remembered by those whose lives they were instrumental in saving.*

Eventually, the first responders had to have their say:

> *We, the undersigned, beg leave to state that, on the morning of April 1, when the steamship Atlantic was wrecked, we with our boat Linnet were the first at the scene and were instrumental in saving about one hundred and fifty lives before others were there—some of whom are claiming more credit than they are justly entitled to.*

It was signed by James Coolen, Dennis Ryan, John Blackburn, Patrick Dollard, Francis Ryan, and Benjamin Blackburn, adding a postscript: "In company with the above was the lifeboat manned by Samuel Blackburn Jr. and Stephen Ryan."[14]

Finally, an April 19, 1873, letter to the *New York Daily Graphic*, opens with the words, "The recent disaster to the White Star Line is not, as most people suppose, the first one that has befallen it." It goes on to relate the author's experience aboard the *Atlantic*'s sister, *Baltic*. After striking a French barque at anchor while leaving New York on October 7, 1871, the ship made a record crossing to Liverpool and grounded at the entrance to the Mersey River. Everybody had to spend the night on deck waiting to see if their ship would survive. It did, but the passengers had to be taken off and the *Baltic* spent the next six months at Harland and Wolff getting repaired.

The letter's author then completed his narrative by declaring, "The true policy of the Oceanic Steam Navigation Company was to hush up the whole thing. And they did."[15]

CHAPTER 28

DIVING THE ATLANTIC

The divers gave thrilling accounts of the sights to be seen below, the bodies in one of the steerages being piled up into heaps, grim and ghastly to look upon, and requiring all the nerve they are masters of to remain in that charnel house unmoved.

Halifax Evening Reporter
April 7, 1873

Salvage of the *Atlantic* began as soon as they could get divers into the water, and divers have been going into those waters ever since. In those days, diving was strictly for work, as many commercial divers do today. Scuba, an acronym for "self-contained underwater breathing apparatus," was still seventy years away, so divers had to wear a canvas suit with a helmet containing tiny windows on the sides and front. On the surface, two men in a boat cranked a manual pump that pushed air down a hose and into the diver's helmet and suit.

After Jacques Cousteau and Emile Gagnan invented the breathing regulator in 1943, freeing divers from the need for air from the surface, diving was dramatically simplified. It brought costs down and opened the door for recreational scuba diving, which is very popular today. Only a scuba diver can appreciate just how many things could go wrong with the old method.

Even so, the old method was such a novelty in 1873 that a couple of newspaper reporters talked the diving companies into taking them down (ignorance is bliss; today, that would be illegal) and they provided detailed descriptions of what they saw.

Because of its somewhat convenient location, the wreck site of the SS *Atlantic* has to be one of the most frequently visited of all major historic wrecks. After many years of being dived on by salvage companies, it became an instant hit with the arrival of recreational diving in the 1960s.

Diving the wreck of the *Atlantic* is like descending a set of giant stairs. It is contained in a small cove that forms a gentle arc on the bottom, a bit like the inside of a bowl. The bottom is at eighty feet and the sides of the bowl are composed of huge boulders. Most of the wreckage is on the sides of the bowl, smashed and flattened, first from being blown up by the salvagers in the summer of 1873 and then from enduring 150 winters with storms that tossed the boulders around and ground the wreckage into smaller and smaller pieces. The site is a very violent place, with a lot of white water much of the time. Strong winds, even in summer, can make the site inaccessible for weeks at a stretch.

The rocks that the stern struck when the ship swung around after hitting Golden Rule Rock rise out of the water and are almost always surrounded by white water. For the past few years, recreational divers have kept a mooring line and float tied to the ship's driveshaft, one of the few recognizable pieces left on the bottom. They tie their small boats to it during the summer and fall diving seasons. The line has to be replaced each spring because it gets beaten to shreds over the winter. It is so frighteningly close to those rocks that sometimes divers fall into white water when they roll off the boat. Once in, they make for the mooring line and pull themselves down. It is about fifty feet down to where the mooring is attached to the shaft.

This is the area where the stern grounded moments after the collision, where the unaccompanied women were the first to lose their lives. At that location, there is wreckage above and strewn down the slope to the deepest part, where the boilers rest. At some point during the salvage, the boilers rolled down the bank and are now sticking up from the sandy bottom eighty feet below the surface. As each year goes by, the toll of the sea is more noticeable and less and less of each boiler remains.

Waves striking the shore above get deflected back to sea, causing constant surge on the bottom when you are diving. It pushes out and then draws you back in again in a steady rhythm. To make any progress, you kick your fins when the surge is in your favour, and when it pulls you back, you relax and save your energy. It is usually easier to stay close to bottom and pull yourself along, but if the surge is particularly strong you can get bounced around, so you have to watch for any sharp pieces sticking up. Bits of brass or lead or glass are common. The iron plates of the hull are mostly corroded and barely recognizable. They corrode in an uneven fashion and sometimes form a series of foot-long rusty needles that are a serious hazard—waiting to ensnare a careless diver.

That is not to imply that it is a particularly dangerous dive. Sometimes it can be quite peaceful, but conditions on the surface are not always a good indicator of conditions on the bottom.

Some like to dive the site on April 1 to commemorate the date of the disaster, but also to see how the wreck has been altered over the winter. The movement of the boulders often exposes small trinkets such as costume jewellery, which is usually bent, dented, or eroded. So much of it has been recovered over the years that it must have been a part of the cargo. Every now and then a coin turns up, or a bolt of cloth, or a bent spoon, or a fork missing a tine or two.

The ashes of at least five divers rest on the site. Those of my long-time dive buddy, Greg Cochkanoff, are in a hollowed-out and engraved granite stone about the size of a basketball. Each time he is sighted is a time of remembrance for those of us who recall the many dives we did together. It may sound odd but it is no different than looking at a headstone in a cemetery or an urn on a mantle in somebody's living room.

When you are comfortable with controlling your buoyancy and managing all the equipment you must wear when diving, and you visit a wreck like the *Atlantic*, you have an experience like none other. As I press the button to vent the air from my suit and begin to sink, a feeling of well-being envelops me as the water pressure squeezes my body and gives me a big welcoming hug. But I am not fooled; the ocean is not my friend and my training and experience always keep me vigilant.

At first there is nothing to see as you look down—just a dark void that gives time for expectation—excitement almost—to build.

On every dive that I've done during thirty years of visiting the wreck, I have always been conscious of the dramatic events of that day. In the clear water, the terrible destruction and waste is everywhere to be seen, intermingled with colourful marine growth swaying gently. All is peace and serenity. How different it was, and how horrifying, for those who got drawn down to where I am. They were probably unconscious before they got down this far. If the ship were here now the way it was that morning it would be overwhelmingly huge compared to my tiny being, towering up out of sight, and if I were to swim under it, I would become so disoriented that there is a better-than-even chance I would not find my way back out. The noise would have been deafening, even after the engines had shut down and the boilers had finished venting their clouds of steam. The groaning and the grinding of the overstressed hull being thrown against the rocks by the huge waves, with the ship's cargo, furniture, belongings, and machinery crashing and banging around inside the disintegrating ship, would have caused a cacophony of terrifying proportions.

Once while I was diving and had my face just inches from the bottom, scrutinizing something, I became aware of a presence on my right. I glanced—and a foot or so from my face was the toe of a man's boot. I had the eerie feeling there was somebody standing there, looking down at me. The boot was in remarkably good condition, sitting upright on the bottom. It had probably washed into position by the ever-active ocean, a very poignant reminder of where I was. On the next dive I happened into the same area and remembered the boot, which was now nowhere to be seen, but when I looked to the left I saw, to my surprise, the mate to the first one I had seen, crushed under a rock. Whether they came off a person in that place or had been laid next to his bed while he slept, I will never know, but I felt a very real connection to that man.

ON MAY 17, 2020, THE SEA AROUND THE WRECK SITE WAS VERY ACTIVE, with ten-foot-high groundswells slamming the shore. I was there with seven other divers. They were interested in the aft part of the wreck, but I wanted to check out the rock and the ledge on which the *Atlantic* had landed minutes after striking. I anchored my boat as closely as I dared to the outside of the rock. I had intended to go around it, but that was out of the question, given the sea state.

I descended to seventy-two feet to make sure the anchor was well hooked. With that settled, I turned to face the shore and the rock. The cliffs seemed to tower above me. Even at this depth, the kelp swayed back and forth, driven by the swells above. I slowly started the climb, knowing that if I went to the surface, the waves would smack me against the rock. There was broken china everywhere, of the type that is now on display at the SS Atlantic Heritage Centre in Terence Bay. It was like going up a set of big, irregular stairs. At about sixty feet I could see above me what looked like a ledge. I swam up to forty-five feet and found a flat area. The surge was much stronger here and I was getting swished around. This ledge was too deep to have been the one on which the *Atlantic* foundered. I looked up and saw another one, so I gingerly went up to thirty feet. Here, as I got closer to the surface, the kelp was really racing back and forth. I stayed close to the rocks to keep from being thrown against them and dumped all the air out of my buoyancy vest to stay heavy. The last thing I wanted was to get pushed to the surface and be tossed against the rock. I grabbed a handhold and took a good look around. This ledge was big enough to hold a ship, and at thirty feet it was at a reasonable depth. The *Atlantic* drew twenty-three feet of water, so with the bottom torn, it would have settled in this area. On the outer part of the ledge near where I was, I saw numerous large rocks, some sawtooth-shaped, jutting up. The inner part of the ledge was lower than where I was, somewhat like a cradle. It all made sense.

In the last minutes before coming ashore, the *Atlantic* grazed several shallow areas of the Grampus shoal, which damaged its bottom.

Then it struck Golden Rule Rock, and because of the taper of the bow's forefoot, slid up on the rock and stopped. Within minutes it sank in the stern because of the earlier strikes and slid to the left off the rock and onto the ledge. After seven or eight minutes, it started to roll to the left, until the rails were under and the decks were swept by the waves, throwing people into the sea. This was the period of the major loss of life. Then, suddenly, the rolling stopped as the ship settled into the position where it remained for eighteen hours or so.

Why did it not roll over? Those outer rocks stopped the rolling. For the rest of the night and the next day, the *Atlantic* rested there. Even though the stern was in deep water, those sawtooth rocks must have stuck into the hull and kept the ship from sliding back. Finally, at 5:00 P.M. the bow broke off, having been weakened by the rocks and the waves. At that point, there was nothing to keep the rest of the ship from continuing to roll, which it did, leaving the broken-off bow on the other side of the rock. For the week that it stayed in that position, people used to walk around on the upper side of the ship's middle, showing off, until a storm finally sank what was left of the *Atlantic*.

CHAPTER 29

MEMORIES

The graves of the Titanic victims buried in Fairview Cemetery in
Halifax are kept up, so why not the graves of the Atlantic?[1]

Percy Baker in 1969
Halifax County Councillor, Terence Bay

here are 150 graves of *Titanic* victims in three Halifax cemeteries. From the beginning, they have been a source of wonder
and fascination. On many days in the summer and fall there are lineups
of tourists who have come from all over the world to see them. Some
weep over them. It is hard to believe that, even though upwards of
five hundred victims of the *Atlantic* are buried in two cemeteries in
Lower Prospect and Terence Bay, very few know where they are or
care that they are there at all.

The worst transatlantic passenger ship disaster of the nineteenth
century and the worst transatlantic passenger ship disaster of the
twentieth century share many similarities—and one big difference. The
difference is that the *Atlantic* story is significantly underrepresented
relative to its historic significance, and the *Titanic* story is the opposite—it is overrepresented. But now, ever so slowly, that is changing.

Salvage activity at the *Atlantic* wreck site continued into the fall of
1873, but summer was the fishing season, during which the livelihood
for the whole year had to be earned, so the people in the three com-

munities had more than enough to keep them busy. With decisions having been made in 1874 about amounts to be paid to those involved in the rescue, the *Atlantic*, while by no means forgotten, soon became part of the folklore.

With the deaths of Michael Clancy (April 15, 1891), Edmund Ryan (July 6, 1894), and others central to the rescue, the story began to fade from memory, and the burial sites began to deteriorate, with scrub and trees stunted by the winds and salt spray overtaking the spaces in Terence Bay and Lower Prospect. Then, in 1905, thirty-two years after the event, Rev. A. F. Dentith, the rector of St. Paul's Church in Terence Bay, decided the site should have a permanent marker to remember those buried there. He wrote to the White Star Line and they sent money for repairs to the gravesite and for the erection of a monument.

At 1:30 P.M. on December 7, 1905, with the sun low in the sky, Reverend Dentith, Rev. Dr. William Armitage, the rector of St. Paul's Church in Halifax, several dignitaries, and a crowd of the local faithful met to unveil a new eight-foot-tall granite monument above the gravesite. Reverend Armitage preached a sermon and then an honoured guest, William Ancient, by then sixty-nine years old, unveiled the memorial after making a few remarks.[2]

Over the decades that followed, newspaper and magazine articles about the *Atlantic* came along on a regular basis. They all bore a common theme—and the reports went something like this: "Guess what? On our shores just outside Halifax, there was a huge shipwreck and hundreds of people died,"—a clear indication that the writer had just discovered the *Atlantic* story and was relating it with as much accuracy as he or she could manage given the article's deadline and the information sources available—but always with the attitude that this was being told to an audience that had never heard of the SS *Atlantic*.

They were right; 95 percent of the people reading the article had indeed never heard of it. It seemed like Nova Scotia had adopted the attitude of the day. The British wanted it forgotten, so the dutiful colonials promptly forgot about it, too.

But the story would not die—and it has not died, thanks to the efforts of a small group of interested people—even though the event and location have no official historical designation. As disasters go, the

Halifax Explosion[3] ranks first and is remembered—as it should be—but after that overarching event, the second most significant tragedy in provincial history is routinely passed over, and smaller events in terms of lives lost take precedence in the minds of the citizens.

It's puzzling, to say the least. The reason lies, perhaps, in the fact that the people who died that morning were not Canadians and the ship was not Canadian-owned. There was nobody local to mourn them then and there is nobody local to remember them now. But that cannot be the whole reason the *Atlantic* gets ignored, because the *Titanic* has even less connection, and yet people line up at Halifax cemeteries to see the grave markers of *Titanic* victims.

And, sadly, the names of Michael Clancy, Sarah Jane O'Reilly, Edmund Ryan, James Coolen, the Blackburns, the O'Briens, and their little group of relatives and neighbours who instinctively left their beds and did whatever it took to snatch four hundred people from the jaws of death, are not honoured by their countrymen and -women.

Perhaps the *Atlantic's* name, like the ship itself, has become swamped by the other Atlantic—the ocean. In 1959, a new school built at nearby Shad Bay was an attempt to remember the disaster. It was called Atlantic Memorial School. The gesture was authentic but "Atlantic Memorial" more readily, in the minds of those with no knowledge of the *Atlantic*, brings forth thoughts of either local people lost at sea or people from the area who were lost in the two world wars.

In a hard-hitting article on November 12, 1969, the *Halifax Mail Star* berated the authorities over the neglect of the gravesite near St. Paul's Cemetery, which for decades had been tended by people who remembered the *Atlantic* or who had been taught by a generation that did. With no first-hand connection to the event, it was forgotten; the gravesite had once again become a tangle of brambles and bushes, and the monument, the article noted, "with a white marble plaque to its side serves as a favourite target for local marksmen who apparently haven't anything better to shoot at. The face of the plaque is scored with many black bullet marks."

After another decade went by with nothing done, the local people decided to take action. Led by Vince Norris, a descendant of Richard Norris, one of the first on site that morning, they called a town meeting, formed the Community Restoration and Development Association of Terence Bay, and went looking for funding.[4] With $16,300 from a Winter Works program, they soon had a project manager and six students hard at work. Between March 27 and June 28, 1981, they cleared a pathway from the new St. Paul's Cemetery through the woods to the site of the monument and common grave.

They refurbished the monument, re-detailed the inscription, and made a new base to surround it. From there, they cleared the historic pioneer cemetery and created a path to the ruins of the little church where Ancient had served, which had been struck by lightning and burned in 1942. (Interestingly, that lightning strike happened on April 1, the sixty-ninth anniversary of the wreck.)

Work was also done to the Star of the Sea Cemetery, where a new monument was erected to honour the 250 Roman Catholic victims interred nearby, and a new plaque was placed on Sarah Jane O'Reilly's grave.

The surrounding area was made accessible for picnicking and paying respects. One of the first visitors was Eleanor Quigley. John Hanley was the son of her great-great-grandparents, Patrick and Mary Hanley, who had perished on the *Atlantic*. John's sister Brigid and her husband, Hugh Towey, had a daughter, Katherine, who was Mrs. Quigley's grandmother.[5] Eleanor Quigley and her husband, Bob, visited from the United States in 1995, the first of many visits to meet descendants of the people who had helped her relative, thought at that time to have been the only surviving child from the disaster.

Mrs. Quigley had always known that she had an ancestor on what was assumed to be the *Titanic*. On their visit, they had no luck with the *Titanic*, but a helpful staff member at the Maritime Museum of the Atlantic advised that there was another White Star Line ship lost near Halifax and that the story was told in the museum. She found the display, which included a picture of John Hanley. The instant she saw it, she started to cry. "He looked just like my Uncle Bill," she declared.

Those small connections have a way of reaching across time. Remember Irving Stuttaford, the steward from Kingston, Ontario, who survived the disaster? In the crew documents I saw his signature where he signed on for the voyage. I sent it to his great-granddaughter,

Elizabeth Church of Halifax, who replied, "I can't believe how much his handwriting looks like my grandmother's." Her grandmother, of course, was Irving's daughter.

Over the years, conditions at the gravesite have continued to deteriorate. One day in 1997, Harbourmaster William Jollimore and companion Bert Reyner discovered that the unrelenting sea had been trying to reclaim her victims. The constant pounding of the waves had badly eroded the shoreline below the site, exposing the bones of those whom Ancient had buried in 1873.

Some local people had found and reburied bones, dogs were seen sniffing around, and even children were curious about the spot. One woman told me that as a thirteen-year-old, she had been unable to resist checking it out, despite a firm warning from her parents. She regularly played along the shoreline, so one evening she slid down the bank and started poking around. After moving some debris she saw what remained of a woman's lace-up boot. Suddenly she realized that the debris she had been moving around was, in fact, the bones of a human hand. She got a good shaking-up that she remembers to this day.

Descendents of Canadian Steward Irving Stuttaford indicate that he was a strong swimmer and probably managed to swim ashore. Many of his children and grandchildren became competitive and long-distance swimmers.

Because the land was the property of the Anglican Church of Canada, the rector of St. Paul's Church, Glen Easson, contacted the local member of the provincial legislative assembly, Bruce Holland, for guidance. It was clear that this was more than a local issue. The situation needed the intervention of the provincial government to remediate the site.

In July 1998, heavy equipment was brought in and workers spent three days overhauling the shore and bank below the graves, at a cost of $20,000.[6] Coincident with that effort, the local citizens formed the SS Atlantic Memorial Committee to determine how the story of the *Atlantic* could be preserved. The group held its first meeting on April 23, 1998. Over the next four years it raised over $200,000 to build the SS *Atlantic* Heritage Park and Interpretation Centre. The SS *Atlantic* Heritage Park Society was incorporated on August 10, 2001, and on June 10th of the following year a park and interpretation centre opened for visitors, with the official opening ceremony on July 28, 2002, coinciding with the annual Blessing of the Boats.

The Centre now provides a permanent home for an artifact and records collection. The museum was initially open six days a week from 11:00 A.M. to 5:00 P.M., then expanded to seven days a week, opening at 10:00 A.M. Historical research and efforts to track down descendants are ongoing, and annual events take place to commemorate and remember the ship, its occupants, and their rescuers.

At the time the stone barrier was installed, it was estimated that thirty feet of shoreline had already eroded since the bodies had been put into the ground. In the fall of 2019, the archaeology department at Saint Mary's University in Halifax, led by Dr. Jonathan Fowler, conducted a survey of the burial site using ground-penetrating radar. Their work confirmed that the graves were still there, although there has undoubtedly been some loss.

Countless ships have gone to the bottoms of the world's oceans and a few are remembered for one reason or another, but not many are commemorated in the way that the *Atlantic* now is. A scant few get a book, some get a monument, a tiny number get a song, and fewer still get a movie made about them. The *Atlantic* has the SS *Atlantic* Heritage Park Society on the job, meeting monthly, putting on at least three commemorative events annually on behalf of the ship and its people, maintaining the burial site, keeping a museum of artifacts, tracking down descendants of those aboard and preserving their stories, hosting school groups, speaking to historical groups, maintaining a website and social media presence—all in an effort to take the sad, strange, multi-layered story of the SS *Atlantic* to the world.

EPILOGUE

At the time of the disaster, there were four lighthouses marking Halifax Harbour:

+ The Sambro light, the first to be encountered when approaching the harbour, was 114 feet high, with a supposed range of twenty-one miles, but which we now know was less than seventeen miles. The white light was powered by thirteen lamps and there was a foghorn and a cannon that was fired in foggy or snowy weather. Keeper William Gilkie, at £110 per annum, was the highest-paid of the thirty-eight lighthouse keepers in the province in 1858.[1]
+ Chebucto Head, the second light to be seen when a vessel was on course, was a revolving white light, with a range of ten miles in good weather.
+ The Devil's Island light was red, to clearly differentiate it from Sambro Light. It was powered by six lamps and could be seen at a distance of nine miles.
+ Maugher's (pronounced Major's) Beach light, on McNabs Island, was white, powered by six lamps. It was situated at the narrowest point when moving from the outer to the inner harbour, and the last light to be encountered on the way in.[2]

In 1885, Nova Scotian John Boutilier expressed the thoughts of many when he penned these words in *The Atlantic Ballad*, one of the many ballads written about the *Atlantic* disaster:

Oh, never may those cruel rocks another victory gain!
Let lightships guard our rocky coast for those who cross the main.

While the drama of the *Atlantic* wreck and its aftermath was playing out, the Canadian government was in the process of bolstering the navigation aids for Halifax Harbour. Just four months before the *Atlantic* was lost, they contracted with Richardson, Duck, and Company to have a new lightship constructed in England. A lightship has a lighthouse on its deck and is anchored in a place where a light is needed but there is no land nearby where it can be erected. Being a member of the crew of a lightship is very taxing because they are stuck out there in all the weather the North Atlantic can hurl their way—and they can't leave!

Based on the design of an existing lightship anchored in the St. Lawrence River south of Quebec City, the *Halifax* was launched at the South Stockton Iron shipyard in Stockton-on-Tees on May 24, 1873, and departed for Nova Scotia on June 28. On July 12, it was anchored eight miles southeast of the Sambro light, too late for the *Atlantic*—but perhaps its presence would prevent another such disaster.[3]

They soon discovered that the St. Lawrence and the North Atlantic are two very different places. After receiving a severe mauling from the autumn storms, by the end of November the new lightship was leaking badly and in danger of sinking. In a telegram to Ottawa, Henry Johnston, the Nova Scotia manager for the Department of Marine and Fisheries, advised William Smith, the deputy minister of marine and fisheries, that the *Halifax* "must be brought in as soon as weather will permit. Vessel appears unsuitable for her exposed situation. Capt. Scott thinks no chance of her taking station again this winter."

When the *Lady Head* arrived to tow it in (the same *Lady Head* that picked up the *Atlantic* survivors), it was so rough they couldn't get a towing line across between the two vessels, nor could they pull the anchor in, so they put a buoy on it and left it to be picked up when conditions improved. Fortunately, the *Halifax* was rigged as a schooner and the crew managed to sail it into the lee of Chebucto Head, where they finally got the line across to *Lady Head*, which then towed it into the harbour "in an unseaworthy state." The next summer, it found a new home in the less tempestuous waters of the St. Lawrence.

The fact that a lightship was being constructed at the time the *Atlantic*'s lookouts were straining to find the Sambro light is testimony to the fact that, even with four lights, Halifax Harbour was inadequately marked. In 1876, a fifth lighthouse started operating on Georges Island, but for the time being it was decided that a lightship could not survive the Nova Scotia winters.[4] Mariners had to be satisfied with an automatic whistle-buoy, first anchored five and a half miles out to sea from the Sambro light in January of 1891.

However, that did not stop mariners from agitating for one. In 1897, John Taylor Wood, who had been captain of a Confederate commerce raider called the *Tallahassee*, wrote a letter to the *Halifax Chronicle* extolling the virtues of lightships and calling for one to be placed outside Halifax.[5] He had first-hand knowledge of the challenges of coming into Halifax at night, having been chased in by two Union gunboats during the American Civil War. The grandson of US President Zachary Taylor, he settled in Halifax after the war and is buried in Camp Hill Cemetery.

On January 25, 1912, *Lightship No. 15* was put into position about seven miles from the Sambro Light. The authorities then ordered *Lightship No. 19* to be built at Bow, Mclachlan, and Company in Paisley, Scotland, to replace *No. 15*. On April 25, 1914, with a crew of fourteen, the new vessel departed for Halifax, but en route—yes—it ran low on coal and was obliged to put into St. John's, Newfoundland. While continuing on, during the night of May 23, in dense fog off Nova Scotia's Eastern Shore and just a day from its destination, *Lightship No. 19* ran aground and was lost with all hands. People in the nearby village of Liscomb could hear the whistle but were unable to assist because of the fog.[6]

With the war raging, *Lightship No. 15* remained through the summer and winter, after which the practice of having the lightship moved elsewhere during the summer while being replaced by the whistle buoy returned. That went on until *No. 15.* was replaced with *Lightship No.*

24 on July 1, 1926. In 1940, the stalwart *Lightship No. 15* was back for another seventeen years, when *Sambro No. 1* arrived in December 1956.[7]

In the summer of 1966 it was decided that modern navigation equipment made lightships unnecessary.[8] *Sambro No. 1* was removed a few short months before the *Cape Bonnie*, a large fishing vessel with a crew of eighteen, ran aground in shallow water on the other side of Meaghers Island, with the loss of all hands. There was widespread condemnation that eighteen men had died because of the removal of the lightship. Like the *Atlantic*, the *Cape Bonnie* had been heading to Halifax and was woefully off course. Unlike the night the *Atlantic* was lost, it was a wild February storm that sent several other vessels to the bottom in eastern Canadian waters. But, also unlike the *Atlantic*, the *Cape Bonnie* was fitted with modern navigation gear such as Decca and Loran radio navigation systems, as well as radar. As with the *Atlantic*, everybody was mystified that this vessel was where it was. Nobody survived to provide any information, so the question of why was never answered.

The *Atlantic* was lost just before the first Halifax Harbour lightship went into position, and the *Cape Bonnie* was lost a mile away just after the last one was removed. Ironically, descendants of those who had recovered bodies from the *Atlantic* ended up recovering the bodies of the men lost on the *Cape Bonnie*.

The People:
Background and Follow-up

Cornelius Lawrence Brady, the unfaltering third officer, who had helped secure the rope line from the ship to the rock, worked tirelessly throughout the rescue, and then walked to Halifax to report the disaster, was born in 1844 at Runcorn, twelve miles up the Mersey River from Liverpool, England. He went to sea at age nine, earning his Second Mate certificate on October 17, 1864, and his Master's certificate at age twenty-six. In 1869, he married Bridget Catherine Newport.

On February 21, 1874, Brady was aboard the SS *Pennsylvania* when it departed Liverpool for Philadelphia. Three days out, the ship ran into a hurricane that swept away all the lifeboats, the wheelhouse, and part of the bridge, taking the captain, two officers, and two crew members. With nobody capable of handling the ship, Brady was asked by the remaining crew to take command and over the next twelve days he kept the vessel afloat and took it safely to port.

Having saved a valuable ship and cargo along with the passengers and crew, Brady was offered a $1,000 reward. Feeling insulted, he sued for the full salvage value of the vessel. The court quadrupled the award to $4,000 and also awarded him expenses.

He left the sea and became a victualler, supplying ships with provisions. In 1876, his son Cornelius died at just six months of age, and Brady himself died the same year, aged thirty-two. He left an estate of £450.

John Brown, the Fourth Officer who had been second in command of the deck when the ship was lost, survived the dark days following the loss of his certificate and went on to continue his career on the sea. He sailed with the State Line aboard the *State of Nebraska* and the Allan Line, the biggest Canadian steamship line of the time, after it took over the State Line in 1891. That means Brown probably returned to Halifax many times. In 1917 the Allan Line merged with Canadian Pacific Steamships.

He was born on September 27, 1848, at Workington, England. He married Harriet Brown in 1885. He died November 12, 1937.

Henry Dry, a steerage passenger who survived and later wrote three extremely emotional letters to the wife he had left behind in England, suffered greatly after he got to Chicago. In his final letter, written on June 2, 1873, he told her that he was returning to England; we assume he did make it back, although there is no evidence either way. He had been unable to recover physically from the events of April 1, and had only found sporadic work. He was falling into debt and had to write to his sister Ellen for money. "She says her Master has been so kind for he is trying to raise a little money for us. I was to write and tell her if I had made up my mind to come home and then they will send me the money and I wrote and told her I had and as soon as I got the money I will come home."

Nicholas P. Christian, who organized the first boat from Upper Prospect to make it to the wreck site, was born at Upper Prospect, Nova Scotia, on August 22, 1841, the son of William Christian and Nancy Anne Brennan. In 1864, he married Margaret Ross McGuire, daughter of Daniel McGuire and Ann Perrin. Nicholas and Margaret had seven children.

On the day of the wreck he arrived at the site around 8:00 A.M. and assisted with the rescue, and later with the salvage of personal possessions from bodies as they were recovered from the wreck. As a respected community member and Justice of the Peace, he was one of the people to whom valuables from bodies were returned. Mr. Christian was a Halifax County Councillor for Upper Prospect from 1880 to 1883.

He died at Prospect on March 26, 1920.

Michael Clancy, the first Canadian to see the stricken *Atlantic*, died in 1891. After twenty years of marriage, his daughter, **Sarah Jane O'Reilly** became a widow when her husband, John, died in 1888 at fifty-five years of age. She moved to Halifax in 1898 to live with one of her daughters and died at the home of her granddaughter on Sept. 14, 1922, at age seventy-seven. Her obituary in the *Halifax Daily Echo* stated, "Nova Scotia has lost another of her splendid women of the old school, a gentle, true-hearted, firm principled woman of the old pioneer stock, that has made Nova Scotia what it is today."

She is buried next to her husband at the Star of the Sea cemetery in Lower Prospect.

Thomas Dunn, twenty-eight, had been the chief bedroom steward on the *Atlantic*. He spent hours in the rigging of the *Atlantic* and was greatly diminished by the traumatic event, but he went immediately back to work, accompanying and caring for injured saloon passengers Samuel Vick and Simon Comachio when they travelled to New York. He returned to Liverpool from New York on the Inman Line steamship *City of Montreal*. He left the sea and returned to Margate, where he had grown up in the home of his grandfather after his father had died when Thomas was four. In January 1899, The *Whitstable Times* reported his death, at age sixty-four:

> He was for years the collector of Queen's taxes for this district...and also for sixteen years local agent to the General Steam Navigation Company. Paralysis was the cause of death. The deceased in early life followed the sea, and was wrecked in the White Star line steamer Atlantic, off Halifax, Nova Scotia...and, through being many hours in the rigging, and then having swum ashore, he suffered intensely from the cold: and it is supposed that the neuralgia from which he suffered for some years was thus caused.

William Stevens Fielding, born November 24, 1848, was the first journalist on site at the disaster. He had joined the *Halifax Morning Chronicle* at age sixteen and remained there for twenty years, working up to managing editor from 1874 to 1884, when he left the *Chronicle* to become the premier of Nova Scotia. In 1896 he become the minister of finance in Prime Minister Wilfrid Laurier's government, and he later served as finance minister for William Lyon Mackenzie King. He died in 1929 at age eighty.

W. S. Fielding stayed with the Blackburns while reporting from Lower Prospect.

John Hanley, the only child definitely known to have survived the wreck, never recovered from his experience of April 1, 1873. In the short term, he was distracted by all the attention he received, but after settling in with what remained of his family in Newark, he struggled to live with the emotional results of the trauma and loss. There was a lot of interest in him; he even got an offer to travel in the circus, which his sisters would not allow. The *New York Times* reported that he made a "considerable" amount of money from the sale of his pictures.

Some reports say he was married but had no children, and that he died at the age of around thirty-five, in the second violent incident of his short life: while crossing the tracks of the Pennsylvania Railway at 10:00 P.M. on September 16, 1897, he was struck and run over by a locomotive. He died in hospital three hours later.[1] It is a natural temptation to wonder if perhaps he had stepped in front of the train intentionally, in an effort to ease the pain of his existence. It is more likely that he was intoxicated—he had become an alcoholic—and simply made a mistake that cost him his life.

James Kerr, the customs agent who remained for weeks at the disaster site and managed the collection of property belonging to the *Atlantic*'s dead, was born in 1831 and died in 1884. He was the son of Scottish immigrant Robert Kerr, who himself died at sea on a trip to St. George's Bay, Newfoundland, in November 1845. He lived at 38 Pleasant Street, which is now South Barrington Street, in Halifax. His original house, which he had built in 1853, still stands, as does a newer house he had constructed, and a third property that he owned. They were occupied by four generations of his family until 1966.

We know that he once took his son Clifford, who was eighteen, with him to the *Atlantic* site. Clifford later became a businessman in

Halifax, trading to the West Indies, while his father was promoted to Inspector of Customs for Nova Scotia in 1874.

Edmund Mortimer McDonald had been the collector of customs for Halifax for just a year when he was called upon by the Canadian government to convene and lead the Halifax inquiry. He was born at Pictou, Nova Scotia, on September 6, 1825. Married to Annie Stairs, he was the vice-president of the North British Society and a Freemason.

He owned the *New Glasgow Eastern Chronicle* and in 1860 he became the Queen's Printer for Nova Scotia. In 1863 he co-founded the *Halifax Citizen* newspaper, which reported on the *Atlantic* disaster. He had sold it in 1871. He was a member of the provincial legislature and became a member of the Dominion parliament after Confederation.

He died on May 25, 1874, a year after delivering the inquiry report on the *Atlantic* disaster.[2]

Edward Mulligan was the captain of the SS *Carlotta* who provided valuable insights into the challenges faced by a steamship captain when approaching Halifax. He lost his ship in a freak accident four months after he testified to the Halifax inquiry. The *Carlotta* was tied up in Portland, Maine, when a devastating fire destroyed the waterfront, including the *Carlotta*.

Quartermaster **Edward Owens** was the third man to get to the rock. He was born circa 1841 and married Elizabeth Pendleton. He died in the spring of 1911 and a tribute was paid to him in a newspaper in England:

> *On Friday the White Star Company paid their last tribute of respect to one of their oldest servants, viz Edward Owens, who was a very familiar figure on the landing stage where the steamers of the White Star Line sailed. The funeral was attended by a large number of the Masonic brethren and representatives of the White Star Line. Mr J. Bruce Ismay sent a beautiful wreath which took the form of a large white star, while from the marine department came a large anchor.*

The obituary of **Edmund Ryan**, one of the first to arrive at the crash site, reads:

Elsewhere the Echo records the death of Mr. Edmund Ryan, J. P., who died at his residence, 99 Creighton Street, at 3:30 this morning. The deceased was well known and respected in the business community as an honest and upright man. He had held for a long time the position of chief inspector of fish and oils for Halifax County....He also served for a lengthy period as county councillor, representing Lower Prospect, and was a valued member of that body. At the time of the wreck of the steamer Atlantic (being then a resident of Lower Prospect) he rendered such valuable assistance that in recognition of his services he was presented by the Dominion government with a gold watch and chain, and in addition to this he was remembered by many mementoes from the passengers.[3]

Elizabeth Ryan, wife of Edmund Ryan, had fed survivors and arranged for their distribution throughout the community on the night of the disaster. She was the only woman reported to receive an expense reimbursement from the Dominion government. She died February 19, 1914, at age eighty-four. She is buried next to her husband, Edmund Ryan, in Mount Olivet Cemetery, Halifax, not far from nineteen graves of *Titanic* victims.

Death of Mrs. Elizabeth Ryan

The death took place yesterday at the residence of her daughter, 99 Creighton Street, of Mrs. Elizabeth Ryan, widow of Edmund Ryan, J. P....who predeceased her twenty years. The death of Mrs. Ryan removes the last of the generation who lived on Ryan's Island, Lower Prospect, and who took such an active and creditable part in giving assistance to the survivors of the Steamship Atlantic...when so many lives were lost. Three hundred or more were fed and cared for by the late Mrs. Ryan and family. Since that time, many of the survivors have written letters showing their appreciation of the hospitality rendered them, as Mrs. Ryan refused to accept remuneration for her services. At that time, many families inhabited Ryan's Island, but today there remains only one house of the many there then—the old Ryan homestead, in which these people were cared for.[4]

The August 5, 1907, obituary of **John Hooper Slaunwhite**, one of the fishermen who rowed Rev. William Ancient to the wreck, reads:

> *There was laid to rest on Saturday at St. Paul's burial ground, Terence Bay, the mortal remains of a highly respected resident of that village. John Hooper Slaunwhite, aged 80 years. For many years he has been a helpless cripple, and latterly suffered considerable pain—passing away to eternal rest Thursday afternoon. The crowded church testified to the esteem and affection in which Mr. Slaunwhite was held. The Rev. A. F. Dentith officiated both in the church and at the grave. Mr. Slaunwhite was one of the little band of heroes who rowed out the Rev W. J. Ancient (the Anglican clergyman in charge of the mission) to the rescue of Chief Officer [Firth] from the rigging of the steamship Atlantic after her shipwreck off [Lower] Prospect.*[5]

John Speakman, the quartermaster who had helped swim the rescue rope to the nearby rock, was billeted the night of April 1, 1873, with one of the Christian families in Upper Prospect. That would most likely have been the home of Nicholas or his brother, William Christian.

Irving Azariah Stuttaford was a steward and the only Canadian known to be aboard the *Atlantic*. He was born at Kingston, Ontario, on December 19, 1852, the son of English immigrants Irving Stuttaford and Amelia Tutin. He survived the disaster and married Ellen Catherine Griffin in Montreal on October 20, 1887. They had five children. He travelled extensively while working on the Wisconsin Central Railroad. He became a successful caterer and died October 21, 1935. He is buried in Montreal.

Thomas Twohig was the only member of the rescue crew that was not from one of the three communities collectively referred to as "Prospect." He was from Pennant, a tiny community across Terence Bay, and was staying with the O'Briens. What was he doing in Lower

Prospect? Seven months after the event, he and **Kate O'Brien** were married. Kate was later the recipient of a gold locket and reward from the city of Chicago.

Just five months later, on April 9, 1874, and a year after his daring efforts against the wild Atlantic seas, Thomas Twohig died, at age twenty-seven. We don't know the cause of his death. The logical candidates are drowning or tuberculosis.

Kate was twenty-six when she became a widow. Eight years later, she remarried and lived to age eighty-nine, outliving her second husband, Samuel Martin of Herring Cove, by twenty-two years.

Her sister, **Agatha O'Brien,** who also received a gold locket and money from Chicago, married Henry Norris, son of Richard Norris, who had arrived at the wreck site before daylight with Edmund Ryan. She died in 1939 at age eighty-four.

Canadian Men
Mentioned in the Records

The list below states who started in each rescue boat. Throughout the rescue, the men swapped places among themselves and with others from the list who relieved them from time to time.

Table 7. The men of the rescue boats.

Name	Age	From	Boat	Start Time
Dennis Ryan	46	Lower Prospect	James Coolen's boat	6:00 A.M.
Francis Ryan	40	Lower Prospect	James Coolen's boat	6:00 A.M.
James Coolen	49	Lower Prospect	James Coolen's boat	6:00 A.M.
Patrick Dollard		Lower Prospect	James Coolen's boat	6:00 A.M.
John Blackburn	24	Lower Prospect	James Coolen's boat	6:00 A.M.
Stephen Ryan	32	Lower Prospect	Michael Clancy's dory	6:00 A.M.
Samuel Blackburn Jr.	39	Lower Prospect	Michael Clancy's dory	6:00 A.M.
James O'Brien	19	Lower Prospect	Michael Clancy's boat	6:30 A.M.
Michael O'Brien	21	Lower Prospect	Michael Clancy's boat	6:30 A.M.
Benjamin Blackburn	30	Lower Prospect	Michael Clancy's boat	6:30 A.M.
William Lacey	47	Lower Prospect	Michael Clancy's boat	6:30 A.M.
Thomas Twohig	26	Pennant	Michael Clancy's boat	6:30 A.M.

Name	Age	From	Boat	Start Time
Edmund Ryan	48	Lower Prospect	Edmund Ryan's boat	8:00 A.M.
John Purcell	53?	Upper Prospect	Edmund Ryan's boat	8:00 A.M.
William Coolen		Upper Prospect	Edmund Ryan's boat	8:00 A.M.
Alex Brophy	27	Lower Prospect	Edmund Ryan's boat	8:00 A.M.
Samuel White	25	Upper Prospect	Edmund Ryan's boat and William Ancient's rescue boat (James Coolen's)	8:00 A.M. 2:00 P.M.
James Power Jr.	30	Upper Prospect	Edmund Ryan's boat and William Ancient's rescue boat (James Coolen's)	8:00 A.M. 2:00 P.M.
Patrick Duggan	31	Upper Prospect	William Ancient's rescue boat (James Coolen's)	2:00 P.M.
John Hooper Slaunwhite	47	Terence Bay	William Ancient's rescue boat (James Coolen's)	2:00 P.M.

Table 8. Others involved on April 1 and/or immediately afterwards.

Name	Role	From
Rev. Martin Maas	Catholic priest, buried Roman Catholic victims	Upper Prospect
Rev. William J. Ancient	Anglican priest, buried non-Catholic victims	Terence Bay
Edmund Ryan	Justice of the Peace for Lower Prospect	Lower Prospect
George J. Longard	Justice of the Peace for Upper Prospect	Upper Prospect
Nicholas P. Christian	Justice of the Peace for Upper Prospect	Upper Prospect
Simon Harrie	Walked to Halifax with Third Officer Brady	Terence Bay
William Gilkie	Lighthouse keeper, Sambro Island	Sambro
George Head	Signal gun operator, Sambro island	Sambro
Edward Johnston	Lighthouse keeper, Chebucto Head	Sambro
Benjamin Fulker	Lighthouse keeper, Devils Island	Dartmouth
John Christian	Rescue	Upper Prospect
Samuel Christian	Rescue	Upper Prospect
Patrick Christian	Rescue	Upper Prospect
Thomas Duggan	Rescue	Upper Prospect
John Duggan	Rescue	Upper Prospect
William Selig	Rescue	Upper Prospect
Michael Purcell	Rescue	Upper Prospect

Martin Marlin	Rescue	Upper Prospect
Tom Hamm	Nine-year-old, helped at rescue	Upper Prospect
Richard Norris	Rescue	Lower Prospect
Eddie Mullins	Rescue	Lower Prospect

Table 9. Officials and others in Halifax and Ottawa.

Name	Role	From
William S. Fielding	Reporter, *Halifax Morning Chronicle*	Halifax
James Duggan	Mayor of Halifax	Halifax
William H. Neal	City alderman, provided clothing to John Hanley	Halifax
William Annand	Premier of Nova Scotia	Halifax
Lord Dufferin	Governor General of Canada, declared Canada's jurisdiction	Ottawa
Peter Mitchell	Minister of Marine and Fisheries, ordered the Halifax inquiry	Ottawa
Henry W. Johnston	Senior Nova Scotia official for federal Department of Marine and Fisheries	Halifax
William B. Vail	Provincial Secretary	Halifax
Edmund M. McDonald	Collector of Customs, led the Halifax inquiry	Halifax
Daniel MacDonald	Commissioner of Mines and Works	Halifax
Henry B. Reid	Inspector of Works, Department of Mines and Works	Halifax
J. Norman Ritchie	Captain's lawyer	Halifax
Hiram Blanchard	Government lawyer (first premier of new province of Nova Scotia)	Halifax
S.L. Shannon	Government lawyer	Halifax
Henry Pryor	Stipendiary magistrate, City of Halifax	Halifax
Lawrence G. Power	Promovents' lawyer	Halifax
James B. Morrow	Cunard agent	Halifax
Sir Adams Archibald	Lieutenant-Governor of Nova Scotia	Halifax
H.W. Smith	Attorney General of Nova Scotia	Halifax
James Kerr	Collector of Customs	Halifax
William Harrington	Partner in firm of Lawson, Harrington, and Company	Halifax
Archibald Sutherland	Acting marshal of Vice Admiralty Court	Halifax
John Hoyt	Clerk at S. Cunard and Company	Halifax

John Milsom	Clerk at S. Cunard and Company	Halifax
Charles Francklyn	Clerk at S. Cunard and Company	Halifax
J.C. Morrison	Clerk at S. Cunard and Company	Halifax
William D. O'Donnell	Photographer	Halifax
Wellington Chase	Photographer	Halifax
J.R. McLellan	Photographer	Halifax
Henry Hesslein	Halifax Hotel, Hollis and Salter Streets	Halifax
William Doull	International Hotel, Hollis and Sackville Streets	Halifax
George Nichols	Acadian Hotel, 64 Granville Street	Halifax
Charles Ramsay	British Hotel	Halifax
Alexander Peers	Mansion House, 149 Barrington Street	Halifax
Mr. Fleming	Elm House, Upper Water Street	Halifax

APPENDIX C

Details About the Ship

This vessel was built under the special inspection of the Surveyors for the Underwriters' Registry for Iron Vessels, and in her hull, decks, rigging, spars, sails, anchors, and chains, is a First Class vessel, fit to carry dry and perishable cargo, and classed for a period of twenty years from the date of launching, subject to survey every four years if the vessel be in the United Kingdom.

Underwriters' Rooms   Thos. B. Royden, Chairman
June 12, 1871   W. W. Rundell, Secretary[6]

+ **First voyage:** Departed Liverpool June 8, 1871, under the command of Captain Digby Murray
+ **Length overall:** 437 feet
+ **Width:** 40.9 feet
+ **Engines:** Two 2-cylinder compound inverted steam engines, built at Liverpool in 1871 by G. Forrester and Company
  • Indicated horse power: 3,000
  • Each engine had cylinders with diameters of 78 inches and 41 inches, 5-foot stroke, and speed of 50 RPM. The cylinders had different diameters to enable the steam to be reused, first in the 41-inch high-pressure cylinder, and then injected into the low-pressure cylinder. This engine was a step in the

evolution of the triple-expansion engine, the 3-cylinder engine that became the workhorse of steamships for more than half a century.

- The two engines were mounted inline on the crankshaft. Because they were external combustion engines and, therefore, did not rely on compression, if a cylinder malfunctioned it could be disconnected from the crankshaft and the ship still had propulsion with three cylinders.

+ **Boilers:** 10 main coal-fired boilers, built by G. Forrester and Company, with 20 furnaces; 1 donkey boiler for driving deck equipment
+ **Drive system:** 1 screw, with 4 iron blades bolted to a hub, 22 feet in diameter
+ **Shaft:** 18 inches in diameter, 120 feet long, supported every 22 feet
+ **Hull:** Riveted iron plates with 7 water-tight compartments
+ **Masts:** 4 steel masts—fore, main, mizzen, and jigger
+ **Height of mainmast from deck:** 110 feet
+ **Sails:** 2 jibs, 2 fore staysails, 2 foresails, 1 mainsail, 5 topsails, 6 trysails, 2 jiggers
+ **Maximum speed:** 14 knots with optimal conditions and sails set; 13 knots with engines only
+ **Sick bays (called hospitals):** 4 rooms on the upper deck, totalling 404 square feet, able to accommodate 18 people
+ **Number of toilets:** 21, of which 6 were for the exclusive use of women; located on upper deck
+ **Emigrants' cooking hearth:** Located in deckhouse, with 6 boilers holding 528 quarts of water and 6 ovens totalling 46 cubic feet
+ **Steerage Accommodation:**
  - Single men on main deck: 228
  - Single men on lower deck: 336
  - Single women on main deck: 156
  - Single women on lower deck: 64
  - Married couples on main deck: 64
  - Married couples on lower deck: 104
  - Total accommodation: 952
+ **Floatation devices:** 12 lifebuoys and 76 lifebelts

+ **Signalling:** 24 1-lb distress rockets, 24 blue signalling lights, 2 signal guns with 24 charges
+ **Navigation:** 2 azimuth and 16 ordinary compasses (azimuth compasses calculate the magnetic deviation); 1 compass in each lifeboat
  + (The main azimuth compass was atop the No. 2 house, away from interference caused by the iron hull; other compasses located in main wheelhouse amidships, aft wheelhouse, quarterdeck, plus spares)
+ **Draught of water on the last voyage:** Forward, 19 feet, 8 inches; aft, 23 feet, 7 inches
+ **Height from surface of water to top of rail amidships:** 13 feet, 9 inches
+ **Cargo:** Tin, iron, and steel—768 tons; measurement goods in bales and cases—819 tons
+ **Water:** 15,000 gallons for cooking for passengers and crew; distilling capacity of 1,600 gallons per 24 hours
+ **Coal capacity:** 960 tons for 16 days at 60 tons per day
+ **Boats:**

Table 10. Lifeboats.

Quantity	Length in Feet	Width	Depth	Volume in Cubic Feet
4	25	6.9	2.9	1,856
2	32	8.6	3.3	1,768
2	30	8.6	3.3	1,657
2	19	5.9	2.3	504

+ **Anchors:**
  + 1 Bower at 5,237 pounds
  + 2 Bower at 5,042 pounds
  + 3 Bower at 4,425 pounds
  + 4 Bower at 4,374 pounds
  + 5 Stream at 2,816 pounds
  + 6 Kedge at 1,083 pounds
  + 7 Kedge at 541 pounds[7]

Passengers

The White Star Line was interested in the space a person occupied and the resources a person consumed. They used units called "statute adults." One adult or two children made one statute adult. Infants were not counted, presumably because they took up an inconsequential amount of space and ate nothing.

A single adult, child, or infant passenger was a "soul." There were 790 souls aboard, of which 673 were adults, 90 were children and 27 were infants.

I have not been able to reconcile the total of 790 passengers (souls) reported by G. W. Cann of the White Star Line passenger department with any list from the dozens printed in newspapers. I have therefore assumed that White Star Line would have had a better idea of how many were aboard than would a newspaper, and concluded that there were 790 passengers aboard, including steerage and saloon.

The passenger lists created in the North American papers are universally unreliable. They confused crew with passengers and disagreed on who lived and who died. After spending many, many hours trying to reconcile multiple lists from respected sources like the *New York Times*, I simply combined them all, on the premise that at least I would not miss anybody. That gave a list containing more than 1,400 names! Consequently, I am unable to include a comprehensive list of those aboard.

Table 11. Estimated passenger demographics.[8]

	Male	Female	Total
English adults	199	75	274
English children and infants	29	22	51
Total English passengers	228	97	325
Scottish adults	7	4	11
Total Scottish passengers	7	4	11
Irish adults	132	73	205
Irish children	16	12	28
Total Irish passengers	148	85	233
"Foreign" adults	151	32	183
"Foreign" children and infants	19	19	38
Total "foreign" passengers	170	51	221
Total men	489		
Total women		184	
Total adults			673
Total children and infants			117
Total passengers	553	237	790

Saloon Passengers

THIS LIST HAS BEEN CONSOLIDATED FROM MULTIPLE SOURCES. THERE WAS a great deal written about the saloon passengers because they were considered to be of more interest than the steerage folk. I found detailed references to thirty-five saloon people, but the White Star Line reported only thirty-two saloon passengers aboard. There was one—a Miss Rawden—who boarded at Liverpool and supposedly disembarked at Queenstown, Ireland. Another, Aline Hayman, was mentioned in only one place, in which a Halifax reporter gave a detailed description of the recovery of her body.

Table 12. Saloon passengers saved and lost.

Saved	Lost
Charles W. Allen	Agnes Barker
Nicholas Brandt	William Brindley
James Brown	Jane Brodie
Simon Comachie	Lewiston Davidson
W.C. Gardiner	Miss Lillian Davidson
Henry Herzel	Cyrus M. Fisher
P. Hirsch	Mary Fisher
J. Spencer Jones	Aline Hayman
Adolphus Jugla	Henry Hewitt
Daniel Kinnane	Hermann A. Kruger
Lewis Levinson	William H. Merritt
Freeman Marckwald	Louise Merritt
B. B. Richmond	Miss Mary Merritt
Samuel W. Vick	John H. Price
	Annie Scrymser
	J. W. Sheat
	Mrs. Sheat
	Rose Sheat (infant)
	H. Sheat (male child)
	Albert Sumner
	Henry M. Wellington

APPENDIX E

Ship's Company

This table includes details of the crew, provided by two sources: the Board of Trade survey of the ship, and the crew lists created by White Star Line. The 152 individuals' names are from the White Star Line crew list. The crew was never reported as having more than 146 members. When describing the crew size to the Halifax inquiry, Williams said, "The number of the ship's crew, including officers and men, were one hundred and forty-six."[9] It sounds like he did not include the six boys, nor did he separate the women.

All told, the crew consisted of 149 males and 3 females.

Table 13. *Atlantic*'s crew.

Rank	Board of Trade survey says:	Crew list says:	Comments and names from the crew list
Captain	1	1	James Agnew Williams
Chief Officer	1	1	Crew list says William Kidley, but John William Firth was assigned just before sailing
Second Officer	1	1	Henry Ismay Metcalfe
Third Officer	1	1	Cornelius Lawrence Brady
Fourth Officer	1	1	John Brown
Purser	1	1	Ambrose Worthington
Surgeon	1	1	Thomas Cuppage

Rank	Board of Trade survey says:	Crew list says:	Comments and names from the crew list
Boatswain	2	1	John Ryde
Boatswain's Mate		1	Mark Lamb
Quartermaster		6	Charles Roylance, William Purdy, Edward Owens, Robert Thomas, John Speakman, John Williams
Carpenter	2	1	William Hanna
Joiner		1	Thomas McCappin
N. Man		1	David McFarlane
Ship's Cook	1		
Ship's Steward	1		
Baker		1	James Brown
Baker's Mate		1	John Cosgrove
Boy		6	John Lynas, John Davenport, Robert Walker, Hamilton Woodward, George Saunders, David Horn
Butcher		1	William Sunderland
Butcher's Mate		1	Benjamin Peck
Passenger Cook	6	6	Charles Walson, John Monohan, George Yates, John Sheridan, David Daniels, Charles Evans
Chief Steward		1	Hugh Christie
Second Steward		1	Samuel May
Chief Bedroom Steward		1	Thomas Dunn
Chief Saloon Steward		1	Ralph Smith
Passenger Steward	42	27	Frederick Raby, George Cheers, Charles Dudley, John Ellery, Henry Roberts, Robert Atkins, Walter Campbell, Daniel McNeil, Matthew Montgomery, Arthur Wilding, Frank Moffatt, Hugh White, John Baillie, Vincent McDonald, Michael Brennan, Hampton Leedom, George Lowe, Alfred Lowe, William Howley, Anton Fredrickson, James Richards, John Gilbert, Irving Stuttaford, John Bellie, Robert Butler, George Ervine, Henry Edwards
Stewardess	3	3	Frances McNally, Ann Waters, Hannah Shevelin
Storekeeper		7	Andrew Horn, John Kerwin, Thomas Kenley, William Roberts, James Candler, George Stone, James Wright
Interpreter/Steward		1	Robert Greener

Rank	Board of Trade survey says:	Crew list says:	Comments and names from the crew list
Able Bodied Seaman	39	39	Henry Whallen, Michael Canavan, Frederick Dalhm, Patrick Clark, William Walling, John Bolger, William Nicholson, Alexander Norton, John Mahoney, George Anderson, John Murphy, David Davison, William Griffiths, Stuart Thomson, John Kelly, Robert McIntees, Joseph Carroll, Patrick Matthews, William Connolly, James McGrath, Thomas Murphy, Alexander Lindsay, Peter Burns, Robert Payne, John Amos, Daniel Mahoney, Daniel Arrowsmith, Michael Shannon, Patrick Kiely, Eran Roberts, John Doyle, John McElmel, James McMullen, Edward Piggott. George Simpson, John McConnell, Daniel Lanning, John Lorunes, Patrick Evans
Chief Engineer	1	1	John Foxley
Engineer	6	5	2nd: Robert Ewing, 3rd: John Hodgson, 4th: William Pattison, 5th: Peter Urquhart, 6th: Samuel Davis
Boilermaker		1	Robert McFarlane
Engineer's Crew— Fireman	33	19	George Myers, Henry McKenna, John Scott, Patrick Kelly, James Ward, Peter Foreman, James Durnan, Edward Egan, Joseph Burns, John Devine, John Less, Patrick Dagan, John McNamara, William Kieley, John Devine, John Jones, James Houghton, John Fredrickson, William Malone
Trimmer		8	Brian Burns, James McAllister, Thomas McDonald, Henry Newton, Andrew Stevenson, Walter Wynne, John McCormick, John Kelly
Greaser		3	James Denny, Peter Craven, Francis Ganzard
Engineer for Distilling	1		
Total	144	152	

(Sources: Survey Report by W. C. Geary, Emigration Officer, Port of Liverpool[10] *and White Star Line Steamship Atlantic crew list for nineteenth voyage.*[11])

Provisions

ONE OF THE MANDATES OF THE BOARD OF TRADE WAS TO ENSURE THAT crews were protected by the Merchant Shipping Act and emigrants were protected by the Passenger Acts. Saloon passengers needed no protection, so on the pre-voyage survey the Board only inspected the provisions for steerage passengers and crew.

Table 14. Provisions.

Passengers			Crew		Medical Comforts	
Barrels or casks	Item	Weight (in pounds) or quantity	Item	Weight (in pounds) or quantity	Item	Weight (in pounds) or quantity
44	Biscuits	3,575	Bread*	4,500	Carolina rice	96
56	Flour	11,016	Beef	3,200	Arrowroot	71
4	Oatmeal	784	Pork	2,400	Sago	80
4	Rice	784	Flour**	980	Barley	56
4	Peas	784	Peas	684	Tapioca	38
	Potatoes	8,960	Tea	35	Loaf sugar†	348
15	Beef	4,560	Coffee	140	Marine soup	84
15	Pork	3,000	Sugar	560	Beef soup (tins)	72
14	Sugar	3,134	Water	500 gallons	Mutton broth in tins	72
4	Tea	288			Lime juice	6 gallons
	Coffee	448			Vinegar	20 gallons
2	Salt	448			Brandy	7 gallons
	Mustard	70			Milk	256 pints
	Pepper	46			Porter	42 dozen
	Vinegar	95 gallons			Port wine	84 quarts
	Molasses	261				
	Barley	112				
	Ling fish	336				
	Raisins	392				
19	Butter	1,596				

*The bread in the crew's provisions would have been hard bread, sometimes known as ship's biscuit or hardtack. It was standard fare for sailors in British ships for generations and is a classic comfort food in some coastal communities of eastern Canada. It is soaked in water and heated before being consumed with dried cod and salted pork.

**The flour would have been for making duff, a simple pudding similar to a dumpling. The crew agreement spelled out the minimum quantities of staples like meat and duff the sailors were entitled to.

†In the days before the bags of granulated sugar we use today existed, sugar came in large cone-shaped pieces called loaves, wrapped in paper. "Sugar nippers" were used to cut off small pieces for domestic use. Perhaps a patient was given a lump of sugar to suck on.[12]

Vessels Involved in the
Final Voyage of SS *Atlantic*

Table 15. Other vessels involved, in order of appearance.

Name	Description
Traffic	White Star Line 155-ton steam tender; in service from 1872 until 1896. Carried passengers between landing stage and *Atlantic* in Liverpool Harbour.
Jackal	Steam tender; carried passengers from ship to landing stage in Queenstown, Ireland.
Carlotta	Carried passengers and freight between Portland, Maine, and Halifax. Entered Halifax on evening of March 31, 1873. Later that summer, it burned and sank when the Portland waterfront was destroyed by fire.
Linnet	Rescue Boat 1, owned by James Coolen of Lower Prospect, Nova Scotia.
Delta	Captain Shaw. 645-ton steamship owned by S. Cunard and Company that carried survivors to Halifax. Built in Scotland in 1853, it had been used on the Halifax–New York–Bermuda run. *Delta* wrecked in St. Mary's Bay, Newfoundland, in September, 1899.
Lady Head	Captain Matson. 299-ton federal government steamship that carried survivors to Halifax. Built in 1857 by Robert Napier at Govan, Scotland, it was 151 feet long and 24 feet wide and had operated between Quebec and Pictou, Nova Scotia. *Lady Head* was lost near Gaspé, Quebec, on August 10, 1878.
Goliah	Captain Jones. Halifax Harbour steam tug; shuttled between Halifax and wreck site.
Unicorn	Halifax Harbour steam tug; shuttled between Halifax and wreck site. In October 1873, the *Unicorn* was sold to a buyer in Sydney, Nova Scotia.
Henry Hoover	Halifax Harbour steam tug; shuttled between Halifax and wreck site. Charged sightseers $2 for a return trip. It sank in Halifax Harbour November 2, 1903, after colliding with the Gloucester schooner *Victor*.
Amateur	Schooner; carried some two hundred coffins from Halifax to Lower Prospect.
Falmouth	Captain Colby. Steamship of New England and Nova Scotia Steamship Company; carried survivors from Halifax to Portland, Maine. Halifax agent was G. P. Black.
Chase	Captain Bennett. Steamship of New England and Nova Scotia Steamship Company; carried survivors from Halifax to Portland, Maine. Departed Halifax with passengers on April 2.

Name	Description
Newport	Steamship that took survivors to New York from Boston.
William Fletcher	Steam towboat in New York Harbor that took survivors from the SS *Newport* to Castle Garden for processing.
North American	Allan Line steamship that carried crew from Halifax to Liverpool, departing April 8.
City of Montreal	Inman Line steamship on which Steward Thomas Dunn travelled from New York to Liverpool after the disaster.
Nestorian	Allan Line steamship that carried the remaining crew from Halifax to Liverpool; departed Halifax April 22.
J. W. Falt	Schooner owned by Captain John Sheridan, diving operator from Halifax.
Lackawana	Steamship owned by American Wrecking Company. Was involved in the salvage and transportation of cargo to New York.
Napier	55-ton schooner; carried salvaged cargo from the wreck site to Halifax. Shortly afterwards, was advertised for sale in the *British Colonist* newspaper.
Nimble	Schooner; carried salvaged cargo from the wreck site to Halifax.
Daisy	Schooner; carried salvaged cargo from the wreck site to Halifax.
Thistle	Schooner; carried salvaged cargo from the wreck site to Halifax.
John Lawrence	Schooner; carried salvaged cargo from the wreck site to Halifax.
D.W. Hennesey	150-ton brigantine chartered from Port Hawkesbury, Nova Scotia, to carry salvaged goods to New York.
Florence D Towers	American schooner; travelled Halifax to New York with salvaged cargo.
Meta	American schooner; travelled Halifax to New York with salvaged cargo.
Perit	American schooner; travelled Halifax to New York with salvaged cargo.
Meteor	American schooner; travelled Halifax to New York with salvaged cargo.
Annie Brown	Schooner that contained cargo impounded by the Vice Admiralty Court.
Leander	50-ton salvage schooner used by Daniel Pitts.

Principal British-Registered Passenger Steamship Companies

Serving the North Atlantic out of Liverpool in 1873

Table 16. Principal British-registered passenger steamship companies serving the North Atlantic out of Liverpool in 1873, ranked by total tonnage.

Informal Name	Registered Name	Number of Ships	Total Tonnage
Cunard Line	British and North American Royal Mail Steam Packet Company	24	72,000
Allan Line	Montreal Ocean Steamship Company	18	54,000
Inman Line	Liverpool, New York, and Philadelphia Steamship Company	12	36,000
National Line	National Steam Navigation Company	12	36,000
Guion Line	Liverpool and Great Western Steamship Company	8	24,000
White Star Line	Oceanic Steam Navigation Company	6*	22,600
Mississippi and Dominion Line	Mississippi and Dominion Steamship Company	7	8,000

The Atlantic loss took the number down to 5. (Source: Halifax Citizen April 8, 1873)

A Note About Sources

In addition to official documents from governments, the White Star Line, the Halifax Vice Admiralty Court, the British Board of Trade, and others, newspapers and magazines were an important source of information for this book. They fall into three categories, and what they provided is determined by where they were located:

Halifax—Thirteen publications provided first-hand information of the event and its aftermath, including years and decades later. All the information printed in American and European newspapers in the first days after the disaster originated with the Halifax papers, primarily the *Morning Chronicle* and the *Acadian Recorder*. They were also vital in documenting the testimony that would constitute the official inquiry.

United States—New York and Boston papers presented detailed first-hand accounts of passengers arriving in Boston and then in New York, along with speculation on causes of the disaster. Their coverage was immediately negative towards the White Star Line and was based on interviews with passengers and local marine experts who gave opinions based on what they had read in other papers. Some American papers sent correspondents to Halifax, who sent back important details.

England and Ireland—Newspapers were generally supportive of the White Star Line and quick to make the point that the *Atlantic* was a well-built ship that was well stocked with coal and provisions. Their contribution to the historical record originates from interviews with surviving crew members returning to Liverpool.

Bibliography
Newspapers consulted

Belfast News Letter
Belfast Weekly Telegraph
Boston Evening Traveller
Bradford Observer
Burton Chronicle
Canadian Illustrated News
Chicago Tribune
Dartmouth Daily News
Frank Leslie's Illustrated Newspaper
Guernsey Star
Halifax British Colonist
Halifax Chronicle Herald
Halifax Daily Acadian Recorder
Halifax Daily Echo
Halifax Evening Express
Halifax Evening Reporter
Halifax Herald
Halifax Mail
Halifax Mail Star

Halifax Morning Chronicle
Halifax Novascotian
Halifax Presbyterian Witness
Halifax Weekly Citizen
Harper's Weekly
Hobart (Tasmania) Mercury
Irish Times
Liverpool Mercury
Liverpool Mail
Lloyd's List
Lyttleton (New Zealand) Star
New York Daily Graphic
New York Herald
New York Tribune
New York Times
Sydney Morning Herald
The Irishman
Wilmington Journal
Yorkshire Post and Leeds Intelligencer

Books and other sources

Armstrong, Warren. *Atlantic Highway*. London: George E. Harrap and Co., 1961.

Bouteillier, Jill Martin. *Sable Island in Black and White*. Halifax: Nimbus Publishing, 2016.

Bonsor, N. R. P., *North Atlantic Seaway*. West Vancouver, British Columbia: 1975.

Brown, Cassie. *Standing into Danger*. Toronto: Doubleday Canada Limited, 1979.

Burns, Marian and Susan Moxley. *The Beacon on the Hill: The History of St. Paul's Anglican Church, Terence Bay, NS*. Council of St. Paul's Anglican Church, 1993.

Cochkanoff, Greg and Bob Chaulk. *SS Atlantic: The White Star Line's First Disaster at Sea*. Fredericton, New Brunswick: Goose Lane Editions, 2009.

Croil, James. *Steam Navigation*. Toronto: William Briggs, 1898.

Eaton, John P. and Charles A. Haas. *Falling Star: Misadventures of White Star Line Ships*. New York: W. W. Norton & Company, Inc., 1989.

Fischer, David Hackett. *Champlain's Dream*. New York: Simon & Schuster, 2008.

Halifax and Its Business. Halifax: Nova Scotia Printing Company, 1876.

Hatchard, Keith A. *The Two Atlantics*. Halifax: Nimbus Publishing, 1981.

Hyde, Francis E. *Cunard and the North Atlantic*. Basingstoke and London: The MacMillan Press Ltd., 1975.

Kemp, Peter, ed. *The Oxford Companion to Ships and the Sea*. Oxford: Oxford University Press, 1976.

Loss of the Steamship Atlantic, Toronto: McLeish & Co., 1873.

Love, Bob. *Destiny's Voyage*. Bloomington, IN: AuthorHouse, 2006.

MacMechan, Archibald. "The Rise of Samuel Cunard." In *The Dalhousie Review*, Halifax, July 1929.

McCluskie, Tom. *Ships from the Archives of Harland & Wolff*. London: PRC Publishing, 1998.

Milsom, C. H. *The Coal was There for Burning*. London: Marine Media Management, 1975.

Nicholson, A. W. *Memories of James Bain Morrow*. Toronto: Methodist Book and Publishing House, 1881.

Official Guide and Album of the Cunard Steamship Company. London: Sutton, Sharp and Co., 1877.

Papers Relating to the Loss of the Steam Ship Atlantic. Ottawa: Canadian House of Commons, July 31, 1873.

Pullen, Hugh F. *The Sea Road to Halifax*. Halifax: Maritime Museum of the Atlantic Occasional Paper #1, 1980.

The City of Liverpool. Cheltenham and London: J. Burrow & Co., Ltd.

The Nautical Magazine. Vol. XLV. London: Simpkin, Marshall & Co., 1876.

Woodham-Smith, Cecil. *The Great Hunger*. New York: Harper and Row, 1962.

Zinck, Jack. *Shipwrecks of Nova Scotia, Vol II*. Hantsport, Nova Scotia: Lancelot Press, 1977.

Endnotes

Chapter 1: The Ismays

1   *Sydney Morning Herald*, July 14, 1899.
2   *Hobart Mercury*, June 27, 1869.
3   Ibid.
4   C. H. Milsom, *The Coal was There for Burning* (London: Marine Media Management, 1975), 7.
5   *New York Times*, March 30, 1871.
6   *The Nautical Magazine* for 1876, (London: Simpkin, Marshall & Co.), Vol. XLV.
7   Captain's Log of the Barque *Compadre*, March 6, 1872.
8   Ibid.
9   Francis E. Hyde, *Cunard and the North Atlantic* (Basingstoke and London: The MacMillan Press Ltd., 1975), 92.
10 The letter was written in instalments. This was added on Feb. 8, 1872. Since he reported on February 7 and made no mention of it, the accident must have happened on February 8. See p. 153 of the Liverpool Investigation, contained in *Papers Relating to the Loss of the Steam Ship* Atlantic, Canadian House of Commons, Ottawa, July 31, 1873.

Chapter 2: A First-Class Vessel

1   White Star Line ad, November 2, 1872.
2   *Papers Relating to the Loss of the Steam Ship* Atlantic (Ottawa: Canadian House of Commons, July 31, 1873), 120.
3   White Star Line trade card, Ismay, Imrie and Company, Liverpool.
4   White Star Line Memorial Foundation, wslmf.org.
5   *Daily Acadian Recorder,* April 10, 1873.
6   *Burton Chronicle*, May, 1873.
7   *Papers Relating to the Loss,* 79.
8   Ibid., 122.
9   Ibid., 75–76.

10 Ibid., 78.
11 Ibid., 81.
12 Ibid., 118.
13 Letter from Ismay, Imrie and Company quoted in the *Burton Chronicle*, May 1873.
14 *Papers Relating to the Loss*, 117. Testimony of Fourth Officer Brown to the Liverpool Investigation.
15 Ibid., 108.
16 Ibid., 11.
17 Ibid., 83.
18 Ibid.
19 Ibid.

Chapter 3: The Leaving of Liverpool

1 An account of the experiences of Thomas Moffatt during the *Atlantic*'s final voyage, composed by Moffatt some years after the disaster. In 1993, the account was sent to the Fisheries Museum of the Atlantic, Lunenburg, Nova Scotia, by Nancy Jane Faraudo of Livermore, California.
2 *Papers Relating to the Loss*, 127.
3 *Irish Times*, April 5, 1873.
4 *Papers Relating to the Loss*, 153.
5 Ibid., 134.
6 SS *Atlantic* Crew Documents, White Star Line.
7 *Boston Evening Traveller*, April 2, 1873.
8 Thomas Moffatt report.
9 *Papers Relating to the Loss*, 99.
10 Halifax Inquiry, 1.
11 Thomas Moffatt report.
12 Halifax Inquiry, 131.
13 Ibid., 99.
14 Ibid.
15 Ibid., 100.
16 Ibid.
17 The *Atlantic* had eleven boilers, but only ten serviced the engines. The donkey boiler was a smaller one for driving other engines on deck.
18 Nova Scotia Lighthouse Preservation Society, nslps.com.
19 N. R. P. Bonsor, *North Atlantic Seaway Volume 1* (West Vancouver, BC: Douglas, David and Charles Limited, 1975), 226.
20 Halifax Inquiry, 126.

Chapter 4: The Captain's Cocoa

1 *Halifax Evening Reporter*, April 7, 1873.
2 Halifax Inquiry, 14.
3 *New York Herald*, April 7, 1873.
4 *Papers Relating to the Loss*, 14.
5 David Hackett Fischer, *Champlain's Dream* (New York: Simon & Schuster, 2008), 448.
6 Halifax Inquiry, 132. The captain testified that he was awakened when the ship struck, and was heading out the wheelhouse door when he met Metcalfe coming in.

7   *New York Herald*, April 7, 1873.

8   I am indebted to Janet Blunt of Hampshire, England, for historical details of her great-great-great-grandmother, Caroline Wood, and family.

9   *Halifax Evening Reporter*, April 7, 1873.

10 *Belfast News-Letter*, April 22, 1873.

11 *Guernsey Star*, May 6, 1873.

12 *Daily Acadian Recorder*, April 4, 1873.

13 Email from Jean-Pierre Feron of Movelier to SS *Atlantic* Heritage Park, July 3, 2004.

14 Thomas Moffatt Report.

15 Halifax Inquiry, 3.

16 *New York World*, April 6, 1873.

Chapter 5: Angels in the Night

1   Thomas Moffatt Report.

2   Letter from Sarah Jane O'Reilly, *Halifax Herald*, April 3, 1906, 6.

3   Oak Island has captured imaginations and claimed lives for over two centuries. Treasure hunters can't stay away from the place.

4   *British Colonist*, April 8, 1873; testimony of Third Officer Brady.

5   Australian sea captain Penelope Kealy told me about her great-grandfather, William Hoy, who was an Irish steerage passenger. He was supposed to have saved many passengers by pulling them upon the rock—one with his teeth. The story appears in several newspaper reports, including the *New York Herald*, on April 7, 1873. Captain Kealy said he saved a boy by lashing him and his mother to a piece of wreckage. The mother died but the boy survived, leaving the possibility that a second child survived the *Atlantic*'s final voyage.

Chapter 6: So Near and Yet So Far

1   *New York World*, April 6, 1873, quoted in *Wilmington Journal*, April 11, 1873.

2   *Canadian Illustrated News*, April 12, 1873.

3   Thomas Moffatt Report.

4   "Affidavit of Dennis Ryan," Court of Vice Admiralty, Halifax, October 7, 1873.

5   Letter from Captain Williams to Ismay, Imrie and Company, April 2, 1873.

6   "Affidavit of Thomas Twohig," Court of Vice Admiralty, Halifax, December 16, 1873.

7   *New York World*, April 6, 1873.

Chapter 7: I Was a Stranger and You Took Me In

1   *Halifax Morning Chronicle*, April 3, 1873.

2   *Halifax Evening Echo*, September 15, 1922.

3   Thomas Moffatt Report.

4   *Halifax Morning Chronicle*, April 5, 1873.

Chapter 8: The Kindness of Strangers

1   *The Wreck of the Atlantic*, (Philadelphia: Old Franklin Publishing House, 1873), 31.

2   Oral history as recounted by Upper Prospect resident Chris Devanney.

3 "Affidavit of Nicholas Christian."
4 Family history related to me by John Mason, great-nephew of Thomas Hamm, related to him by his father, Gerald Mason, about his uncle Tom.
5 "Affidavit of Dennis Ryan."

Chapter 9: The Long Watch

1 "Affidavit of Thomas Twohig."
2 "Affidavit of Nicholas Christian."
3 *Canadian Illustrated News*, April 12, 1873.
4 "Affidavit of Nicholas Christian."
5 *New York Times*, April 4, 1873.
6 *New York World*, April 6, 1873.
7 *New York Herald*, April 7, 1873.
8 *Guernsey Star*, May 6, 1873.

Chapter 10: The Last Survivor

1 *Halifax Evening Express*, April 3, 1873.
2 *Paterson Daily Express*, quoted in *The Irishman*, May 3, 1873.
3 Eleanor Quigley, great-grand-niece of John, provided the correct spelling.
4 *New York Tribune*, April 7, 1873. Most New York papers provided extensive coverage of Hanley's arrival in New York with the other passengers.
5 Letter of Sarah Jane O'Reilly to *Halifax Herald*, April 3, 1906.
6 Iris Shea, history researcher with the Mainland South Heritage Society. Mary Ann Umlah was her great-aunt.
7 *Halifax Morning Chronicle*, April 2, 1873.

Chapter 11: Stop the Presses!

1 *Halifax Daily Acadian Recorder*, April 1, 1873.
2 Courtesy of SS *Atlantic* Heritage Park Society. Henry Dry's letters provided to the Society by Jean Cameron-Francis of Poole, England, whose children are the great-great-great-grandchildren of Henry Dry.
3 *Guernsey Star*, May 6, 1873.
4 *Halifax Morning Chronicle*, April 2, 1873.
5 Ibid., April 3, 1873.
6 Henry Dry wrote to his wife: "They said it was the anchor dropt down but the terrible crash was heard the second time." May 18, 1873.
7 *Irish Times*, April 22, 1873.
8 "Affidavit of William J. Ancient," Court of Vice Admiralty, Halifax, December 31, 1873.
9 "Affidavit of James B. Morrow," Court of Vice Admiralty, Halifax, December 27, 1873.
10 Thomas Moffatt Report.
11 *Halifax Daily Reporter*, April 4 1873.
12 *Halifax Morning Chronicle* April 3, 1873.

Chapter 12: The Hill of Death

1   Tom Hughes, *The Blue Riband of the Atlantic* (Cambridge: Patrick Stephens, 1873), 32.

2   *Halifax Morning Chronicle*, April 5, 1873.

3   Ibid.

4   *Halifax Evening Reporter*, April 7, 1873.

5   *Halifax Daily Acadian Recorder*, April 5, 1873.

6   Edmund Ryan's mother was Elizabeth Fenton, aged seventy. His mother and his wife had the same first name.

7   *Halifax Daily Acadian Recorder*, April 5, 1873. An early book about the *Atlantic* disaster took this account and inserted Edmund Ryan and his wife eating breakfast when a mob of survivors stormed into their house, ravenously eating anything in sight, including unrisen bread dough. It purports to be the first indication that the *Atlantic* was on the rocks. In fact, Ryan had been at the wreck site for several hours and these survivors, after being rescued, were taken to his home to convalesce. They would never have found his house as it was on another island. The story, though untrue, lives on.

8   *Halifax Daily Acadian Recorder*, April 5.

9   Nova Scotia Hospital for the Insane, Dartmouth, NS, Admittance Records 1126 and 1146. I am indebted to Nathan Smith for providing this item.

10   *SS Atlantic*, produced and directed by Christopher Devanney (independent short documentary, 2020).

11   *Halifax Daily Acadian Recorder*, April 7, 1873.

12   Connie Drew, SS *Atlantic* Heritage Park Society Oral History Project, Terence Bay, NS, Recorded by Krystal Harrie, July 11, 2019.

13   *Halifax Novascotian*, April 28, 1873.

14   "Affidavit of Nicholas Christian."

15   *Halifax Evening Express*, April 10, 1873.

16   *Halifax Evening Reporter*, April 5, 1873.

17   Correspondence with Adaire Gibb, great-grandson of David Boswell, April 2018.

18   *Halifax Evening Reporter*, April 8, 1873.

19   Penelope Kealy. See Chapter 5, note 5.

20   *Halifax Evening Reporter*, April 4, 1873, 2.

Chapter 13: Farewell to Nova Scotia, Your Sea-Bound Coast

1   *Halifax Evening Reporter*, April 4, 1873.

2   *Halifax Evening Express*, April 3, 1873.

3   *Daily Acadian Recorder*, April 4, 1873.

4   *New York Times*, April 4, 1873.

5   *New York Herald*, April 7, 1873.

6   *Wilmington Journal*, April 11, 1873.

7   *Halifax Evening Reporter*, April 5, 1873.

8   *New York Tribune*, April 8, 1873.

9   *Halifax Evening Reporter*, April 10, 1873.

10   *New York Tribune*, April 8, 1873.

Chapter 14: Lead Us Not Into Temptation

1   *Halifax Evening Reporter*, April 7, 1873.
2   Lost in 1797; with some 240 deaths, HMS *Tribune* represented the biggest loss of life among the wrecks near Halifax before the *Atlantic*.
3   Jack Zinck, *Shipwrecks of Nova Scotia, Vol. II* (Hantsport, Nova Scotia: Lancelot Press, 1977), 144.
4   Williams's letter to Ismay, Imrie and Company, April 2, 1873.
5   Associated Press in *Chicago Tribune*, April 4, 1873.
6   "Affidavit of Nicholas Christian."
7   Halifax Inquiry, 124.
8   *Halifax Evening Express*, April 10, 1873.
9   *Halifax Evening Reporter*, April 15, 1873.

Chapter 15: Dust to Dust

1   *New York Daily Graphic*, April 3, 1873.
2   Ibid., April 7, 1873.
3   *New York Daily Graphic*, April 5, 1873.
4   Ibid., April 5, 1873.
5   *Daily Standard*, April 5, 1873.
6   *Halifax Evening Reporter*, April 8.
7   *Halifax Evening Express*, April 12, 1873.
8   *Halifax Morning Chronicle*, April 3, 1873.
9   *Acadian Recorder*, April 3, 1873.
10 *Halifax Morning Chronicle*, April 8, 1873.
11 *Daily Acadian Recorder*, April 4, 1873.
12 *Halifax Daily Reporter*, April 5, 1873.
13 *Halifax Evening Reporter*, May 8 and 10, 1873.
14 *Halifax Citizen*, April 26, 1873.
15 *Halifax Evening Reporter*, April 14, 1873.
16 *Wilmington Journal*, April 11, 1873.
17 *New York Tribune*, April 8, 1873.
18 *Daily Acadian Recorder*, April 7, 1873.
19 Ibid., April 8, 1873.
20 Marian Burns and Susan Moxley, *The Beacon on the Hill: The History of St. Paul's Anglican Church, Terence Bay, NS*, Council of St. Paul's Anglican Church, 1993, 2.
21 *Halifax Evening Reporter*, July 15, 1873.
22 *Halifax Daily Acadian Recorder*, April 7, 1873.
23 I am indebted to Mary Casteleyn and Bernie Kirwan, genealogists transcribing the memorial stones in the Roman Catholic cemetery of Tigeaghna, County Kilkenny, Ireland, for this information about Bridget Mary Brown.
24 *Halifax Evening Express*, April 4 1873.

Chapter 16: The Five Hundred–Pound Promise

1   "Affidavit of Edmund Ryan," Court of Vice Admiralty, Halifax, December 2, 1873.
2   *Halifax Daily Reporter* April 5, 1873.
3   Ibid., May 15, 1873.
4   *Halifax Evening Reporter*, April 9, 1873.

5   *Daily Acadian Recorder*, May 21, 1873.
6   *Halifax Evening Reporter*, May 23, 1873.
7   Ibid., April 15 and 17, 1873.
8   *Halifax Novascotian*, April 21, 1873.
9   The watch is on display at the Maritime Museum of the Atlantic in Halifax. The inscription is clearly legible.
10   Letter of James H. Sparks to Edward Owens, October 29, 1873. Courtesy Nova Scotia Archives and Records Management.
11   *New York Tribune*, April 8, 1873.
12   *Halifax Evening Reporter*, June 26 1873.
13   In a letter to the *Shipping and Mercantile Gazette* on April 24, 1873, the company valued the loss of the ship at £50,000, which would be $3–$4 million today. The *New York Times* reported that the ship and cargo were insured in London for $150,000.
14   In a letter to Ismay, Imrie and Company on April 2, 1873, Williams reported that arrangements had been made to transfer passengers to New York for $17 ($350 today) per person, including "victualling" (meals).
15   *Papers Relating to the Loss*, 53.
16   *New York Times*, December 1, 1875. Marckwald sued the Oceanic Steam Navigation Company in December, 1873, seeking $5,000 in damages for lost luggage and loss of business. The courts ruled in his favour but White Star appealed. The appeal was denied in July 1877.
17   *Irish Times*, June 27, 1873.
18   Ibid., June 19, 1873.
19   *Liverpool Mercury*, April 12, 1873.
20   *Halifax Citizen*, April 8, 1873.
21   whitestarhistory.com/tropic.
22   wikivisually.com/wiki/ss_asiatic_(1870).
23   "Affidavit of J. N. Ritchie," Court of Vice Admiralty, Halifax, June 27, 1873.
24   *Halifax Morning Chronicle*, April 4, 1873.
25   *Daily Acadian Recorder*, April 9, 1873.
26   *Halifax Evening Reporter*, April 14, 1873.
27   Ibid., April 14, 1873.

Chapter 17: The Lawsuit

1   *Loss of the Steamship Atlantic* (Toronto: McLeish & Co., 1873), 11.
2   *Halifax Evening Reporter*, May 10, 1873.
3   *Court of Vice Admiralty*, Halifax, June 27, 1873.
4   *Halifax and Its Business* (Halifax: Nova Scotia Printing Company, 1876), 69.
5   *Halifax Evening Reporter*, June 7, 1873.
6   "Affidavit of James Kerr," Court of Vice Admiralty, Halifax, December 31, 1873.
7   A. W. Nicholson, *Memories of James Bain Morrow* (Toronto: Methodist Book and Publishing House, 1881).

Chapter 18: Medals, Money, and Watches

1   *Seventh Annual Report of the Department of Marine and Fisheries for fiscal year ended 30th June, 1874* (Ottawa: MacLean Roger & Co., 1875), 201.
2   "Affidavit of Nicholas Christian"

3   *Halifax Evening Reporter*, April 10, 1873.
4   *Halifax Evening Reporter*, June 18, 1873.
5   *Seventh Annual Report of the Department of Marine and Fisheries*, 201.
6   Ibid., 200.

Chapter 19: Cargo and Artifacts

1   *Halifax Herald*, April 28, 1934.
2   *Halifax Evening Reporter*, April 30, 1873.
3   Ibid., May 1.
4   Ibid., May 1.
5   Ibid., April 14, April 22, June 13, June 18.
6   Hesta MacDonald of Charlottetown, Prince Edward Island, provided a 1925 newspaper article describing her grandfather Leonard Lyons's diving work on the *Atlantic* before he became a grocer.
7   Williams's great-grandson Andrew Thomas carried what is believed to be the *Atlantic*'s flag back to Halifax aboard the Cunard Liner *Queen Mary 2*. The event is covered in the *Halifax Mail Star*, September 5, 2006.
8   *Halifax Mail Star*, July 5, 1986.

Chapter 20: The Halifax Inquiry

1   Milsom, 50.
2   *Belfast Weekly Telegraph*, April 12, 1873.
3   *Halifax Evening Reporter*, Apr 18, 1873, quoting an unnamed Plymouth newspaper.
4   *Halifax Citizen*, April 5, 1873.
5   Halifax Inquiry, 53.
6   *Halifax Evening Express*, April 8, 1873.
7   *Liverpool Mail*, April 26, 1873.
8   *New York Herald*, April 7, 1873.
9   *Liverpool Mercury*, May 14, 1873.
10   Halifax Inquiry, 130.

Chapter 21: Coal

1   Hyde, *Cunard and the North Atlantic*, 92.
2   *Papers Relating to the Loss*, 49.
3   Ibid.
4   Ibid.
5   Ibid., 51.
6   Ibid., 49.
7   Ibid., 50.
8   Ibid., 53.
9   Ibid., 52.
10   Ibid., 55.
11   Ibid., 69.

Chapter 22: The Final Verdict

1   *Papers Relating to the Loss*, 94.
2   Ibid., 178.

3 Ibid., 90.
4 Ibid., 86.
5 Ibid., 94.
6 Ibid., 182.
7 Ibid., 529.
8 Ibid., 530.
9 Ibid., 99.

Chapter 23: The Hero of Our Song

1 *Halifax Novascotian*, April 21, 1873.
2 Halifax Inquiry, 31.
3 Henry Greenbaum, "Lines to Captain Williams," handwritten poem, Jan 24, 1868, courtesy of Andrew Thomas.
4 *New York Tribune*, April 3, 1873.
5 *Papers Relating to the Loss*, 100.
6 Halifax Inquiry, 13.
7 *Halifax Novascotian*, April 21, 1873.
8 Halifax Inquiry, 19.
9 Halifax Inquiry, 22.
10 Halifax Inquiry, 26.
11 *Papers Relating to the Loss*, 172.
12 *Chicago Tribune*, April 1873.
13 *Irish Times*, March 31, 1873.
14 *New York Daily Graphic*, April 7, 1873.
15 *Halifax Evening Express*, April 18, 1873.
16 *Halifax Evening Reporter*, April 7, 1873.
17 *Halifax Evening Reporter*, April 4, 1873.
18 *Halifax Evening Reporter*, May 15, 1873.
19 Williams told the Halifax inquiry, "Having no officer at hand, I detailed the boatswain and eight men to prevent wreckers."
20 *Papers Relating to the Loss*, 100.
21 Halifax Inquiry, 8.
22 Ibid., 14.
23 *Papers Relating to the Loss*, 47.
24 *Papers Relating to the Loss*, 532.
25 *Halifax Evening Reporter*, April 22, 1873.
26 Ibid., May 8, 1873.
27 *Papers Relating to the Loss*, 47.
28 Ibid., 47.
29 *Halifax Novascotian*, April 21, 1873.
30 *Agreement and Account of Crew*, SS *Calabar*, October 26, 1874.
31 Correspondence with Andrew Thomas, July 28, 2018. In another exchange, Mr. Thomas adds a note related to him by a relative: "Thereafter (presumably in the late 1870s) Capt. Williams went to Japan to help train the Japanese Imperial Navy, which was being rapidly expanded and westernized at that time. They were ordering modern warships from British yards, and were eager to train a new cadre of seamen with the appropriate skills, that they would use to great effect against the Chinese in 1894 and the Russians in 1905."

Chapter 24: Driving the Atlantic

1   Cassie Brown, *Standing into Danger*, (Toronto: Doubleday Canada, 1979).
2   Halifax Inquiry, 53.
3   *Papers Relating to the Loss*, 112.
4   *Halifax Evening Express*, April 14, 1873.

Chapter 25: The Elusive Light

1   *Halifax Chronicle*, April 28, 1873.
2   Halifax Inquiry, 120.
3   Ibid., 102.
4   Greg Cochkanoff and Bob Chaulk, *SS Atlantic: The White Star Line's First Disaster at Sea* (Fredericton, New Brunswick: Goose Lane Editions, 2009), 129.
5   Halifax Inquiry, 118.
6   Ibid., 99.
7   Ibid., 116.
8   Ibid., 112.
9   Ibid., 115.
10 Nova Scotia Lighthouse Preservation Society, nslps.com.
11 Halifax Inquiry, 115.

Chapter 26: The Ancient Story

1   *Halifax Evening Reporter*, May 16, 1873.
2   The watch was made by E. D. Johnson of London, England. It is on display at the Maritime Museum of the Atlantic in Halifax, Nova Scotia.
3   *Acadian Recorder*, October 8, 1873.
4   *Acadian Recorder*, Dec. 8, 1905.
5   "Affidavit of James Coolen," Court of Vice Admiralty, Halifax, October 7, 1873.
6   *Halifax Herald*, December 8, 1905.
7   Cecil Woodham-Smith, *The Great Hunger* (New York: Harper and Row, 1962), 18.
8   *Halifax Daily Acadian Recorder*, April 2, 1873.
9   *New York Tribune*, April 8, 1873.
10 *Daily Acadian Recorder*, July 21, 1908.
11 Jill Martin Bouteillier, *Sable Island in Black and White*, 33.

Chapter 27: Myths, Lies, and Other Untruths

1   Phyllis R. Blakely, *W. J. Ancient—Hero of Shipwreck Atlantic* (Petheric Press, September 1973), The Nova Scotia Historical Quarterly, Vol. 3 No. 3.
2   John Malcolm Brinnin, *The Sway of the Grand Saloon* (New York: Barnes & Noble, 2000), 253.
3   *Papers Relating to the Loss*, 100.
4   *Irish Times*, June 27, 1873.
5   *The Nautical Magazine for 1876* (London: Simpkin, Marshall & Co.), Vol. 45, 321.
6   *Lyttleton* (New Zealand) *Star*, March 10, 1906.
7   *Carrie Clancy: The Heroine of the Atlantic* (Philadelphia: Old Franklin Publishing House, 1873), 4.
8   *New York Times*, April 4, 1873.

9   *Halifax Evening Reporter*, April 4, 1873.
10 *Halifax Morning Chronicle*, April 21.
11 Milsom, 44.
12 *New York Herald*, April 7, 1873.
13 *Burton Chronicle*, May 1873.
14 *Halifax Morning Chronicle*, April 26, 1873.
15 *Halifax Evening Reporter*, May 2, 1873.

Chapter 29: Memories

1 *Halifax Mail Star*, November 12, 1969.
2 *Halifax Herald*, December 8, 1905.
3 On December 6, 1917, two ships collided in Halifax Harbour and one, loaded with explosives, blew up, causing widespread carnage, including two thousand deaths.
4 Other members were Florence Harrison, Terry Thomas, Connie Drew, and Patricia Avery. Source: Meeting minutes.
5 *Halifax Chronicle Herald*, July 26, 1998.
6 *Halifax Sunday Herald*, July 12, 1998.

Epilogue

1 *Report of Committee on Navigation Securities,* Office of Board of Works, Halifax, March 15, 1858.
2 *Halifax Evening Reporter*, April 8, 1873.
3 Ibid., July 12, 1873.
4 *Government of Canada, Seventh Report of the Select Standing Committee on Public Accounts 2nd April, 1875; Papers Relating to Light Ship "Halifax,"* Ottawa, October 25, 1872, to December 26, 1873.
5 *Halifax Morning Chronicle*, November 10, 1897, 3.
6 *Halifax Morning Chronicle*, May 25, 1914.
7 Hugh F. Pullen, *The Sea Road to Halifax*, (Halifax: Maritime Museum of the Atlantic Occasional Paper #1, 1980).
8 *Halifax Mail Star*, July 28, 1966.

Appendices

1 *New York Times*, September 18, 1897.
2 *Dictionary of Canadian Biography.*
3 *Halifax Daily Echo*, July 6, 1894.
4 Halifax newspaper February 19, 1914.
5 *Halifax Herald* August 5, 1907.
6 *Papers Relating to the Loss*, 130.
7 *Papers Relating to the Loss*, 7–11, 119, 121, 122, 126, 130.
8 *Yorkshire Post and Leeds Intelligencer*, April 3, 1873.
9 Halifax Inquiry, 125.
10 *Papers Relating to the Loss*, 11.
11 Maritime History Archive, Memorial University of Newfoundland.
12 *Papers Relating to the Loss*, 78.